Mastering CentOS 7 Linux Server

Configure, manage, and secure a CentOS 7 Linux server to serve a variety of services provided in a sustainable computer's infrastructure

Mohamed Alibi

Bhaskarjyoti Roy

BIRMINGHAM - MUMBAI

Mastering CentOS 7 Linux Server

Copyright © 2016 Packt Publishing

First published: January 2016

Production reference: 1250116

Published by Packt Publishing Ltd.
Livery Place
35 Livery Street
Birmingham B3 2PB, UK.

ISBN 978-1-78528-239-3

www.packtpub.com

Credits

Authors

Mohamed Alibi

Bhaskarjyoti Roy

Reviewers

Sayyed Mehdi Poustchi Amin

Benjamin KRAFT

Frank Lemmon

Commissioning Editor

Sarah Crofton

Acquisition Editor

Shaon Basu

Content Development Editor

Merwyn D'souza

Technical Editor

Utkarsha S. Kadam

Copy Editors

Joanna McMahon

Merilyn Pereira

Vikrant Phadke

Project Coordinator

Nikhil Nair

Proofreader

Safis Editing

Indexer

Rekha Nair

Graphics

Jason Monteiro

Abhinash Sahu

Production Coordinator

Melwyn Dsa

Cover Work

Melwyn Dsa

About the Authors

Mohamed Alibi is a Linux System administrator at the training team of the European Bio-informatics Institute EMBL-EBI at the Wellcome Trust Genome Campus. He got his master's degree in Network System and Telecom from the Faculty of Sciences of the Tunis El Manar University, with an internship held at the University of Illinois Urbana-Champaign at the National Center for Supercomputer Applications and the Carl R. Woese Institute for Genomic Biology.

He started his career as a system and network administrator at Institut Pasteur de Tunis from 2011 to 2015. During this time, he got associated with the network project H3ABioNet. He held the title of the co-chair of the Infrastructure Working Group, helping the development and enhancement of the computer infrastructure of project nodes. Between 2014 and 2015, he started his career as a part-time professor at Superior Institute of Biotechnology of Sidi Thabet, then, as a system administrator trainer with the University of Pretoria as part of the project H3ABioNet. At the end of 2015, Mohamed got his current position as a Linux system administrator with the European Bio-informatics Institute.

He reviewed a book about CentOS 7 troubleshooting in late 2014 and early 2015.

I would like to acknowledge my family for their constant support and my friends and colleagues for their help and their guiding advices. Special thanks go to my fiancée for her enormous love and daily encouragement to move forward in my career, and finally, I would like to thank all my work colleagues and supervisors for giving me the opportunity to expand my knowledge and my experience.

Bhaskarjyoti Roy is a Linux and open source enthusiast with more than 12 years of experience in Linux system administration, virtualization, and cloud computing.

He provides his services to many companies and organizations on a daily basis. He learns from his experience, which he has gained through self-learning and serving clients regularly. He has built more than 100 servers based on various CentOS versions running different types of services such as virtualization, web-server, e-mail, DNS, and many more.

He is currently working with gotcha! Mobile Solutions, a Dallas based digital marketing agency specializing in local SEO, mobile web apps, and custom web development projects.

I am thankful to my wife Hema, without whom this would never have been possible. I am grateful to my mom, my sis, and other family members and friends who have always stood beside me. I would like to thank Mr. Krishnendu Paul (KP), Mr. Indranil Dasgupta (IDG) and Mr. Chanchal Debnath for their support and encouragement. Special thanks go to Mr. Christopher Jenkin, CEO, and Mr. Hassan Khawaja, Director of Operations, gotcha! Mobile Solutions, who always encouraged me to achieve and perform better.

About the Reviewers

Sayyed Mehdi Poustchi Amin (RHCE, RHCSA, CCNA, MCITP, MCTS, MCSE, MCSA, and MCP) has 15 years of experience in the information technology industry. He is a senior datacenter system administrator in a reputed company in Toronto. He worked as a developer, and later as a system administrator at Islamic Azad University of Mashhad, Iran from 2000 to 2010. He was a PhD research student in computer science at SIU, India before moving to Canada. In early 2008, he founded the Iran Honeynet Project website, which provides security-related information regarding the latest attacks observed by a network of honeypots.

> Mehdi strongly appreciates his wife Hediyeh's constant support of his career endeavors. He wants to thank her for all of her support through this project.

Benjamin KRAFT is a system administration team leader in a major internet service provider based in Luxembourg. Benjamin Kraft also operates for a well-known European DNS registrar, a VoIP operator, and a SaaS platform provider.

Passionate and curious about everything related to IT, he specializes in virtualization, storage, Linux systems, and monitoring.

Frank Lemmon has been a practicing software quality engineer for more than three decades. He has broad experience in systems ranging from legacy mainframe computers, to contemporary Windows, Macintosh, Android, and Linux based systems.

He has worked at a number of companies including start-ups and big-name players. Currently, he's working for a public company in the student services sector, where he enjoys enabling new generations of students to attain their higher education in a cost-effective and productive fashion.

Frank acted as a reviewer for CentOS 6 Linux Server Cookbook by Packt Publishing and also helped review OWASP Developer's Guide, second edition.

www.PacktPub.com

Support files, eBooks, discount offers, and more

For support files and downloads related to your book, please visit www.PacktPub.com.

Did you know that Packt offers eBook versions of every book published, with PDF and ePub files available? You can upgrade to the eBook version at www.PacktPub.com and as a print book customer, you are entitled to a discount on the eBook copy. Get in touch with us at service@packtpub.com for more details.

At www.PacktPub.com, you can also read a collection of free technical articles, sign up for a range of free newsletters and receive exclusive discounts and offers on Packt books and eBooks.

https://www2.packtpub.com/books/subscription/packtlib

Do you need instant solutions to your IT questions? PacktLib is Packt's online digital book library. Here, you can search, access, and read Packt's entire library of books.

Why subscribe?

- Fully searchable across every book published by Packt
- Copy and paste, print, and bookmark content
- On demand and accessible via a web browser

Free access for Packt account holders

If you have an account with Packt at www.PacktPub.com, you can use this to access PacktLib today and view 9 entirely free books. Simply use your login credentials for immediate access.

Table of Contents

Preface

CentOS 7 Linux is one of the most reliable Linux operating systems to be used for multiple functionalities in a computer infrastructure. It is like Pandora's box for any system administrator in that he can shape it to perform any task for his environment.

Having a CentOS 7 server in any infrastructure can help deploy a number of useful services to maintain, secure, and manage the infrastructure in a smart and automated way.

What this book covers

Chapter 1, Advanced User Management, teaches you how to manage users and groups on CentOS 7 to get a better understanding of how it is organized.

Chapter 2, Security, shows the best practices to secure your CentOS 7 and some of its valuable services from many attacks that could disable the services or expose some critical data.

Chapter 3, Linux for Different Purposes, enumerates and introduces a step-by-step tutorial on how to set up a list of very useful services that your computer infrastructure should have.

Chapter 4, Mail Server with Postfix, introduces you to Postfix as a common open source mail server to have it installed and configured for advanced usage.

Chapter 5, Monitoring and Logging, monitors your infrastructure and follows your machine's issues via user-friendly monitoring and logging tools.

Chapter 6, Virtualization, initiates your virtual environment and explores the possibilities and benefits all the virtual technologies can offer.

Chapter 7, Cloud Computing, explores Cloud computing by building your own Cloud environment using OpenStack and its amazing components.

Chapter 8, Configuration Management, takes your infrastructure to an advanced level where everything runs on configuration management using Puppet, as it is one of the most famous configuration management tools in this field.

Chapter 9, Some Additional Tricks and Tools, teaches you the small tricks and tools that can make your life easier when administrating the CentOS 7 server for any use.

What you need for this book

To follow this book properly, we recommend that you have one CentOS 7 server to hold most of these services with the following characteristics:

- CPU: 4 Core 3.00 GHz
- Memory: 6 GB RAM
- Hard Disk: 150 GB
- Network: 1 Gbit/s

Also, you will need some machines with the following characteristics to test the services on:

- CPU: 2 Core 3.00 GHz
- Memory: 2 GB RAM
- Hard Disk: 50 GB
- Network: 1Gbit/s

A good Internet connection and a Gigabit network switch are also required.

Who this book is for

If you are a Linux system administrator with an intermediate administration level, this is your opportunity to master the brand new distribution of CentOS. If you wish to possess a fully sustainable Linux server, with all its new tools and tweaks, that serves a variety of services to your users and customers, this book is ideal for you. It is your ticket to easily adapting to all the changes made in the latest shift.

Conventions

In this book, you will find a number of text styles that distinguish between different kinds of information. Here are some examples of these styles and an explanation of their meaning.

Code words in text, database table names, folder names, filenames, file extensions, pathnames, dummy URLs, user input, and Twitter handles are shown as follows: "We can include other contexts through the use of the include directive."

A block of code is set as follows:

```
<html>
    <title>
  Test page
    </title>
    <body>
  <h1>This is a test page</h1>
    </body>
</html>
```

Any command-line input or output is written as follows:

```
testuser:x:1001:1001::/home/testuser:/bin/bash
```

New terms and **important words** are shown in bold. Words that you see on the screen, for example, in menus or dialog boxes, appear in the text like this: "Then we define the fields asked to fill **Country Name**, **State or Province Name**, **Locality Name**, **Organization Name**, **Organizational Unit Name**, **Common Name**, and **Email Address**."

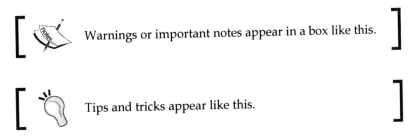

Warnings or important notes appear in a box like this.

Tips and tricks appear like this.

Reader feedback

Feedback from our readers is always welcome. Let us know what you think about this book—what you liked or disliked. Reader feedback is important for us as it helps us develop titles that you will really get the most out of.

To send us general feedback, simply e-mail feedback@packtpub.com, and mention the book's title in the subject of your message.

If there is a topic that you have expertise in and you are interested in either writing or contributing to a book, see our author guide at www.packtpub.com/authors.

Customer support

Now that you are the proud owner of a Packt book, we have a number of things to help you to get the most from your purchase.

Downloading the color images of this book

We also provide you with a PDF file that has color images of the screenshots/diagrams used in this book. The color images will help you better understand the changes in the output. You can download this file from `https://www.packtpub.com/sites/default/files/downloads/MasteringCentOS7LinuxServer_ColorImages.pdf`.

Errata

Although we have taken every care to ensure the accuracy of our content, mistakes do happen. If you find a mistake in one of our books—maybe a mistake in the text or the code—we would be grateful if you could report this to us. By doing so, you can save other readers from frustration and help us improve subsequent versions of this book. If you find any errata, please report them by visiting `http://www.packtpub.com/submit-errata`, selecting your book, clicking on the **Errata Submission Form** link, and entering the details of your errata. Once your errata are verified, your submission will be accepted and the errata will be uploaded to our website or added to any list of existing errata under the Errata section of that title.

To view the previously submitted errata, go to `https://www.packtpub.com/books/content/support` and enter the name of the book in the search field. The required information will appear under the **Errata** section.

Piracy

Piracy of copyrighted material on the Internet is an ongoing problem across all media. At Packt, we take the protection of our copyright and licenses very seriously. If you come across any illegal copies of our works in any form on the Internet, please provide us with the location address or website name immediately so that we can pursue a remedy.

Please contact us at `copyright@packtpub.com` with a link to the suspected pirated material.

We appreciate your help in protecting our authors and our ability to bring you valuable content.

Questions

If you have a problem with any aspect of this book, you can contact us at
questions@packtpub.com, and we will do our best to address the problem.

1
Advanced User Management

In this chapter, we will introduce some advanced user and group management scenarios along with some examples on how to handle advanced level options such as password aging, managing sudoers, and so on, on a day to day basis. Here, we are assuming that we have already successfully installed CentOS 7 along with a root and user credentials as we do in the traditional format. Also, the command examples, in this chapter, assume you are logged in or switched to the root user.

The following topics will be covered:

- User and group management from the GUI and the command line
- Quotas
- Password aging
- Sudoers

Managing users and groups from GUI and the command line

We can add a user to the system using `useradd` from the command line with a simple command, as follows:

```
useradd testuser
```

This creates a user entry in the `/etc/passwd` file and automatically creates the home directory for the user in `/home`. The `/etc/passwd` entry looks like this:

```
testuser:x:1001:1001::/home/testuser:/bin/bash
```

But, as we all know, the user is in a locked state and cannot log in to the system unless we add a password for the user using the command:

```
passwd testuser
```

This will, in turn, modify the /etc/shadow file, at the same time unlock the user, and the user will be able to log in to the system.

By default, the preceding set of commands will create both a user and a group for the testuser user on the system. What if we want a certain set of users to be a part of a common group? We will use the -g option along with the useradd command to define the group for the user, but we have to make sure that the group already exists. So, to create users such as testuser1, testuser2, and testuser3 and make them part of a common group called testgroup, we will first create the group and then we create the users using the -g or -G switches. So, we will do this:

```
# To create the group :
groupadd testgroup

# To create the user with the above group and provide password and unlock
user at the same time :

useradd testuser1 -G testgroup
passwd testuser1

useradd testuser2 -g 1002
passwd testuser2
```

Here, we have used both -g and -G. The difference between them is: with -G, we create the user with its default group and assign the user to the common testgroup as well, but with -g, we create the user as part of the testgroup only. In both cases, we can use either the gid or the group name obtained from the /etc/group file.

There are a couple more options that we can use for an advanced level user creation; for example, for system users with uid less than 500, we have to use the -r option, which will create a user on the system, but the uid will be less than 500. We also can use -u to define a specific uid, which must be unique and greater than 499. Common options that we can use with the useradd command are:

- -c: This option is used for comments, generally to define the user's real name, such as -c "John Doe".
- -d: This option is used to define home-dir; by default, the home directory is created in /home such as -d /var/<user name>.

- -g: This option is used for the group name or the group number for the user's default group. The group must already have been created earlier.

- -G: This option is used for additional group names or group numbers, separated by commas, of which the user is a member. Again, these groups must also have been created earlier.

- -r: This option is used to create a system account with a UID less than 500 and without a home directory.

- -u: This option is the user ID for the user. It must be unique and greater than 499.

There are few quick options that we use with the passwd command as well. These are:

- -l: This option is to lock the password for the user's account

- -u: This option is to unlock the password for the user's account

- -e: This option is to expire the password for the user

- -x: This option is to define the maximum days for the password lifetime

- -n: This option is to define the minimum days for the password lifetime

Quotas

In order to control the disk space used in the Linux filesystem, we must use quota, which enables us to control the disk space and thus helps us resolve low disk space issues to a great extent. For this, we have to enable user and group quotas on the Linux system.

In CentOS 7, the user and group quotas are not enabled by default so we have to enable them first.

To check whether quota is enabled or not, we issue the following command:

```
mount | grep ' / '
```

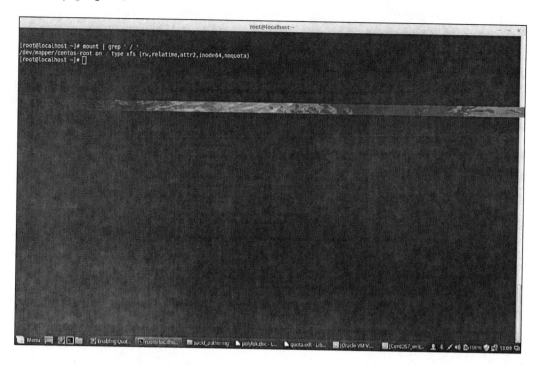

The image shows that the root filesystem is enabled without quota as mentioned by the noquota in the output.

Now, we have to enable quota on the root (/) filesystem, and to do that, we have to first edit the file /etc/default/grub and add the following to GRUB_CMDLINE_ LINUX:

```
rootflags=usrquota,grpquota
```

In file GRUB_CMDLINE_LINUX line should read as follows:

```
GRUB_CMDLINE_LINUX="rd.lvm.lv=centos/swap vconsole.font=latarcyrheb-sun16
rd.lvm.lv=centos/root crashkernel=auto  vconsole.keymap=us rhgb quiet
rootflags=usrquota,grpquota"
```

The output of cat `/etc/default/grub` command should look like the following screenshot:

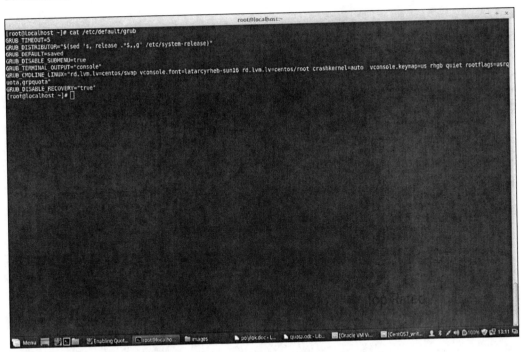

Since we have to reflect the changes we just made, we should backup the grub configuration using the following command:

```
cp /boot/grub2/grub.cfg /boot/grub2/grub.cfg.original
```

Now, we have to rebuild the grub with the changes we just made using the command:

```
grub2-mkconfig -o /boot/grub2/grub.cfg
```

Next, reboot the system. Once it's up, log in and verify that the quota is enabled using the command we used before:

```
mount | grep ' / '
```

It should now show us that the quota is enabled and will show us an output as follows:

```
/dev/mapper/centos-root on / type xfs (rw,relatime,attr2,inode64,usrquota
,grpquota)
```

Add the following lead-in before image and apply CIT style to **mount | grep '/'**

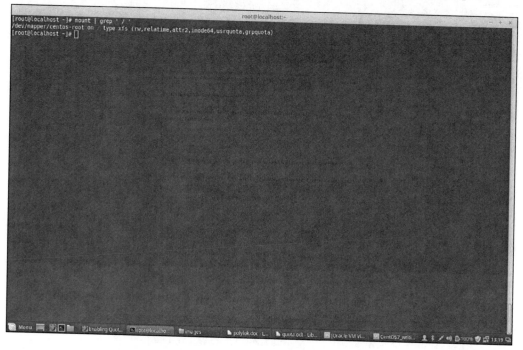

Now, since quota is enabled, we will further install quota using the following to operate quota for different users and groups, and so on:

```
yum -y install quota
```

Once quota is installed, we check the current quota for users using the following command:

```
repquota -as
```

The preceding command will report user quotas in a human-readable format.

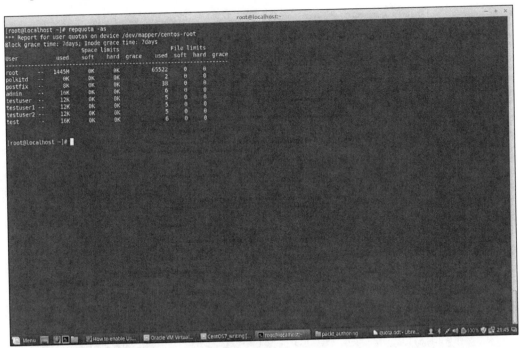

From the preceding screenshot, there are two ways we can limit quota for users and groups; one is setting soft and hard limits for the size of disk space used, and another is limiting the user or group by limiting the number of files they can create. In both cases, soft and hard limits are used. A soft limit is something that warns the user when the soft limit is reached, and the hard limit is the limit that they cannot bypass.

We will use the following command to modify a user quota:

```
edquota -u username
```

The preceding command output shall look like the following screenshot:

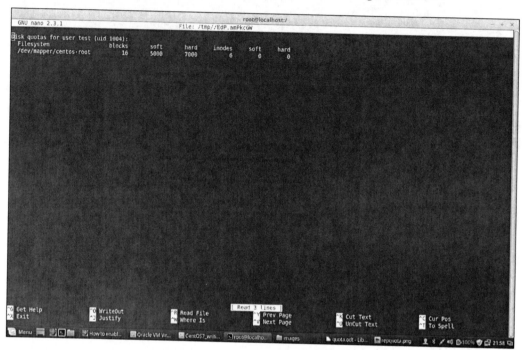

Now, we will use the following command to modify the group quota:

```
edquota -g groupname
```

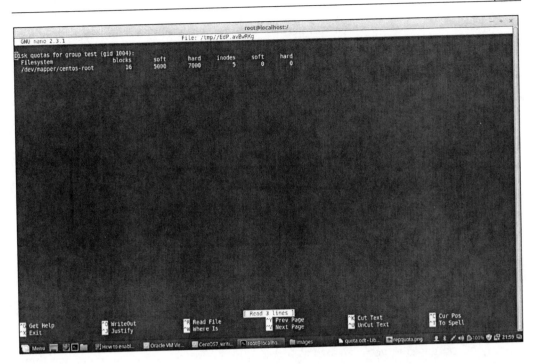

If you have other partitions mounted separately, you have to modify the /etc/fstab file command to enable quota on the filesystem by adding usrquota and grpquota after the defaults for that specific partition as in the following screenshot, where we have enabled the quota for the /var partition:

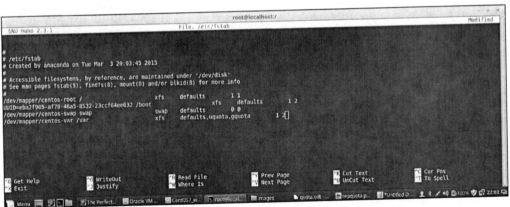

Once you are finished enabling quota, remount the filesystem and run the following commands:

```
To remount /var :
mount -o remount /var
To enable quota :
quotacheck -avugm
quotaon -avug
```

Quota is something all system admins use to handle disk space consumed on a server by users or groups and limit over usage of the space. It thus helps them manage the disk space usage on the system. In this regard, it should be noted that you plan before your installation and create partitions accordingly as well so that the disk space is used properly. Multiple separate partitions such as /var and /home etc are always suggested, as generally these are the partitions which consume most space on a Linux system. So, if we keep them on a separate partition, it will not eat up the root (/) filesystem space and will be more failsafe than using an entire filesystem mounted as only root.

Password aging

It is a good policy to have password aging so that the users are forced to change their passwords at a certain interval. This, in turn, helps to keep the security of the system as well.

We can use chage to configure the password to expire the first time the user logs in to the system.

 Note: This process will not work if the user logs in to the system using SSH.

This method of using chage will ensure that the user is forced to change the password right away.

 If we use only chage <username>, it will display the current password aging value for the specified user and will allow them to be changed interactively.

The following steps need to be performed to accomplish password aging:

1. Lock the user. If the user doesn't exist, we will use the useradd command to create the user. However, we will not assign any password to the user so that it remains locked. But, if the user already exists on the system, we will use the usermod command to lock the user:

    ```
    Usermod -L <username>
    ```

2. Force immediate password change using the following command:

```
chage -d 0 <username>
```

3. Unlock the account. This can be achieved in two ways. One is to assign an initial password and the other is to assign a null password. We will take the first approach as the second one, though possible, is not good practice in terms of security. Therefore, here is what we do to assign an initial password:

   ○ Use the Python command to start the command-line Python interpreter:

     ```
     import crypt; print
     crypt.crypt("Q!W@E#R$","Bing0000/")
     ```

   ○ Here, we have used the `Q!W@E#R$` password with a salt combination of the alphanumeric character: `Bing0000` followed by a / character. The output is the encrypted password, similar to `BiagqBsi6gl1o`.

   ○ Press *Ctrl* + *D* to exit the Python interpreter.

4. At the shell, enter the following command with the encrypted output of the Python interpreter:

   ```
   usermod -p "<encrypted-password>" <username>
   ```

   So, here, in our case, if the username is `testuser`, and the encrypted output is " `BiagqBsi6gl1o`" we will do:

   ```
   usermod -p "BiagqBsi6gl1o" testuser
   ```

Now, upon initial login using the `Q!W@E#R$` password, the user will be prompted for a new password.

Setting the password policy

This is a set of rules defined in some files, which have to be followed when a system user is setting up. It's an important factor in security because one of the many security breach histories was started with hacking user passwords. This is the reason why most organizations set a password policy for their users. All users and passwords must comply with this.

A password policy usually is defined by the following:

- Password aging
- Password length
- Password complexity
- Limit login failures
- Limit prior password reuse

Configuring password aging and password length

Password aging and password length are defined in `/etc/login.defs`. Aging basically means the maximum number of days a password might be used, minimum number of days allowed between password changes, and number of warnings before the password expires. Length refers to the number of characters required for creating the password. To configure password aging and length, we should edit the `/etc/login.defs` file and set different PASS values according to the policy set by the organization.

Note: The password aging controls defined here do not affect existing users; it only affects the newly created users. So, we must set these policies when setting up the system or the server at the beginning. The values we modify are:

- PASS_MAX_DAYS: The maximum number of days a password can be used
- PASS_MIN_DAYS: The minimum number of days allowed between password changes
- PASS_MIN_LEN: The minimum acceptable password length
- PASS_WARN_AGE: The number of days' warning to be given before a password expires

Let's take a look at a sample configuration of the `login.defs` file:

```
root@localhost:~
# Please note that the parameters in this configuration file control the
# behavior of the tools from the shadow-utils component. None of these
# tools uses the PAM mechanism, and the utilities that use PAM (such as the
# passwd command) should therefore be configured elsewhere. Refer to
# /etc/pam.d/system-auth for more information.
#

# *REQUIRED*
#   Directory where mailboxes reside, or name of file, relative to the
#   home directory. If you _do_ define both, MAIL_DIR takes precedence.
#   QMAIL_DIR is for Qmail
#
#QMAIL_DIR      Maildir
MAIL_DIR        /var/spool/mail
#MAIL_FILE      .mail

# Password aging controls:
#
#       PASS_MAX_DAYS   Maximum number of days a password may be used.
#       PASS_MIN_DAYS   Minimum number of days allowed between password changes.
#       PASS_MIN_LEN    Minimum acceptable password length.
#       PASS_WARN_AGE   Number of days warning given before a password expires.
#
PASS_MAX_DAYS   99999
PASS_MIN_DAYS   0
PASS_MIN_LEN    5
PASS_WARN_AGE   7

#
# Min/max values for automatic uid selection in useradd
#
UID_MIN              1000
UID_MAX             60000
# System accounts
SYS_UID_MIN           201
SYS_UID_MAX           999

#
# Min/max values for automatic gid selection in groupadd
#
GID_MIN              1000
GID_MAX             60000
# System accounts
```

Configuring password complexity and limiting reused password usage

By editing the `/etc/pam.d/system-auth` file, we can configure the password complexity and the number of reused passwords to be denied. Password complexity refers to the complexity of the characters used in the password, and the reused password deny refers to denying the desired number of passwords the user used in the past. By setting the complexity, we force the usage of the desired number of capital characters, lowercase characters, numbers, and symbols in a password. The password will be denied by the system until and unless the complexity set by the rules is met. We do this using the following terms:

- **Force capital characters in passwords**: `ucredit=-X`, where X is the number of capital characters required in the password.

- **Force lower case characters in passwords**: `lcredit=-X`, where X is the number of lowercase characters required in the password.

- **Force numbers in passwords**: `dcredit=-X`, where X is the number of numbers required in the password.

- **Force the use of symbols in passwords**: `ocredit=-X`, where X is the number of symbols required in the password. For example:

  ```
  password requisite pam_cracklib.so try_first_pass retry=3 type=
  ucredit=-2 lcredit=-2 dcredit=-2 ocredit=-2
  ```

- **Deny reused passwords**: `remember=X`, where X is the number of past passwords to be denied. For example:

  ```
  password sufficient pam_unix.so sha512 shadow nullok try_first_
  pass use_authtok remember=5
  ```

Let's now take a look at a sample configuration of /etc/pam.d/system-auth:

```
[root@localhost ~]# cat /etc/pam.d/system-auth                          root@localhost:~                                    - + x
#%PAM-1.0
# This file is auto-generated.
# User changes will be destroyed the next time authconfig is run.
auth        required      pam_env.so
auth        required      pam_tally2.so file=/var/log/tallylog deny=3 no_magic_root unlock_time=300
auth        sufficient    pam_unix.so nullok try_first_pass
auth        requisite     pam_succeed_if.so uid >= 1000 quiet_success
auth        required      pam_deny.so

account     required      pam_unix.so
account     required      pam_tally2.so
account     sufficient    pam_localuser.so
account     sufficient    pam_succeed_if.so uid < 1000 quiet
account     required      pam_permit.so

#password   requisite     pam_pwquality.so try_first_pass local_users_only retry=3 authtok_type=
password    requisite     pam_cracklib.so try_first_pass retry=3 type= ucredit=-2 lcredit=-2 dcredit=-2 ocredit=-2
password    sufficient    pam_unix.so sha512 shadow nullok try_first_pass use_authtok
password    required      pam_deny.so

session     optional      pam_keyinit.so revoke
session     required      pam_limits.so
-session    optional      pam_systemd.so
session     [success=1 default=ignore] pam_succeed_if.so service in crond quiet use_uid
session     required      pam_unix.so
[root@localhost ~]#
```

Configuring login failures

We set the number of login failures allowed by a user in the /etc/pam.d/password-auth, /etc/pam.d/system-auth, and /etc/pam.d/login files. When a user's failed login attempts are higher than the number defined here, the account is locked and only a system administrator can unlock the account. To configure this, make the following additions to the files. The following deny=X parameter configures this, where X is the number of failed login attempts allowed.

Add these two lines to the /etc/pam.d/password-auth and /etc/pam.d/system-auth files and only the first line to the /etc/pam.d/login file:

```
auth           required      pam_tally2.so file=/var/log/tallylog deny=3 no_
magic_root unlock_time=300

account        required      pam_tally2.so
```

The following screenshot is a sample /etc/pam.d/system-auth file:

The following is a sample /etc/pam.d/login file:

To see failures, use the following command:

```
pam_tally2 -user=<User Name>
```

To reset the failure attempts and to enable the user to log in again, use the following command:

```
pam_tally2 -user=<User Name> --reset
```

Sudoers

Separation of user privileges is one of the main features in Linux operating systems. Normal users operate in limited privilege sessions to limit the scope of their influence on the entire system. One special user exists on Linux that we know already is root, which has super-user privileges. This account doesn't have any restrictions that are present to normal users. Users can execute commands with super-user or root privileges in a number of different ways.

There are mainly three different ways to obtain root privileges on a system:

- Log in to the system as root.
- Log in to the system as any user and then use the su - command. This will ask you for the root password and once authenticated, will give you the root shell session. We can disconnect this root shell using *Ctrl + D* or using the command exit. Once exited, we will come back to our normal user shell.
- Run commands with root privileges using sudo without spawning a root shell or logging in as root. This sudo command works as follows:
  ```
  sudo <command to execute>
  ```

Unlike su, sudo will request the password of the user calling the command, not the root password.

The sudo doesn't work by default and requires to be set up before it functions correctly.

In the following section, we will see how to configure sudo and modify the /etc/sudoers file so that it works the way we want it to.

visudo

The sudo is modified or implemented using the /etc/sudoers file, and visudo is the command that enables us to edit the file.

> Note: This file should not be edited using a normal text editor to avoid potential race conditions in updating the file with other processes. Instead, the `visudo` command should be used.

The `visudo` command opens a text editor normally, but then validates the syntax of the file upon saving. This prevents configuration errors from blocking `sudo` operations.

By default, `visudo` opens the `/etc/sudoers` file in vi editor, but we can configure it to use the `nano` text editor instead. For that, we have to make sure `nano` is already installed or we can install `nano` using:

```
yum install nano -y
```

Now, we can change it to use `nano` by editing the `~/.bashrc` file:

```
export EDITOR=/usr/bin/nano
```

Then, source the file using:

```
. ~/.bashrc
```

Now, we can use `visudo` with `nano` to edit the `/etc/sudoers` file. So, let's open the `/etc/sudoers` file using `visudo` and learn a few things.

We can use different kinds of aliases for different sets of commands, software, services, users, groups, and so on. For example:

```
Cmnd_Alias NETWORKING = /sbin/route, /sbin/ifconfig, /bin/ping, /sbin/
dhclient, /usr/bin/net, /sbin/iptables, /usr/bin/rfcomm, /usr/bin/wvdial,
/sbin/iwconfig, /sbin/mii-tool
```

```
Cmnd_Alias SOFTWARE = /bin/rpm, /usr/bin/up2date, /usr/bin/yum
```

```
Cmnd_Alias SERVICES = /sbin/service, /sbin/chkconfig
```

We can use these aliases to assign a set of command execution rights to a user or a group. For example, if we want to assign the NETWORKING set of commands to the group `netadmin` we will define:

```
%netadmin ALL = NETWORKING
```

Otherwise, if we want to allow the wheel group users to run all the commands, we will do the following:

```
%wheel   ALL=(ALL)   ALL
```

If we want a specific user, `john`, to get access to all commands, we will do the following:

```
john   ALL=(ALL)   ALL
```

We can create different groups of users, with overlapping membership:

```
User_Alias       GROUPONE = abby, brent, carl
User_Alias       GROUPTWO = brent, doris, eric,
User_Alias       GROUPTHREE = doris, felicia, grant
```

Group names must start with a capital letter. We can then allow members of GROUPTWO to update the `yum` database and all the commands assigned to the preceding software by creating a rule like this:

```
GROUPTWO     ALL = SOFTWARE
```

If we do not specify a user/group to run, `sudo` defaults to the root user.

We can allow members of GROUPTHREE to shut down and reboot the machine by creating a command alias and using that in a rule for GROUPTHREE:

```
Cmnd_Alias        POWER = /sbin/shutdown, /sbin/halt, /sbin/reboot, /sbin/
restart
GROUPTHREE   ALL = POWER
```

We create a command alias called POWER that contains commands to power off and reboot the machine. We then allow the members of GROUPTHREE to execute these commands.

We can also create Runas aliases, which can replace the portion of the rule that specifies to the user to execute the command as:

```
Runas_Alias       WEB = www-data, apache
GROUPONE     ALL = (WEB) ALL
```

This will allow anyone who is a member of GROUPONE to execute commands as the www-data user or the apache user.

Just keep in mind that later, rules will override previous rules when there is a conflict between the two.

There are a number of ways that you can achieve more control over how sudo handles a command. Here are some examples:

The updatedb command associated with the mlocate package is relatively harmless. If we want to allow users to execute it with root privileges without having to type a password, we can make a rule like this:

```
GROUPONE      ALL = NOPASSWD: /usr/bin/updatedb
```

NOPASSWD is a tag that means no password will be requested. It has a companion command called PASSWD, which is the default behavior. A tag is relevant for the rest of the rule unless overruled by its twin tag later down the line.

For instance, we can have a line like this:

```
GROUPTWO      ALL = NOPASSWD: /usr/bin/updatedb, PASSWD: /bin/kill
```

In this case, a user can run the updatedb command without a password as the root user, but entering the root password will be required for running the kill command. Another helpful tag is NOEXEC, which can be used to prevent some dangerous behavior in certain programs.

For example, some programs, such as `less`, can spawn other commands by typing this from within their interface:

```
!command_to_run
```

This basically executes any command the user gives it with the same permissions that `less` is running under, which can be quite dangerous.

To restrict this, we could use a line like this:

```
username     ALL = NOEXEC: /usr/bin/less
```

You should now have clear understanding of what `sudo` is and how we modify and provide access rights using `visudo`. There are many more things left here. You can check the default `/etc/sudoers` file, which has a good number of examples, using the `visudo` command, or you can read the `sudoers` manual as well.

One point to remember is that root privileges are not given to regular users often. It is important for us to understand what these commands do when you execute with root privileges. Do not take the responsibility lightly. Learn the best way to use these tools for your use case, and lock down any functionality that is not needed.

Reference

Now, let's take a look at the major reference used throughout the chapter:

```
https://access.redhat.com/documentation/en-US/Red_Hat_Enterprise_
Linux/7/html/System_Administrators_Guide/index.html
```

Summary

In this chapter, you learned about some advanced user management and how to manage users through the command line, along with password aging, quota, exposure to `/etc/sudoers`, and how to modify them using `visudo`. User and password management is a regular task that a system administrator performs on servers, and it has a very important role in the overall security of the system.

In the next chapter, we will look into advanced security features called **Security-Enhanced Linux (SELinux)**, which comes integrated with CentOS or RedHat Linux operating systems.

2
Security

In this chapter, we will find different tools and utilities that we can use to secure the CentOS system we are using. Security is the most important part for a system or server and thus, a System Administrator's job is always to keep the system up to date and secure from different kind of attacks that happen on a regular basis on servers.

We will discuss several tools here starting from SELinux to other security tools and measures that we can take on a CentOS 7 system. Let's dive into them one by one.

In this chapter, we will look into:

- SELinux and its tools
- Installing SELinux
- Domain transition
- SELinux users
- SELinux audit logs and troubleshooting

Introducing SELinux

Security Enhanced Linux (SELinux) is a set of kernel modifications and user-space tools that have been present in CentOS for quite a long time. It is a kind of mechanism that supports Mandatory Access Control security policies, which were initially developed by the US National Security Agency and later released in the public domain to protect computer systems from malicious intrusion and tampering.

Not many System Administrators use SELinux. Commonly, people are reluctant to learn about SELinux and just disable it directly. However, a properly configured SELinux system can reduce the security risks to a great extent.

SELinux implements **Mandatory Access Control (MAC)**, which works on top of already available **Discretionary Access Control (DAC)** on CentOS 7. DAC is the traditional security model that we have on Linux systems where we have three entities: User, Group, and Others who can have a combination of read, write, and execute permission for files and directories. By default, if a user creates any file in his home directory, the user and his group will have the read access and the user will have write access to the file but the other entity might also have read access to it.

The user who owns the file can change this access policy and grant or revoke access as well as ownership of the file. This might leave critical files exposed to accounts that don't need access to these files and thus pose as a security threat to the running system. It confines every process to its own domain and makes sure that it can interact only with a defined type of files and processes and thus protect the system from a hacker hijacking a script or process and gaining system-wide control through it.

To check what SELinux packages are installed on your system, run the following command:

```
rpm -qa | grep selinux
```

The command will display the following output:

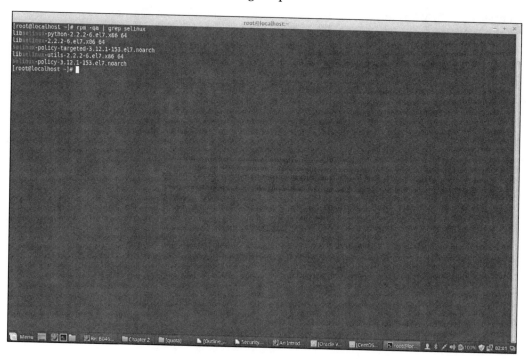

Installing SELinux

Install all the packages with the following command; this will install the rest of the packages and update the already installed packages on the system:

```
yum install policycoreutils policycoreutils-python selinux-policy
selinux-policy-targeted libselinux-utils setroubleshoot-server setools
setools-console mcstrans
```

Now, we will have all the packages required by SELinux installed on the system. Let's install two more services apache (`httpd`) for the web server and FTP (`vsftpd`) server on the system, so that we can test the SELinux with them:

```
yum install httpd vsftpd
```

Run the apache service now using either of the following commands:

```
systemctl start httpd
```

```
service httpd start
```

Check the status of httpd using either of the following commands:

```
service status httpd
```

```
systemctl status httpd
```

These commands will show that it's running, as seen in the following screenshot:

Also, `start vsftpd` using either of the following commands and then check the status of `vsftp` in the same way:

```
systemctl start vsftpd
```

```
service vsftpd start
```

Check the status of ftpd using either of the following commands:

```
service status ftpd
```

```
systemctl status ftpd
```

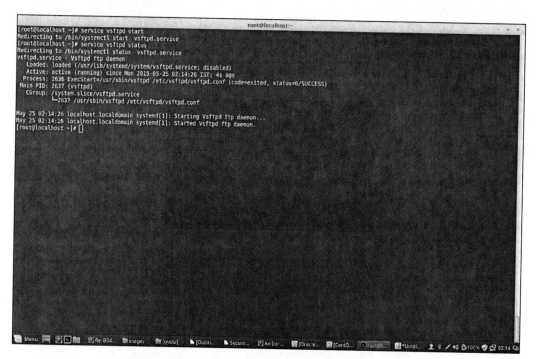

SELinux mode

There are three types of SELinux modes; they are as follows:

- **Enforcing**: In this mode, SELinux enforces its policies onto the system and makes sure that all access by unauthorized users or processes are denied. These access denial events are also logged in to the system as well, which we will look into later on in this chapter.

- **Permissive**: This is like a semi-enabled mode state where SELinux doesn't deny any access as the policies are in permissive mode. This is the best mode to test the SELinux policies.

- **Disabled**: In this mode, the SELinux is in a completely disabled state and no logs are created or permissions are denied.

We can run the following commands to get the present SELinux status:

```
getenforce
```

```
sestatus
```

The outputs from the preceding commands are shown in the following image when SELinux is enabled on the system:

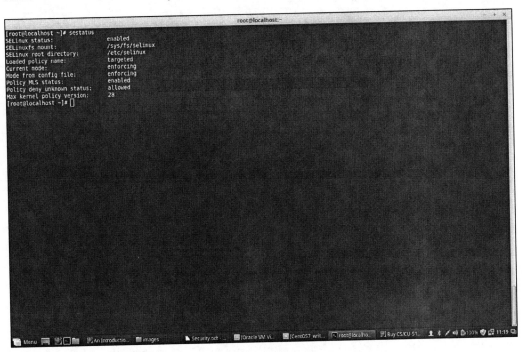

The main SELinux configuration file is `/etc/selinux/config`. We will now enable SELinux by setting up `SELINUX=permissive` in this file, and then saving and rebooting the system.

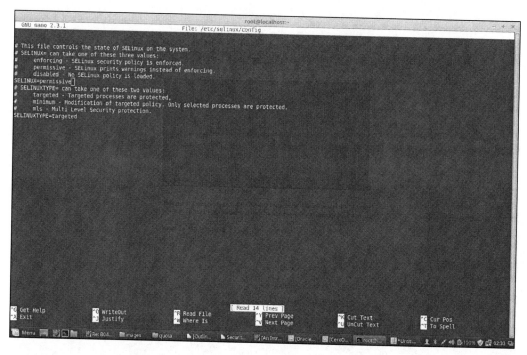

The `SELINUXTYPE` parameter in the `config` file also has three options, as follows:

- **Targeted**: This is the default value that allows you to customize and fine-tune your policies
- **Minimum**: In this mode, only the selected processes are protected
- **MLS**: Multi Level Security is an advanced mode of protection and you need an additional package to install it as well

We will keep the `SELINUXTYPE` at the default value (that is, targeted).

This is necessary to set the SELinux into the permissive mode the first time it runs, as it's required to label all files on the system. Otherwise, processes running under confined domains might fail as they can't access the files with correct contexts.

Once we are set and we reboot the system, it will label all the files, which will take some time depending on the system with SELinux contexts. Since it's in the permissive mode, only failures and access denials will be reported.

We must check the system once it is up for any errors using the following command:

```
grep 'SELinux' /var/log/messages
```

This will show you outputs such as the following if the SELinux is running in permissive mode:

```
May 25 01:54:46 localhost kernel: SELinux:  Disabled at runtime.
```

```
May 25 03:06:40 localhost kernel: SELinux:  Initializing.
```

```
May 25 03:06:58 localhost systemd[1]: Successfully loaded SELinux policy
in 2.863609s.
```

```
May 27 06:31:39 localhost kernel: SELinux:  Initializing.
```

```
May 27 06:31:55 localhost systemd[1]: Successfully loaded SELinux policy
in 1.944267s.
```

Now, since all the rules are loaded and the files are labeled, we have to enable the SELinux enforcing mode instead of the permissive mode. So, edit the SELinux config file once again and set the following to enforcing:

```
SELINUX=enforcing
```

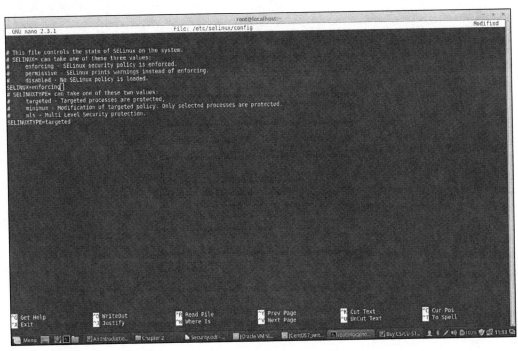

Now, reboot the server once again.

Once it is back, check the SELinux status with the `sestatus` command and it will show you an output similar to the following:

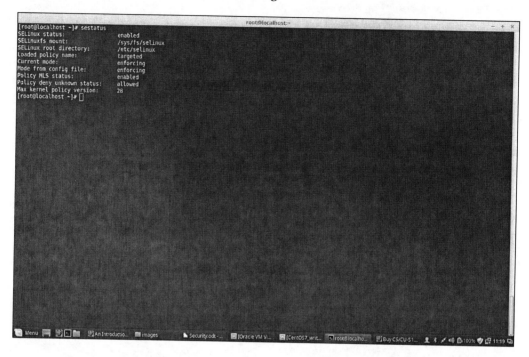

Now, if you `grep` SELinux in `/var/log/messages` you will find the following:

```
May 27 11:18:21 localhost kernel: SELinux: Initializing.
```

```
May 27 11:18:34 localhost systemd[1]: Successfully loaded SELinux policy
in 715.664ms.
```

To check the SELinux enforcing status, run the `getenforce` command, and it will display the status as `enforcing`.

The `sestatus` command will display more details about the operating SELinux configuration as follows:

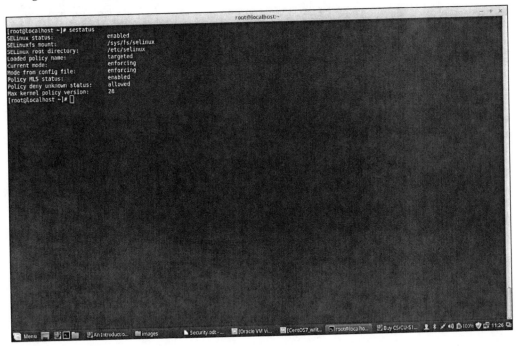

If we want to change the SELinux mode temporarily while running SELinux, we can do that using the `setenforce` command as follows:

```
setenforce permissive
```

Now, `sestatus` will show you the following screen:

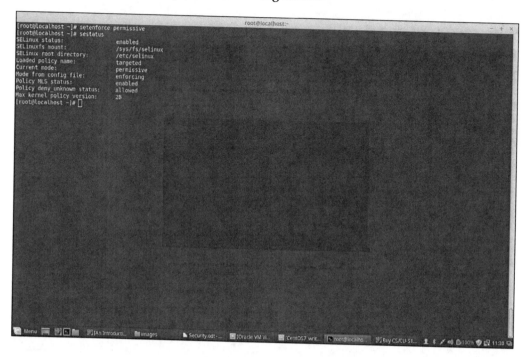

Switch back to the enforcing mode using the following command:

```
setenforce enforcing
```

SELinux policy

You must have noticed from the previous SELinux outputs in `/var/log/messages` that it is based on Policy. Policy means a set of rules that defines the relation, security and access rights to the following:

- **User**: All regular Linux users are defined by one or more SELinux users. However, please note that SELinux users are different from Linux users. Also, note that a running process or a program is defined as subject in the SELinux.

- **Role**: They are like filters that define which user can access a process and so on. It's like a gateway between a user and a process. A user can only run a specific process if the role grants it and the user has access to the role. SELinux is based on **Role Based Access Control (RBAC)**.

- **Subject** and **Object**: Subject is like a process or a program and object is anything than can be acted on; like a file, port, directory, and so on. The actions that are performed by a subject on an object depend on the subject's permissions.

- **Domain**: This is like a wrapper around the Subject (process), which tells the process what it can or can't do. For example, the domain will define the directories, folders, files, ports, and so on a process can access. Domains are related to subject in SELinux.

- **Type**: A file's context is called its type. For example, the context of a file describes whether it's only accessible to the local web server process or it's available to any process within any other directory such as / and so on or which specific SELinux user is the owner of the file. Type is related to the object in SELinux.

In SELinux, policy defines rules for users access to roles, role access to domains, and domain access to types.

There are three forms of access control in SELinux defined by the `SELINUXTYPE` in the `/etc/selinux/config` file:

- **Type Enforcement (TE)**: This is the primary mechanism of access control used in the targeted policy

- **Role-Based Access Control (RBAC)**: This is based around SELinux users (not necessarily the same as the Linux user), but not used in the default targeted policy

- **Multi-Level Security (MLS)**: This is not commonly used and often hidden in the default targeted policy.

The targeted policy is used by default in SELinux and we will continue our discussion based on it here.

Also, remember that SELinux doesn't replace the traditional DAC policy in the Linux system. Instead, if a file access is prohibited by the DAC policy, the SELinux policy will not be evaluated and will not grant access to the file even if is allowed by SELinux.

SELinux policies are loaded in a modular format much like a kernel module into the memory and can be viewed using the following command:

```
semodule -l | more
```

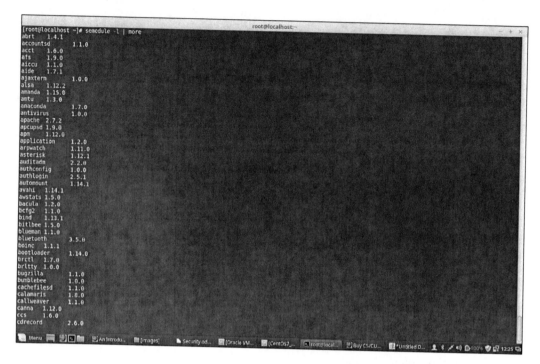

The `semodule` command can be used for installing, removing, reloading, upgrading, enabling, and disabling SELinux policy modules as well.

The module files are located in `/etc/selinux/targeted/modules/active/ modules/` with the `.pp` extension and are not human readable. But, if you look into them closely, you will surely find that they are actually related to different applications in Linux.

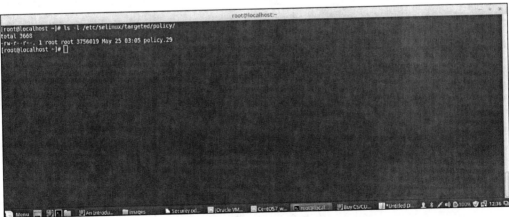

These policy modules are combined into an active policy and are then loaded into the memory. This combined binary policy can be found in the `/etc/selinux/targeted/policy/` directory:

We cannot modify these rules directly but can manage them using the `semanage boolean` command. The output of the `semanage boolean -l | less` command will show us this:

It is clearly evident in the second line of the preceding output that the FTP service access to user home directories is turned off at this moment. We can also see just the status of the `ftpd` service policies using the following command pipeline:

```
semanage boolean -l | grep ftpd
```

Now, to allow FTP users to access their home directories and allow read-write access we have to issue the following commands. First check the status of the `ftp_home_dir` policy using the following command:

getsebool ftp_home_dir

This will display the following output:

ftp_home_dir --> off

Now, enable access to the user home directory using `setsebool -P` for permanent:

setsebool -P ftp_home_dir on

Now, check the status again:

getsebool ftp_home_dir

This will show the following output:

ftp_home_dir --> on

Now, users will be allowed to access their home directories via the FTP provided; the FTP protocol is allowed in the firewall.

SELinux files and processes

So far, we have looked into the basics of SELinux and how to allow a service like vsftpd to allow users to access their files from ftp. Let's look into the details of the context of files and how they are defined in SELinux. Context in SELinux is a collection of information related to security, which helps SELinux determine access control policies. In Linux, everything can have a security context such as files, directories, services, or ports but security context means different type of things for different objects.

We can display the SELinux file context for any file by using the `ls -Z` parameter like this:

```
ls -laZ /home/test/*
```

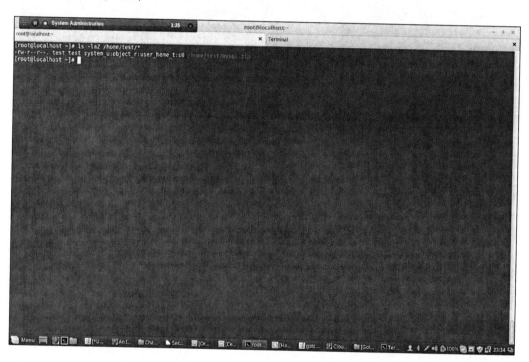

In the preceding output, this part is the SELinux context for that specific file:

```
system_u:object_r:user_home_t:s0
```

There are four parts, each separated by a colon (`:`). The first part is the SELinux user context, which is shown as `system_u` here. As you already know, each Linux system user is mapped to a SELinux user and here it is `system_u`.

The second part is the SELinux role, which is `object_r` here.

The most important part here is the third part, which is mentioned as `user_home_t`. This is the one that defines the type of file, and from this, we can understand that it belongs to the user's home directory.

The fourth part (s0) actually explains the sensitivity of the file and it actually works with the Multi-Level Security. The first three parts are more important, so we will only work with them.

Now, let's look at the SELinux process context using the `httpd` file that we installed before. Let's start the `httpd` process first using:

```
systemctl httpd start
```

Now let's run the `ps` command with the additional `-z` flag to see the process context:

```
ps -efZ | grep httpd
```

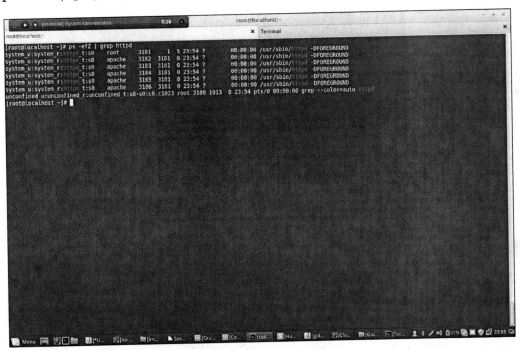

The security context in the preceding output is as follows:

```
system_u:system_r:httpd_t:s0
```

In SELinux, users are suffixed by `_u`, roles are suffixed by `_r`, and types are suffixed by `_t`.

For a process to run like `httpd`, it needs to access its files and action them. We already have seen that each process can only have access to certain types (files, directories, ports, and so on).

SELinux defines these access rules in a policy. These access rules follow the standard `allow` statement as follows:

```
allow <domain> <type>:<class> { <permissions> };
```

A generic `allow` statement indicates:

- Whether a process is of a certain domain
- That the resource object the process is trying to access is of a certain class and type
- Whether it can allow access or deny access

Let's see how this works in consideration with the security context of the https process that we have already looked into.

The document root or the default directory for `httpd` is `/var/www/html`. Now, let's create a file in there and check its security context:

```
touch /var/www/html/index.html
ls -Z /var/www/html/*
```

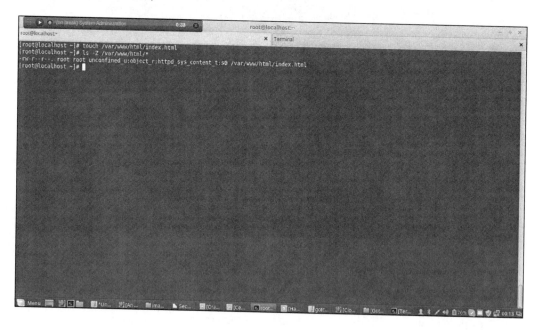

The file context for the `index.html` file we created is shown to be `httpd_sys_content_t`.

We will use the `sesearch` command in the following way to check the type of access allowed for the `httpd` daemon:

```
sesearch --allow --source httpd_t --target httpd_sys_content_t --class
file
```

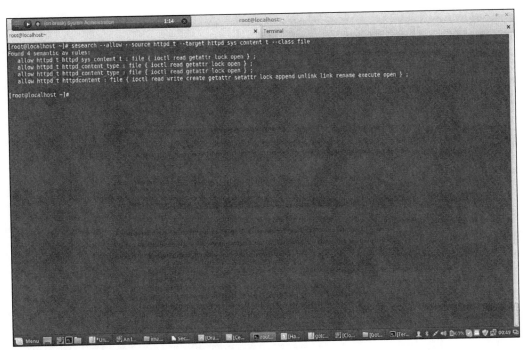

The flags used in the preceding command are easily understandable; source domain is `httpd_t`, which the domain apache is running within. We wanted to list the target resources that are files and have the type context `httpd_sys_content_t`.

Notice the first line of context output in the preceding screenshot is:

```
allow httpd_t httpd_sys_content_t : file { ioctl read getattr lock open }
;
```

Now, if you relate it with the generic allow statement previously, we will clearly understand that the `httpd` service has I/O control, read, get attribute, lock, and open access to the files of the `httpd_sys_content_t` type. And, in our case, the `index.html` file that we created is also of the same type, which means the `httpd` service will have access to this `index.html` file.

Let's create a test web page modifying the `index.html` file so that we can check its output from the browser. Add the following lines into the `index.html` file using your favorite editor and save it:

```
<html>
    <title>
   Test page
    </title>
    <body>
   <h1>This is a test page</h1>
    </body>
</html>
```

We will change the permission of the /var/www folder followed by `httpd restart` using the following commands:

```
chmod -R 755 /var/wwwsystemctl restart httpd
```

You might have to allow the http port in the firewall if you are doing it for the first time using the following commands:

```
firewall-cmd --permanent --add-port=80/tcp

firewall-cmd --permanent --add-service=http

firewall-cmd -reload
```

Now try to access it from the browser. It will show you the output as in the following screenshot:

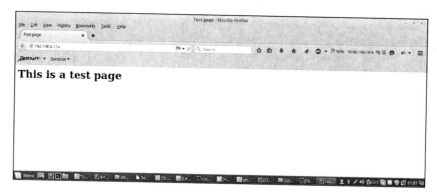

Now, let's see if we change the type context of the `index.html` file and whether we will still be able to access it or not. We will use the `chcon` command to change the type context and will use the `-type` flag for this purpose as shown here:

```
chcon --type var_t /var/www/html/index.html
```

If we check the context of the file using `ls -Z` , it will show us:

```
-rwxr-xr-x. root root unconfined_u:object_r:var_t:s0    /var/www/html/
index.html
```

It is visible that the type has been changed to `var_t` here.

Now, if you try to access the web page again, it will show you an error or you might see a default page but not the same page that we saw before. This is because we have changed the type context for the `index.html` file.

To revert it, we will use the following command:

```
restorecon -v /var/www/html/index.html
```

Now, if we access the site again, we will see that it works again as before.

The SELinux enforcing mode guarantees that unless otherwise specified by the policy, processes and files are created with the same context as their parents. What this means is that if process A is spawning process B, the spawned process B will run in the same domain as process A unless specified differently by the SELinux policy, and similarly, if we have a directory with some `context_t` type, unless defined otherwise, the files or directories under it will inherit the same `context_t` type.

In CentOS 7, the contexts of all files that exist in the system are listed in the `/etc/selinux/targeted/contexts/files/file_contexts` file and contexts of new directories and files are recorded in the `/etc/selinux/targeted/contexts/files/file_contexts.local` file. Since `chcon` is used to change context temporarily and `restorecon` is used to restore the context, `restorecon` actually looks into this file to restore the original context of a file.

Let's create `/www/html`:

```
mkdir -p /www/html
```

Now, we copy the contents from `/var/www/html` to `/www/html` using the following command:

```
cp /var/www/html/index.html /www/html/
```

If we check the context of the file, we will find that it's different from what we have for `/var/www/html/index.html` and its `default_t` because that is the context of its parent directory.

Further, even if we change the `httpd` configuration file to an open `index.html` file from this new location, we will still face errors because the contexts are not right yet. While copying the `index.html` file from `/var/www/html` to `/www/html`, it inherited the context from its parent directory, which is `default_t`.

To resolve this issue we will have to change its context.

To permanently change the context of the `index.html` file under `/www/html` that we created before, we will follow two steps:

```
semanage fcontext --add --type httpd_sys_content_t "/www(/.*)?"
semanage fcontext --add --type httpd_sys_content_t "/www/html(/.*)?"
```

Now, we check the context database from the `/etc/selinux/targeted/contexts/files/file_contexts.local` file:

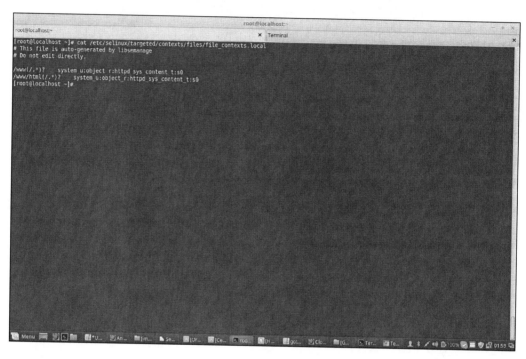

Now, we will run the `restorecon` command to relabel the file or directory to what has been recorded in the previous step:

```
restorecon -Rv /www
```

This will work in three levels; first it will relabel the `/www` directory, then the `/www/html` directory, and finally, the `/www/html/index.html` file.

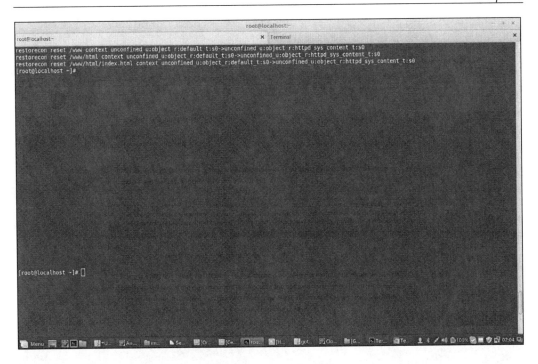

Now, if we try to access the web page it should work.

There is also a command called `matchpathcon`, and it is very handy to troubleshoot context related issues. It can compare the context of a current resource with what's under the SELinux context database and report back. If the match is different, it suggests the changes required. We can run the command using the `-V` flag for `/www/html/index.html` in the following way:

```
matchpathcon -V /www/html/index.html
```

Domain transition

Now, let's find out how a process accesses other processes.

Let's consider that the `vsftpd` process is running; if it's not started, we can start it using the following command:

```
systemctl start vsftpd
```

The `vsftpd` process is started by the `systemd` process; this is a replacement of the `Sys V init` process and runs within a context of `init_t`:

```
ps -eZ | grep init
```

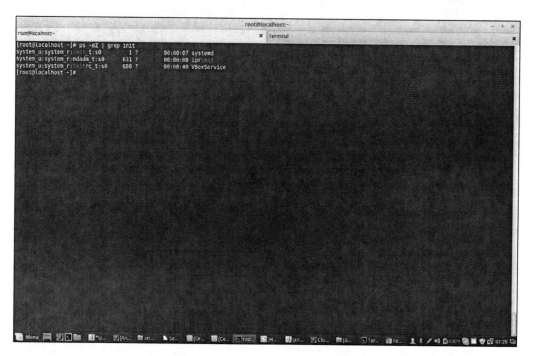

The `systemd` process running under the `init_t` domain is very short lived; it invokes `/usr/sbin/vsftpd`, which has a type context `ftpd_exec_t`, and when this binary executable starts, it becomes the `vsftpd` service itself and runs in the `ftpd_t` domain.

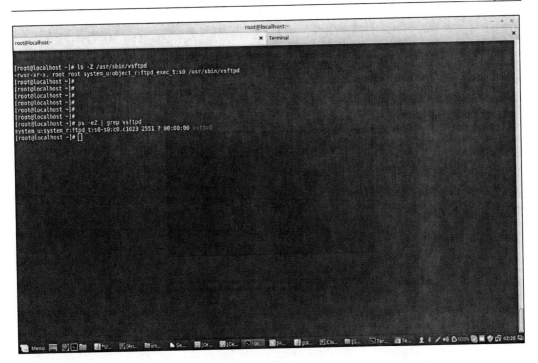

So, here's the `systemd` process running under the `init_t` domain executing a binary file with the `ftpd_exec_t` type. The binary file then starts a service within the `ftpd_t` domain.

Domain transition is followed by three strict rules:

- The parent process of the source domain must have the permission to execute the application between both the domains
- The file context for that application must be identified as an entry point for the target domain
- The original domain must be allowed to transit to the target domain

Let's run the `sesearch` command for the `vsftpd` service to check whether it follows these rules:

1. First, the source domain `init_t` must have permission to execute the application in the `ftpd_exec_t` context. So we run:

   ```
   sesearch -s init_t -t ftpd_exec_t -c file -p execute -Ad
   ```

   We found the following output:

   ```
   allow init_t ftpd_exec_t : file { read getattr execute open } ;
   ```

So, the `init_t` can read, get attribute, execute, and open files of the `ftpd_exec_t` context.

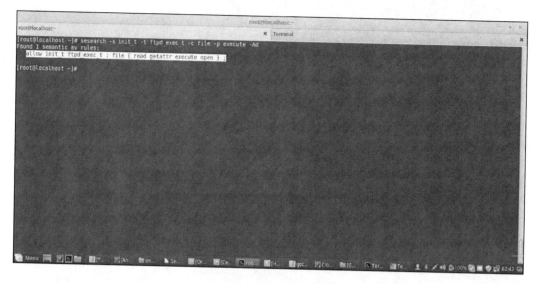

2. Next, we check whether the binary file is the entry point for the target domain `ftpd_t`:

```
sesearch -s ftpd_t -t ftpd_exec_t -c file -p entrypoint -Ad
```

We found that it is:

```
allow ftpd_t ftpd_exec_t : file { ioctl read getattr lock execute
execute_no_trans entrypoint open } ;
```

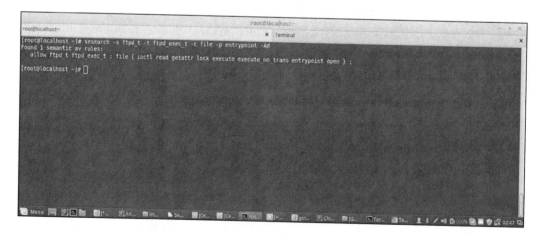

3. Finally, the source domain `init_t` needs to have permission to transit to the target `ftpd_t` domain:

```
sesearch -s init_t -t ftpd_t -c process -p transition -Ad
```

We can see that the source domain has that permission as well:

```
allow init_t ftpd_t : process transition ;
```

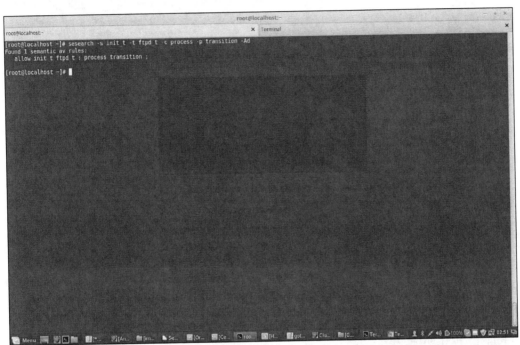

SELinux also supports processes that run under unconfined domains; for example, `unconfined_t`. This is the domain where logged in users run their processes by default.

SELinux users

As explained before, SELinux users are different from normal Linux users. SELinux users are defined in the policy that's loaded into the memory at boot time, and there are only a few of these users.

After SELinux is enforced, each regular user account is mapped to a SELinux user account. There can be multiple user accounts mapped to the same SELinux user. This enables the normal user account to inherit the permission of its SELinux counterpart.

To view the mapping, we will run the following command:

```
semanage login -l
```

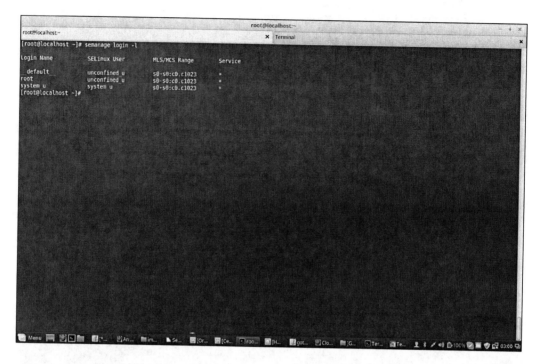

Here, we will find that there are only three Login Names as shown in the preceding screenshot representing the Linux user accounts. Any Linux user is mapped to the entry shown as __default__ here. The user root is not mapped to default, instead it has its own entry and there is system_u for the running processes or services. The second column indicates the SELinux user they are mapped to. Normal user accounts and roots are mapped to unconfined_u, whereas the processes and services are mapped to the system_u SELinux user. For now, ignore the third column, which shows the **Multi-Level Security (MLS) Multi Category Security** (MCS) class for the user, and the last column (service) as well.

To see the SELinux users that are available in the system, use the `semanage user` command as follows:

```
semanage user -l
```

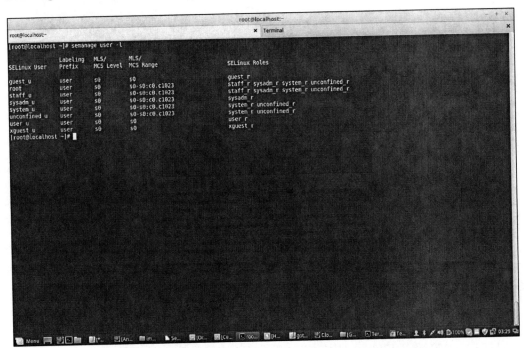

The table in the preceding screenshot shows the SELinux users available in the system and the roles they have access to. We already discussed that SELinux roles are like gateways between a user and a process. We also compared them to filters, where a user can enter a role, provided the role grants it. If a role is authorized to access a process domain, the users associated with that role will be able to enter that process domain.

Now, run the id -z command as the root user. It will show the SELinux security context for the root:

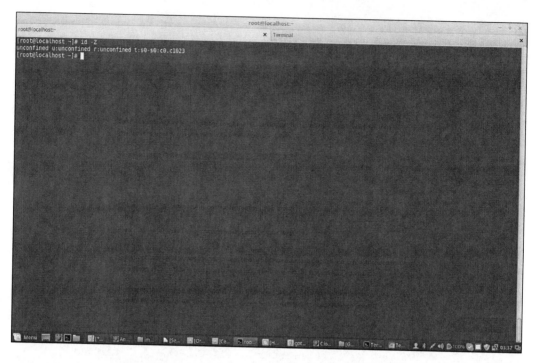

So, the root user is mapped to the unconfined_t SELinux user, which is authorized to the unconfined_r role, which in turn is authorized to run processes in the unconfined_t domain.

We already saw that there are several SELinux users available in the system. Let's discuss some of them here:

- guest_u: This type of user doesn't have access to the X Windows system or networking and also cannot execute the su or sudo commands

- xguest_u: This type of user has access to GUI and the network via the browser only

- user_u: This type of user has general access to GUI and the network but cannot run su or sudo

- staff_u: This is the same as user_u except that they can run sudo.

- system_u: This is meant for system services and are not mapped with regular user accounts

Restricting access to su or sudo

We can restrict a user from running the `su` or `sudo` commands by changing the user's SELinux user mapping like this:

```
semanage login -a -s user_u test
```

The preceding command will change the Linux `test` user's mapping to `user_u` and will not allow the `su` or `sudo` commands access.

 This will only take effect when the user is not logged in.

Restricting permissions to run scripts

To restrict the Linux `test` user's ability to run scripts we have to do two things. First, we change the user's mapping to `guest_u`, the same way as we did previously:

```
semanage login -a -s guest_u test
```

By default, SELinux allows users mapped to `guest_t` to execute scripts from their home directories. We can confirm the same using the following command:

```
getsebool allow_guest_exec_content
```

It will show that `guest_exec_content` is on. So, the second step is that we disable the `guest_exec_content` using this:

```
setsebool allow_guest_exec_content off
```

Now, the test user for whom we changed the mapping won't be able to execute any scripts even if he has full access to his home directory and the files that he creates there.

If we do a grep to see what SELinux is preventing `/var/log/messages`, it will show us the access denial along with an alert ID. We can note the alert ID and run:

```
sealert -1 <alert id>
```

It will show us full details about the access denial along with some suggestions to remove it as well.

Restricting access to services

Assume we have a user admin with access to sudo so that it can run commands with sudo to start and stop services like httpd. Now, even if the user has sudo accesses, we can stop him from management access to services by changing his user mapping to user_u, the same way we did before:

```
semanage login -a -s user_u admin
```

This will restrict the user admin from restarting or stopping services.

We can verify the user_u access info by running the seinfo command as the root:

```
seinfo -uuser_u -x
```

This output shows the roles user_u can have access to; they are object_r and user_r.

Let's go one step further and run the same command to find out what domains the user_r role is authorized to enter:

```
seinfo -ruser_r -x
```

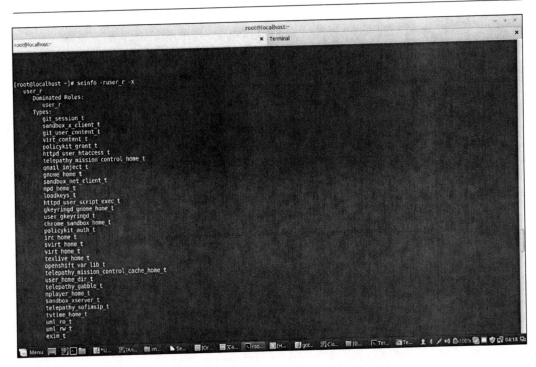

There is a long list of domains the role can enter. Now, let's find out whether the role can enter the domain `httpd_t` by just filtering the output with grep:

```
seinfo -ruser_r -x | grep httpd_t
```

This will return nothing, which means that the `user_r` role is not authorized to enter the `httpd_t` domain, and therefore, it is unable to start the `httpd` process or daemon.

SELinux audit logs

In CentOS 7, we should look into two files for SELinux-related errors and alerts; they are as follows:

- `/var/log/audit/audit.log`
- `/var/log/messages`

SELinux troubleshooting

SELinux comes with some tools that are very useful for checking errors and troubleshooting. We already saw one, `sealert -l <alert id>`, where we gather the alert ID by looking into `/var/log/messages`. There is another command called `ausearch`, which is also very helpful in checking errors if the `auditd` service is running, which is as follows:

```
ausearch -m avc -c httpd
```

Summary

In this chapter, we looked into various aspects of SELinux and how to configure it; we also demonstrated how to use it according to our needs. However, be cautious and never test SELinux on a production system. It is better to use a production replica and test everything there first. The SELinux facility will enhance the security of a system when it's properly configured, but it's best used when strict security controls are necessary and only when it is deployed with care.

In the next chapter, we will look at how Linux can be used for a variety of purposes.

3
Linux for Different Purposes

The plans we make to set up a server infrastructure or a data center are generally the same. We always try to organize services between the servers that we are running, respecting our needs. Servers operating on a Linux system can be used to run multiple services at once or just one depending on how much processing power that service will need and its position inside the network. Following the needs of the users, system administrators should always be ready to set up or to take down services in their infrastructure. Usually, for a basic system installation, there will be a number of services already installed but not well configured.

This chapter will cover some of the main Linux services that most users are in need of, and also how to set up, configure, and operate them. Then we are going to explore some of those service's aspects, how to secure them, and how to operate them in the best way possible.

In this chapter, we are going to learn to:

- Configure a Gateway server using iptables and IP masquerading
- Install a VPN server
- Implement BIND as a DNS server
- Set up and use a web server using Apache-MySQL-PHP with ModSecurity
- Install an FTP server
- Implement OpenSSL in Apache and FTP

Configuring a gateway server

In many network infrastructures, system administrators need to separate their servers and workstation inside multiple subnetworks. Others use private network addresses that can be associated with public addresses using the **Network Address Translation (NAT)** technology. A Linux gateway server is one of the common solutions that can help set up this kind of configuration. The following screenshot is a presentation of an example of an architecture where the Gateway server serves to pass through both local and external networks:

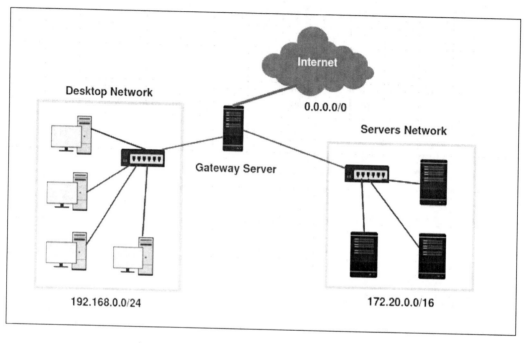

As per the requirement, we are in need of a Linux server with at least two network interfaces (as a best practice). We then need to make a bridge between the two networks associated with them. During this section, we will be working on setting up a gateway between public (external) and private (local) addresses using IP forwarding and NAT rules to route the traffic from the private network to the public network. We will call the external network **Wide Area Network (WAN)** and the local network **Local Area Network (LAN)**.

> The traffic generated from the local network will appear to originate from the Gateway server to the external network. In this example, we will need another machine to present a server inside the LAN network.

First, we will set up the network configuration of the WAN interface. To do so, there will be two options: either the interface will take its IP configuration via DHCP (automatic) or we set it ourselves manually (static). In our case, we will do the automatic configuration since our WAN network is provided by a router that serves DHCP configuration.

We will start by editing the configuration file of the designated interface eth0:

```
$ sudo nano /etc/sysconfig/network-scripts/ifcfg-eth0
```

The file will contain the following lines:

```
HWADDR="XX:XX:XX:XX:XX:XX"
TYPE="Ethernet"
BOOTPROTO="dhcp"
DEFROUTE="yes"
PEERDNS="yes"
PEERROUTES="yes"
IPV4_FAILURE_FATAL="no"
IPV6INIT="yes"
IPV6_AUTOCONF="yes"
IPV6_DEFROUTE="yes"
IPV6_PEERDNS="yes"
IPV6_PEERROUTES="yes"
IPV6_FAILURE_FATAL="no"
DEVICE="eth0"
UUID="01f7dbb3-7ac8-406d-a88b-76082e0fa6eb"
ONBOOT="yes"
```

We should focus on the line where BOOTPROTO is written, which is the protocol to use for the network configuration, and we need to make sure that it is set on dhcp.

The default installation sets all the interfaces to the DHCP configuration unless they have been modified during the installation or later.

Also, we need to make sure that the DEVICE is set to the interface name that we are going to use to serve the DHCP server and as named in our server (for our case it is eth0). Then the option ONBOOT is set to yes.

 After editing the file, if needed, make sure to save the modifications before leaving the text editor.

After making sure that all changes are successfully set, we need to restart the network manager so the machine can take the DHCP configuration:

```
$ sudo systemctl restart network.service
```

During the execution of this step, the network connection may be lost. We need to make sure that we do not need it in the meantime.

Now we can move to the configuration of the second network interface of the gateway server connected to the LAN. For this configuration, we need to use a static IP address.

In a similar way to the first interface, we are going to edit the configuration file of this interface `eth1`:

```
$ sudo nano /etc/sysconfig/network-scripts/ifcfg-eth1
```

Also, this file will contain some configuration files, but we will be interested in only some of them:

```
HWADDR="XX:XX:XX:XX:XX:XX"
TYPE="Ethernet"
BOOTPROTO="dhcp"
DEFROUTE="yes"
PEERDNS="yes"
PEERROUTES="yes"
IPV4_FAILURE_FATAL="no"
IPV6INIT="yes"
IPV6_AUTOCONF="yes"
IPV6_DEFROUTE="yes"
IPV6_PEERDNS="yes"
IPV6_PEERROUTES="yes"
IPV6_FAILURE_FATAL="no"
DEVICE="eth1"
UUID=" b3fcc00e-a7d9-4b55-a32c-1e88e394aaf6"
ONBOOT="yes"
```

This is the default configuration, so we need to change it from a dynamic configuration to a static one.

The modification will consist of modifying some lines and adding others.

We start by changing the configuration protocol from dhcp to static to look like this:

```
BOOTPROTO="static"
```

Then we add the static IP address with this line: IPADDR="10.0.1.1".

Then the network mask, NETMASK="255.255.255.0".

And, finally, we make sure that the option DEVICE is set to eth1 and the option ONBOOT is set to yes.

Again, to make sure that this configuration is successfully applied, we need to restart the network service:

```
$ sudo systemctl restart network.service
```

> If the configuration does not take effect when typing ifconfig, to check the interfaces' configuration we need to run this command:
> ```
> $ sudo systemctl restart network.service
> $ sudo systemctl status network.service
> ```

Now we move on to the configuration of a client, the machine that will be using the gateway server. So we need to configure its interface for the LAN network. Since we are not limited to one specific client, if we have a graphical interface we can just go to the connected interface and enter these configurations:

IP address: 10.0.1.2

Network Mask: 255.255.255.0

Gateway: 10.0.1.1

For the DNS server, we will go with Google DNS, which is very reliable:

DNS server: 8.8.8.8

> It is not an obligation to enter the Google DNS server address. Some sites may be blocking it, others may be using their local DNS server. Depending on the need and if we don't have any, Google DNS will be fine.

If we need to use another CentOS 7 server, we may need to do the same steps during the static server configuration.

We edit the configuration file of the interface:

```
$ sudo nano /etc/sysconfig/network-scripts/ifcfg-eth1
```

By changing the configuration protocol to `static` and add these two lines:

```
IPADDR="10.0.1.2"
NETMASK="255.255.255.0"
```

We also sure that `ONBOOT=yes` and `DEVICE=eth0`.

To use the Google DNS server, we can edit the `/etc/resolv.conf` file:

```
$ nano /etc/resolv.conf
```

To add these two lines:

```
nameserver 8.8.8.8
nameserver 8.8.4.4
```

Then restart the network service:

```
$ sudo systemctl restart network.service
```

We go back to our Gateway server, then start doing the configuration of the IP forwarding. First, we need to enable it for the IPv4 packet forwarding:

```
$ sudo sysctl -w net.ipv4.ip_forward=1
```

To hold maintain configuration on every system restart we need to make a modification to the IP forwarding configuration file:

```
$ sudo nano /etc/sysctl.conf
```

Then add this line and save:

```
net.ipv4.ip_forward = 1
```

To reload the configuration made to the file, we need to run this command:

```
$ sudo sysctl -w
```

The current configuration can be visualized via this command:

```
$ sudo cat /proc/sys/net/ipv4/ip_forward
```

Now we go to enabling NAT configuration. Using `iptables`, we need to enable the IP masquerading. `firewalld` is a service that allows easy configuration of `iptables` easily. To use `firewalld` we will rely on the command `firewalld-cmd`, then we enter the required configuration.

We start by configuring the NAT in `firewalld`. First, we will set the LAN network as a trusted zone:

```
$ sudo firewall-cmd --permanent --zone=trusted --add-source=10.0.1.0/24
```

Then we integrate the LAN interface `eth1` to a zone called `internal`:

```
$ sudo firewall-cmd --change-interface=eth1 --zone=internal --permanent
```

We do the same for the WAN interface `eth0` to a zone called `external`:

```
$ sudo firewall-cmd --change-interface=eth0 --zone=external --permanent
```

Then we configure the `masquerade` option for the external WAN:

```
$ sudo firewall-cmd --zone=external --add-masquerade --permanent
```

For an optional DNS configuration, we can make it pass through the `internal` zone:

```
$ sudo firewall-cmd --zone=internal --add-service=dns --permanent
```

Before we finish, we make sure that the NAT is configured to pass through traffic from the LAN to the WAN interface:

```
$ sudo firewall-cmd --permanent --direct --passthrough ipv4 -t nat -I
POSTROUTING -o eth0 -j MASQUERADE -s 10.0.1.0/24
```

Finally, we need to reload the firewall service so that the configuration takes effect:

```
$ sudo firewall-cmd –reload
```

After this point, the Gateway server should be running well. To test the configuration, we need to ping any website from any machine located on the LAN network:

```
$ ping www.google.com
```

Then we need to see the following kind of output to know that our Gateway server is working correctly:

```
PING www.google.com (216.58.210.196): 56 data bytes
64 bytes from 216.58.210.196: seq=0 ttl=50 time=55.799 ms
64 bytes from 216.58.210.196: seq=1 ttl=50 time=65.751 ms
64 bytes from 216.58.210.196: seq=2 ttl=50 time=54.878 ms
64 bytes from 216.58.210.196: seq=3 ttl=50 time=54.186 ms
```

```
64 bytes from 216.58.210.196: seq=4 ttl=50 time=93.656 ms
--- www.google.com ping statistics ---
5 packets transmitted, 5 packets received, 0% packet loss
round-trip min/avg/max = 54.186/64.854/93.656 ms
```

We would recommend the use of a DHCP server to set up the configuration for all the clients if we are using a desktop machine and are not in need of static configuration. Even for a more advanced DHCP configuration we can associate specific IP addresses to the servers via their interfaces' MAC address.

Setting up a VPN server

OpenVPN is an opensource software application that implements **virtual private network (VPN)** techniques for creating secure point-to-point or site-to-site connections in routed or bridged configurations and remote access facilities.

As a requirement for this section, we are in need for a CentOS 7 server with the capacity to install some packages and make some changes to the network configuration files (internet and root access). At a later stage, we may need to create some authentication certificates. We will cover how to do that too.

First, we will start with the installation of the required packages. And before we do that, OpenVPN isn't available in the default CentOS standard repository, so we need to add the EPEL repository that contains the popular additional packages:

```
$ sudo yum install epel-release
```

After this command is done, we can start OpenVPN. We also need to install an RSA generator to generate the SSL key pairs that we will use to secure the VPN connection:

```
$ sudo yum install openvpn easy-rsa
```

By the end of the execution of the command, the OpenVPN and the easy-rsa are successfully installed on the system.

Now we move to the configuration part of the OpenVPN. Since OpenVPN has an example of a configuration file in its documentation directory, we are going to use the `server.conf` file as our initial configuration and build on that. To do so, we need to copy it to the `/etc` directory:

```
$ sudo cp /usr/share/doc/openvpn-*/sample/sample-config-files/server.conf
/etc/openvpn/
```

Then we can edit it to suit our needs:

```
$ sudo nano /etc/openvpn/server.conf
```

After opening the file, we need to remove some commented lines and make some little changes as follows (using `nano` to look for the lines to change, we should use *Ctrl + w*, then type the word we are looking for).

First, we need to set the RSA encryption length to be 2048 bytes, so we need to make sure that the option line that indicates the filename is going to be used like this.

```
dh dh2048.pem
```

 Some articles suggest that a DH key with 1024 bytes is vulnerable, so we recommend using a DH key with 2048 bytes or more for better security. The vulnerability is called Logjam and for more details, you can read more about it at: `http://sourceforge.net/p/openvpn/mailman/message/34132515/`

Then we need to uncomment the line `push redirect-gateway def1 bypass-dhcp""`, which tells the client to redirect all traffic to OpenVPN.

Next we need to set a DNS server to the client, since it will not be able to use the one provided by the ISP. Again, I will go with the Google DNS `8.8.8.8` and `8.8.4.4`:

```
push "dhcp-option DNS 8.8.8.8"
push "dhcp-option DNS 8.8.4.4"
```

Finally, to lead a smooth run for the OpenVPN, we need to run it through no privileges first. To do so we need to run it through a user and group called `nobody`:

```
user nobody
group nobody
```

Then save the file and exit.

By now, the configuration part of the OpenVPN service is done. We'll move on to the certificate and key generation part, where we need to create some script using Easy RSA. We start by creating a directory of Easy RSA in the configuration folder of the OpenVPN:

```
$ sudo mkdir -p /etc/openvpn/easy-rsa/keys
```

Then we need to populate the folder with the predefined scripts of Easy RSA that generate keys and certificates:

```
$ sudo cp -rf /usr/share/easy-rsa/2.0/* /etc/openvpn/easy-rsa/
```

To perform an easy VPN setup, we will start by typing our information once and for all in the vars file:

```
$ sudo nano /etc/openvpn/easy-rsa/vars
```

We are basically changing the lines that start with export KEY_ to update their values to match the ones of the organization desired, and at some point we may need to uncomment them:

```
export KEY_COUNTRY="UK"

export KEY_PROVINCE="GL"

export KEY_CITY="London"

export KEY_ORG="City-Center"

export KEY_EMAIL="user@packt.co.uk"

export KEY_OU="PacktPublishing"


# X509 Subject Field
export KEY_NAME="server"


export KEY_CN="openvpn.packt.co.uk"
```

Then save the file and exit.

The field KEY_NAME represents the name of the files .key and .crt.

The field KEY_CN is where we should put the domain or the sub-domain that leads to our VPN server.

To make sure that no issues arise during our use of the OpenSSL configuration file due to a version update, we will remove the version from the filename:

```
$ sudo cp /etc/openvpn/easy-rsa/openssl-1.0.0.cnf /etc/openvpn/easy-rsa/
openssl.cnf
```

Now we move to the creation of certificate and keys creation. We need to be in the /etc/openvpn/easy-ras folder to run the scripts:

```
$ cd /etc/openvpn/easy-rsa
```

Then we start the source in the variables:

```
$ sudo source ./vars
```

After that we clean any old generated keys and certificates:

```
$ sudo ./clean-all
```

Then we build the certification authority, which has its information already defined as default options:

```
$ sudo ./build-ca
```

Now we create the keys and certificates for our VPN server. We skip the challenge password phase by pressing *Enter*. Then we make sure to validate by typing Y for the last step:

```
$ sudo ./build-key-server server
```

When running this command, we should see the following message if it is running correctly:

```
Check that the request matches the signature
Signature ok
The Subject's Distinguished Name is as follows
countryName              :PRINTABLE:'UK'
stateOrProvinceName     :PRINTABLE:'GL'
localityName             :PRINTABLE:'London'
organizationName         :PRINTABLE:'City-Center'
organizationalUnitName:PRINTABLE:'PacktPublishing'
commonName               :PRINTABLE:'server'
name                     :PRINTABLE:'server'
emailAddress             :IA5STRING:'user@packt.co.uk'
```

Also, we need to generate the Diffie-Hellman (dh) key exchange. This may take a while longer, as compared to the other commands:

```
$ sudo ./build-dh
```

After finishing this step, we will have all our keys and certificates ready. We need to copy them so they can be used by our OpenVPN service:

```
$ cd /etc/openvpn/easy-rsa/keys
$ sudo cp dh2048.pem ca.crt server.crt server.key /etc/openvpn
```

All the clients of this VPN server need certificates to get authenticated. So we need to share those keys and certificates with the desired clients. It is best to generate separate keys for each client that needs to connect.

For this example, we will only generate keys for one client:

```
$ cd /etc/openvpn/easy-rsa
$ sudo ./build-key client
```

With this step, we can say that we are done with the certificates.

Now for the routing step. We will do the routing configuration using `iptables` directly without the need of using `firewalld`.

If we want to only use the `iptables` configuration, we will first make sure that its services are installed:

```
$ sudo yum install iptables-services
```

Then disable the `firewalld` service:

```
$ sudo systemctl mask firewalld
$ sudo systemctl enable iptables
$ sudo systemctl stop firewalld
$ sudo systemctl start iptables
$ sudo iptables --flush
```

Then we add the rule to `iptables` that does the forwarding of the routing to the OpenVPN subnet:

```
$ sudo iptables -t nat -A POSTROUTING -s 10.0.1.0/24 -o eth0 -j
MASQUERADE
$ sudo iptables-save > /etc/sysconfig/iptables
```

Then we need to enable IP forwarding in `sysctl` by editing the file `sysctl.conf`:

```
$ sudo nano /etc/sysctl.conf
```

Then add the following line:

```
net.ipv4.ip_forward = 1
```

Finally, restart the network service so this configuration can take effect:

```
$ sudo systemctl restart network.service
```

We can now start the OpenVPN service, but before we do this, we need to add it to `systemctl`:

```
$ sudo systemctl -f enable openvpn@server.service
```

Then we can start the service:

```
$ sudo systemctl start openvpn@server.service
```

If we want to check whether the service is running, we can use the command
`systemctl`:

```
$ sudo systemctl status openvpn@server.service
```

We should see this message with the activity status `active (running)`:

```
openvpn@server.service - OpenVPN Robust And Highly Flexible Tunneling
Application On server
    Loaded: loaded (/usr/lib/systemd/system/openvpn@.service; enabled)
    Active: active (running) since Thu 2015-07-30 15:54:52 CET; 25s ago
```

After this check, we can say that our VPN server configuration is done. We can now
go to the client configuration regardless of the operating system. We need to copy the
certificates and the keys from the server. We need to copy these three files:

```
/etc/openvpn/easy-rsa/keys/ca.crt
```

```
/etc/openvpn/easy-rsa/keys/client.crt
```

```
/etc/openvpn/easy-rsa/keys/client.key
```

There are a variety of tools to copy these files from the server to any client. The easiest
one is scp, the shell copy command between two Unix machines. For Windows
machines we can use folder sharing tools such as Samba, or we can use another tool
equivalent to SCP called **WinSCP**.

From the client machine, we start by copying the desired files:

```
$ scp user@openvpn.packt.co.uk:/etc/openvpn/easy-rsa/keys/ca.crt /home/
user/
$ scp user@openvpn.packt.co.uk:/etc/openvpn/easy-rsa/keys/client.crt /
home/user/
$ scp user@openvpn.packt.co.uk:/etc/openvpn/easy-rsa/keys/client.key /
home/user/
```

After the copying is done we should create a file, `client.ovpn`, which is a
configuration file for the OpenVPN client that helps set up the client to get connected
to the VPN network provided by the server. The file should contain the following:

```
client
dev tun
proto udp
remote server.packt.co.uk 1194
resolv-retry infinite
nobind
persist-key
```

```
persist-tun

comp-lzo

verb 3

ca /home/user/ca.crt

cert /home/user/client.crt

key /home/user/client.key
```

We need to make sure that the first line contains the name of the client typed in the keys and certificate. After this, remote should be the public IP address of the server or its domain address. In the end, the correct location of the three client files should be copied from the server.

The file `client.ovpn` could be used with multiple VPN clients (OpenVPN client for Linux, Tunnelblick for MAC OS X, OpenVPN Community Edition Binaries for Windows) to get them configured to connect to the VPN.

On a CentOS 7 server we will use the OpenVPN client. To use this configuration, we use the command `openvpn --config`:

```
$ sudo openvpn --config ~/path/to/client.ovpn
```

By getting the client connected to the VPN server, we can confirm that our VPN service is working well.

Implementing BIND as a DNS server

BIND is the most widely used open source name server application. It helps implement the **Domain Name System (DNS)** protocols for the Internet. It provides a robust and stable platform on which to build a distributed computing system, with knowledge that those systems are fully compliant with published DNS standards. It helps resolve queries about names by sending those questions to the appropriate servers and responding appropriately to the servers' replies.

As an example of the implementation of BIND, we will set up an internal DNS server to resolve some public IP addresses inside the network to simplify the mapping inside a large environment.

We need the following prerequisites to implement BIND:

- One server to have BIND installed and configured on it
- Two machines, either servers or simple workstations, to test the DNS service
- Root privilege to be able to set up BIND and configure the network to resolve from our internal DNS server

First, we will start by installing BIND on our DNS server:

```
$ sudo yum install bind bind-utils
```

After getting BIND installed, we start configuring our DNS server.

The BIND service has a bunch of configuration files that get included from its main configuration file, `named.conf`, which is associated with the process that BIND runs:

```
$ sudo nano /etc/named.conf
```

At the beginning of the file we need to add a block just before the `options` block, the `acl "trusted"` block, where we are going to define the list of clients allowed to do recursive DNS queries. Since our server will be serving two subnets we will add its two addresses:

```
acl "trusted" {
    192.168.8.12;  # Our DNS server inside the subnet 192.168.8.0/24
    10.0.1.1;  # Our DNS server inside the subnet 10.0.1.0/24
    192.168.8.5;    # Webserver
    10.0.1.2;    # client host
};
```

We need to make some modifications inside the `options`. Since we are using IPv4 only, we need to comment the IPv6 line:

```
# listen-on-v6 port 53 { ::1; };
```

And to make sure that the DNS server will listen in both subnets, we will add the following two addresses:

```
listen-on port 53 { 127.0.0.1; 192.168.8.12; 10.0.1.1; };
```

With the IP address `192.168.8.12` as the IP address of the DNS server.

Then we change the line `allow-query` from pointing to the `localhost` to point to the `trusted` clients ACL:

```
allow-query { trusted; };
```

> If we don't fully rely on our DNS server to respond to all queries, we can use a secondary DNS server by typing this command inside the `options`:
>
> ```
> allow-transfer { localhost; 192.168.8.1; };
> ```

And finally, at the end of the file we need to add the line that includes the local file configuration:

```
include "/etc/named/named.conf.local";
```

Then we save the file and move to the local file configuration to set the DNS zones:

```
$ sudo nano /etc/named/named.conf.local
```

The file will be empty since we are the ones who created it, so we need to fill it with the necessary zones.

First, we will add the forward zone. To do so we need to enter the following lines:

```
zone "packt.co.uk" {

type master;

file "/etc/named/zones/db.packt.co.uk";   # The location of the zone
configuration file.
};
```

Now we will add the Reverse zone. Since our first LAN is at `192.168.8.0/24` we start with the Reverse zone name, which will be `8.168.192`, the reverse of `192.168.8`:

```
zone "8.168.192.in-addr.arpa" {

type master;

file "/etc/named/zones/db.8.168.192";   # The subnet of 192.168.8.0/24
};
```

Now we do same with our second LAN on `10.0.1.0/24`, so its reverse zone name `1.0.10`:

```
zone "1.0.10.in-addr.arpa" {

type master;

file "/etc/named/zones/db.1.0.10";   # The subnet of 10.0.1.0/24
};
```

We need to do the same thing for all the subnets in the network, then we save the file.

After finishing with setting the zones and the Reverse zones, we move on to create and fill up their corresponding files.

We start by creating the forwarding file, which is where we define DNS records for forward DNS lookups. We create the folder in which we are going to put all the zone files. Then we start creating our zone files inside it:

```
$ sudo chmod 755 /etc/named
$ sudo mkdir /etc/named/zones
```

Then we create the Forward zone file and fill it up:

```
$ sudo nano /etc/named/zones/db.packt.co.uk
```

We need to add the following lines. Starting with the SOA record by adding the domain of the DNS server, we need to increment the serial value every time we edit the zone file so the change can take effect after restarting the service:

```
$TTL    604800
@  IN  SOA  server.packt.co.uk.  admin.packt.co.uk.   (
3     ; Serial
604800      ; Refresh
86400      ; Retry
2419200  ; Expire
604800 )  ; Negative Cache TTL
```

For the serial, we can make it more understandable by making it look like a `date:` `{yyyymmmddss}` `yyyy = year`, `mm = month`, `dd = day`, `ss = a` sequence number.

Then we add the name server records:

```
; name servers - NS records
IN  NS  server.packt.co.uk.
```

Then we add the `A records` for the hosts that belong to this zone, which will include every machine, either a server or a workstation, which we want to address with our DNS server:

```
; name servers - A records
server.packt.co.uk.  IN  A  192.168.8.12

; 192.168.8.0/24 - A records
server2.packt.co.uk.  IN  A  192.168.8.5

; 10.0.1.0/24 - A records
client1.packt.co.uk.  IN  A  10.0.1.2
server.packt.co.uk.  IN  A  10.0.1.1
```

Now we create the Reverse zone files. It is where we define DNS PTR records for reverse DNS lookups.

We start with the first Reverse zone `db.1.0.10`:

```
$ sudo nano /etc/named/zones/db.1.0.10
```

As we have done for the first zone file, we need to define the SOA domain:

```
$TTL    604800
@  IN  SOA  server.packt.co.uk.  admin.packt.co.uk.  (
                            3            ; Serial
                       604800            ; Refresh
                        86400            ; Retry
                      2419200            ; Expire
                       604800 )          ; Negative Cache TTL
```

Then the name-server records:

```
; name servers - NS records
IN  NS  server.packt.co.uk.
```

Finally, we add the PTR records that list all the machines with IP addresses that are on the subnet of the zone file:

```
; PTR Records
1   IN   PTR   server.packt.co.uk.   ; 10.0.1.1
2   IN   PTR   client1.packt.co.uk.  ; 10.0.1.2
```

Then we do the second Reverse zone file `db.8.168.192`:

```
$ sudo nano /etc/named/zones/db.8.168.192
```

We add the SOA domain:

```
$TTL    604800
@  IN  SOA  server.packt.co.uk.  admin.packt.co.uk.  (
                            3            ; Serial
                       604800            ; Refresh
                        86400            ; Retry
                      2419200            ; Expire
                       604800 )          ; Negative Cache TTL
```

Then we add the name-server records:

```
; name servers - NS records
IN  NS  server.packt.co.uk.
```

And we finish with the PTR records:

```
; PTR Records
12  IN  PTR  server.packt.co.uk.     ; 192.168.8.12
5  IN  PTR  webserver.packt.co.uk.   ; 192.168.8.5
```

We save all files. And we check the BIND configuration by checking the syntax of the files `named.conf*`:

```
$ sudo named-checkconf
```

If no errors are shown, it means that all configuration files are well written with no syntax mistakes. Otherwise, try to track the errors and fix them using the error message.

Then check the zone files using the command `named-checkzone` in each zone if we have many:

```
$ sudo named-checkzone packt.co.uk /etc/named/zones/db.packt.co.uk
```

If the zone is successfully set we should see this kind of message:

```
zone packt.co.uk/IN: loaded serial 3
OK
```

We should see the same thing for the Reverse zones:

```
$ sudo named-checkzone 1.0.10.in-addr.arpa /etc/named/zones/db.1.0.10
$ sudo named-checkzone 8.168.192.in-addr.arpa /etc/named/zones/
db.8.168.192
```

We should also see the same message if everything is well configured. Otherwise, we need to troubleshoot the following error message:

```
zone 8.168.192.in-addr.arpa/IN: loaded serial 3
OK
```

After checking all configurations, we are now ready to start the BIND service.

And just before that we need to make sure that our firewall allows us to do so. We need to open port 53 using the `Firewalld` service:

```
$ sudo firewall-cmd --permanent --add-port=53/tcp
$ sudo firewall-cmd --permanent --add-port=53/udp
$ sudo firewall-cmd --reload
```

After reloading the Firewall, the change will take effect and now we can start the DNS service:

```
$ sudo systemctl start named
```

Then we enable it so it can start at the system boot:

```
$ sudo systemctl enable named
```

With this step the DNS server is now ready to receive and respond to DNS queries.

Let's now do a client configuration to test the DNS server. On a Linux server, we only need to modify the `resolv.conf` file by adding the name-server IP address and the search domain:

```
$ sudo nano /etc/resolv.conf
```

By adding the following lines, then saving:

```
search nyc3.example.    # Our domain
nameserver 10.0.1.1    # The DNS server IP address
```

Now we can start the test. We will use a simple ping and the command `nslookup`. The ping will only test whether we can reach the machine giving its domain name:

```
$ ping webserver.packt.co.uk
PING webserver.packt.co.uk (192.168.8.5): 56 data bytes
64 bytes from 192.168.8.5: icmp_seq=0 ttl=64 time=0.046 ms
64 bytes from 192.168.8.5: icmp_seq=1 ttl=64 time=0.092 ms
64 bytes from 192.168.8.5: icmp_seq=2 ttl=64 time=0.117 ms
64 bytes from 192.168.8.5: icmp_seq=3 ttl=64 time=0.092 ms

--- webserver.packt.co.uk ping statistics ---
4 packets transmitted, 4 packets received, 0.0% packet loss
round-trip min/avg/max/stddev = 0.046/0.087/0.117/0.026 ms
```

There are also other tools that can give more detailed results when testing the DNS service such as `dig` and `nslookup` to do a simple DNS lookup:

```
$ nslookup webserver.packt.co.uk
Server:     10.0.1.1
Address:    10.0.1.1#53

Name:       webserver.packt.co.uk
```

```
Address:      192.168.8.5 webserver.packt.co.uk
```

After running the DNS lookup, we will try a reverse DNS lookup:

```
$ nslookup webserver.packt.co.uk
Server:      10.0.1.1
Address:      10.0.1.1#53


5.8.168.192.in-addr.arpa   name = webserver.packt.co.uk.
```

After running all these tests, we should check whether all the values are `true`, to confirm that we have a fully-working DNS server.

Setting up a web server using Apache-MySQL-PHP

One of the common services that a Linux server offers is being a web server, to give its user the capacity to host their web content in a secure, fast, and reliable location, browsable from all over the world. In this section, we are going to show you how to set up a reliable web server on a CentOS 7 server with some security modules that will secure the website, and we will do an implementation of a **Content Management System (CMS)**: Joomla.

Our web server will host dynamic websites and web applications. So we will install a LAMP (Stack) server, represent a Linux operating system with the Apache web server, where the site data will be stored in MySQL databases (using MariaDB, which is a community-developed fork of the MySQL relational database management system intended to remain free under the GNU GPL), and dynamic content processed by PHP.

We will start with the installation of the Apache web server, which is the most popular web server in the world:

```
$ sudo yum install httpd
```

By the end of the command, the Apache web server is successfully installed. We can start it using the command `systemctl`:

```
$ sudo systemctl start httpd.service
```

Before testing the service, we need to make sure that the server firewall allows web access. So, we need to open the ports that Apache is serving from, HTTP (80) and HTTPS (443):

```
$ sudo firewall-cmd --permanent --add-service=http
$ sudo firewall-cmd --permanent --add-service=https
$ sudo firewall-cmd --reload
```

We can now test the web server by typing in any other machine web browser inside the same network IP address of the server (`http://Server_IP_Address`). We should see something like this:

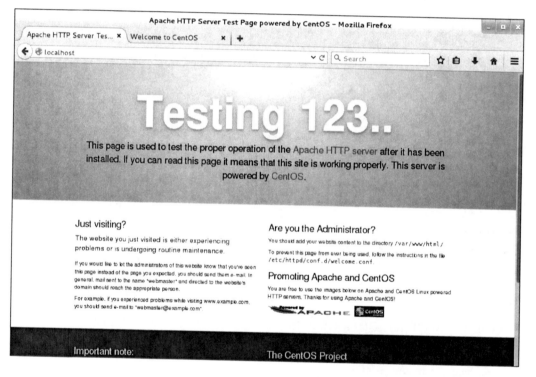

After making sure that the service is working fine, we need to add it to the system startup services:

```
$ sudo systemctl enable httpd.service
```

Now we will set up two virtual hosts on Apache to show Apache's capacity to support multiple websites.

For the next part, we will make a number of changes to the Apache configuration file, so we will create a backup file:

```
$ sudo cp /etc/httpd/conf/httpd.conf /etc/httpd/conf/httpd.conf.backup
```

Apache has the capacity to separate its functionality and components into units that can be customized and configured independently. These units are called **virtual hosts**. Virtual hosts allow us to host multiple domains. Each configured domain will direct the visitors to a specific folder specified to the website, which holds its information. This technique is extendable as long as the server can handle the traffic attracted by the websites stored inside it.

First, we need to make the folders where we are going to store our websites. The directory /var/www/ is our web server root directory:

```
$ sudo mkdir -p /var/www/packt.co.uk/home
$ sudo mkdir -p /var/www/packt2.co.uk/home
```

Then we grant these folders permission to be accessible by changing the ownership from the root (the user who just created them) to the $USER (the user that is currently logged in):

```
$ sudo chown -R $USER:$USER /var/www/packt.co.uk/home
$ sudo chown -R $USER:$USER /var/www/packt2.co.uk/home
```

To fully test the virtual hosts, we need to create an example HTML page to be opened at the client web browser:

```
$ nano /var/www/packt.co.uk/home/index.html
```

Then we add some HTML code to populate the page:

```
<html>
  <head>
    <title>Packt Home Page</title>
  </head>
  <body>
    <h1>Welcome to the home page of the Packt Publishing 1st
       example web server </h1>
  </body>
</html>
```

Similarly, for the second host, we need to create the same file with different content to tell the difference:

```
$ nano /var/www/packt2.co.uk/home/index.html
```

And then we put in the following HTML code:

```
<html>
  <head>
    <title>Packt2 Home Page</title>
  </head>
  <body>
    <h1>Welcome to the home page of the Packt Publishing 2nd
      example web server </h1>
  </body>
</html>
```

Now we need to create the virtual host files in the Apache configuration folder. We start by creating the folders where we need to put our files:

```
$ sudo mkdir /etc/httpd/sites-available
$ sudo mkdir /etc/httpd/sites-enabled
```

Then we need to tell the Apache service to use the configuration provided at the `sites-enabled` directory by editing the Apache main configuration file. This configuration can also be obtained as the configuration directory `/etc/httpd/conf.d`.

```
$ sudo nano /etc/httpd/conf/httpd.conf.
```

Then we add the following line to the end of the file:

```
IncludeOptional sites-enabled/*.conf
```

We save the file, then we move to the virtual host file creation in the folder `sites-available`. The file should always end with `.conf` so the Apache service can use it:

```
$ sudo nano /etc/httpd/sites-available/packt.co.uk.conf
```

Then we put the following configuration inside it:

```
<VirtualHost *:80>


    ServerName www.packt.co.uk
    ServerAlias packt.co.uk
    DocumentRoot /var/www/packt.co.uk/home
    ErrorLog /var/log/httpd/packt.co.uk_error.log
    CustomLog /var/log/httpd/packt.co.uk_requests.log combined


</VirtualHost>
```

We save the file, and then do the same thing for the second virtual host:

```
$ sudo nano /etc/httpd/sites-available/packt2.co.uk.conf
```

And we put the following commands inside it:

```
<VirtualHost *:80>

    ServerName www.packt2.co.uk
    ServerAlias packt2.co.uk
    DocumentRoot /var/www/packt2.co.uk/home
    ErrorLog /var/log/httpd/packt2.co.uk_error.log
    CustomLog /var/log/httpd/packt2.co.uk_requests.log combined


</VirtualHost>
```

After configuring both sites, we can now activate the Virtual Hosts to be usable:

```
$ sudo ln -s /etc/httpd/sites-available/packt.co.uk.conf /etc/httpd/
sites-enabled/packt.co.uk.conf
$ sudo ln -s /etc/httpd/sites-available/packt2.co.uk.conf /etc/httpd/
sites-enabled/packt2.co.uk.conf
```

To make sure that all the configurations we have done will be effected, we need to restart the Apache service by using either of these commands:

```
$ sudo apachectl restart
$ sudo systemctl restart httpd.service
```

 If we ever get any error related to our server host name, try to use this command to change it and get rid of the error:
```
$ sudo hostnamectl set-hostname --static packt.co.uk
```

In our case, those domains are not public and they are not defined by any DNS server. So we can either add them to our local DNS server or we can just add them to the /etc/hosts file in our client machine (the machine where we are going to open the web browser). This step is only to do the test. Usually we should define them with the DNS server of the ISP or at the local DNS server:

```
$ sudo nano /etc/hosts
```

Then we add the two lines that associate our web server IP address to the two domains that we have created:

```
Server_IP_Address       packt.co.uk
Server_IP_Address       packt2.co.uk
```

Then we go to the client web browser and we type the domain in the address bar:

```
http://packt.co.uk
```

We should see the page associated with the first domain. We do the same thing for the second domain. If the test is valid, we confirm that our virtual hosts have been created properly.

Now we can move to secure Apache against one of the most common attacks that is affect the world's websites. A brute-force attack or **Distributed Denial of Service (DDoS)** attack is a kind of attack that sends multiple requests to the same web server to overload it and make it unreachable. Now we are going to set up modules that help secure our web server from the kinds of attack. Mod_Security and Mod_evasive are the basic modules that will help detect and prevent intrusions, and help reinforce the web server protection against brute-force or DDoS attacks. First, we need to install the modules using the package manager. We require that the system already has the EPEL repository installed:

```
$ sudo yum install mod_security mod_evasive
```

So to verify that the installation is complete we need to see whether there are two files that have been created in the /etc/httpd/conf.d/ folder:

```
$ sudo ls /etc/httpd/conf.d/mod_*
/etc/httpd/conf.d/mod_evasive.conf
/etc/httpd/conf.d/mod_security.conf
```

To make sure that Apache loads these two modules when it starts, we need to add some configuration options to the two configuration files, which have been created after the installation:

```
$ sudo nano /etc/httpd/conf.d/mod_evasive.conf
$ sudo nano /etc/httpd/conf.d/mod_security.conf
```

And we add the following lines respectively or we make sure that they are uncommented:

```
LoadModule evasive20_module modules/mod_evasive24.so
LoadModule security2_module modules/mod_security2.so
```

Now we can restart Apache so the configuration can take effect:

```
$ sudo service httpd restart
```

We start by configuring the Mod_Security module. So we need to set up a **Core Rule Set (CRS)**. We will download a free CRS (OWASP) to have it configured for our web server. We need to create a directory to put the rules inside before downloading its package:

```
$ sudo mkdir /etc/httpd/crs-tecmint
$ cd /etc/httpd/crs-tecmint
$ sudo wget https://github.com/SpiderLabs/owasp-modsecurity-crs/tarball/
master
```

After that we can extract the package there and we can change its name to an appropriate one:

```
$ sudo tar -xzvf master
$ sudo mv SpiderLabs-owasp-modsecurity-crs-c63affc/ owasp-modsecurity-crs
```

Now we can start configuring the Mod_Security module. We need to copy the sample file configuration into another file without the .example extension:

```
$ cd owasp-modsecurity-crs
$ sudo cp modsecurity_crs_10_setup.conf.example modsecurity_crs_10_setup.
conf
```

Then tell Apache to use this module by inserting the following line into the Apache main configuration file:

```
$ sudo nano /etc/httpd/conf/httpd.conf
<IfModule security2_module>
    Include crs-tecmint/owasp-modsecurity-crs/modsecurity_crs_10_
setup.conf
    Include crs-tecmint/owasp-modsecurity-crs/base_rules/*.conf
</IfModule>
```

Now we need to create a configuration file in the /etc/httpd/modsecurity.d/ directory to make it easier to upgrade the CRSs if there are newer versions:

```
$ sudo nano /etc/httpd/modsecurity.d/tecmint.conf
```

After creating the new file, we need to add the following line and save the file:

```
<IfModule mod_security2.c>
    SecRuleEngine On
    SecRequestBodyAccess On
    SecResponseBodyAccess On
    SecResponseBodyMimeType text/plain text/html text/xml
        application/octet-stream
    SecDataDir /tmp
</IfModule>
```

With this step we can say that the Mod_Security module is successfully installed and configured. We can now move to the next module, Mod_Evasive. To configure this module, we need to make sure that some lines are not commented in the main configuration file:

```
$ sudo nano /etc/httpd/conf.d/mod_evasive.conf
```

And then check the IfModule options are successfully set:

```
<IfModule mod_evasive24.c>
        DOSHashTableSize    3097
        DOSPageCount        2
        DOSSiteCount        50
        DOSPageInterval     1
        DOSSiteInterval     1
        DOSBlockingPeriod   10
</IfModule>
```

Let's go through the previous code in some detail:

- DOSHashTableSize: This option specifies the size of the hash table used to keep track of the IP's activities
- DOSPageCount: The legitimate number of identical requests to one resource from one IP address
- DOSSiteCount: The same as the DOSPageCount, but for all the requests that can be made
- DOSBlockingPeriod: The blacklisting period for an IP that excludes the options on top

Those numbers are an example of configuration. We can change them as per our need.

An extra option that can be useful is DOSSystemCommand, which helps to run some script that can block IP addresses. To do so we need to add it to the configuration file.

```
DOSSystemCommand "sudo /etc/httpd/scripts/ban_ip.sh %s".
```

And we need to create the script at an appropriate location:

```
$ sudo nano /etc/httpd/scripts/ban_ip.sh
```

And we should add the following code inside it:

```
#!/bin/sh
IP=$1
IPTABLES="/sbin/iptables"
MOD_EVASIVE_LOGDIR=/tmp
$IPTABLES -I INPUT -s $IP -j DROP
echo "$IPTABLES -D INPUT -s $IP -j DROP" | at now + 2 hours
rm -f "$MOD_EVASIVE_LOGDIR"/dos-"$IP"
```

This script requires some system modifications to run properly. Let's make it executable:

```
$ sudo chmod +x /etc/httpd/scripts/ban_ip.sh
```

We need to add a line to the Sudoers rule file:

```
$ sudo nano /etc/Sudoers
apache ALL=NOPASSWD: /usr/local/bin/scripts/ban_ip.sh
Defaults:apache !requiretty
```

For security reasons, editing the file directly may be harmful. We recommend using the following command:

```
$ sudo visudo
```

Second, this script works with iptables so we need to deactivate Firewalld and install and activate iptables:

```
$ sudo yum update && yum install iptables-services
$ sudo systemctl enable iptables
$ sudo systemctl start iptables
$ sudo systemctl status iptables
```

Then apply the new configuration we need to restart the Apache service:

```
$ sudo systemctl restart httpd
```

Finally, our web server is well secured and configured.

As a small tip, the Apache server by default shows what operating system and version it has been running on. Sometimes it shows what modules are installed. That information can be very valuable for attackers to use as a vulnerability, so we need to disable the display of that information:

```
$ sudo nano /etc/httpd/conf/httpd.conf
```

And then we change the following two lines to look like this:

```
ServerSignature Off

ServerTokens Prod
```

We can now move to database installation. The database in a server is essential for the execution of a dynamic website to be used as a medium to store its data. Usually, on old Linux versions, we install MySQL as our default database server but recently most Linux distros have migrated to the MariaDB database server. To do so, we need to use the package manager to install it:

```
$ sudo yum install mariadb-server mariadb
```

We are going to install some modules that are not available in the default repository. So we need to install the EPEL repository to make sure that we are covered for this part:

```
$ sudo yum install epel-release
```

Then we start the service and enable it for the next startup:

```
$ sudo systemctl start mariadb
$ sudo systemctl enable mariadb.service
```

To have a well-secured database server, we need to use the MariaDB secure installation command. This command is very useful to customize the level of security of the database server with a variety of options:

```
$ sudo mysql_secure_installation
```

 We should make sure to specify a powerful root password for the database during the execution of the command.

To make sure that our database server is working correctly we can just run the CLI interface and run some basic SQL commands:

```
$ sudo mysql -u root -p
```

We type the password already set during the secure installation and we will have the MariaDB CLI. To quit it just type `quit`.

In order not to type the password each time, we can write the password in a file located in our home directory `~/.my.cnf` and add the following line:

```
[mysql] \npassword=password
```

We can now move to the PHP5 installation. In the future, we will add `phpmyadmin`, which is a program that allows the management of the MariaDB database via a graphical interface accessible via the web browser. First, we start by installing PHP5 and the library that supports MySQL for PHP:

```
$ sudo yum install php php-mysql
```

We can edit `/etc/php/php.ini` to configure where to put error messages, the maximum size to upload a file to the website (very useful for dynamic websites that handle files), and so on.

We can do some minor configuration to make PHP more secure. First, we can remove the information and errors message and log them to a log file. Then turn off remote code execution. Also, if we are not in need of a file upload in the website, we can disable it. We need to use a safe SQL mode. Finally, we disable dangerous PGP functions:

```
$ sudo nano /etc/php.d/secutity.ini
```

Then, change the following lines:

```
expose_php=Off
display_errors=Off


log_errors=On
error_log=/var/log/httpd/php_scripts_error.log


allow_url_fopen=Off
allow_url_include=Off


sql.safe_mode=On
magic_quotes_gpc=Off


disable_functions =exec,passthru,shell_exec,system,proc_open,popen,curl_
exec,curl_multi_exec,parse_ini_file,show_source
```

To protect PHP from known and unknown flows, we consider installing the Suhosin advanced protection system:

```
$ sudo yum install php-devel
$ sudo cd /usr/local
$ sudo wget -c https://download.suhosin.org/suhosin-0.9.38.tar.gz
$ sudo tar -xzvf suhosin-0.9.38.tar.gz
$ sudo cd suhosin-0.9.38
$ sudo phpize
$ sudo ./configure
$ sudo make
$ sudo make install
```

Now we configure it so Apache starts using it:

```
$ sudo echo 'extension=suhosin.so' > /etc/php.d/suhosin.ini
```

Then we restart Apache:

```
$ sudo systemctl restart httpd
```

Now, we move to the installation of the packages required for the phpmyadmin installation:

```
$ sudo yum install php-gd php-pear php-mbstring
```

After installing them, we install the phpmyadmin package:

```
$ sudo yum install phpMyAdmin
```

We need to do a little configuration to enable outside access to the interface of phpmyadmin other than from the server itself. We need to edit its configuration file:

```
$ sudo nano /etc/httpd/conf.d/phpMyAdmin.conf
```

Then we need to comment the old configuration:

```
#<Directory /usr/share/phpMyAdmin/>
#    <IfModule mod_authz_core.c>
#       # Apache 2.4
#       <RequireAny>
#          Require ip 127.0.0.1
#          Require ip ::1
#       </RequireAny>
#    </IfModule>
```

```
#    <IfModule !mod_authz_core.c>
#       # Apache 2.2
#       Order Deny,Allow
#       Deny from All
#       Allow from 127.0.0.1
#       Allow from ::1
#    </IfModule>
#</Directory>
```

And add the new configuration that grants access:

```
<Directory /usr/share/phpMyAdmin/>
          Options none
          AllowOverride Limit
          Require all granted
</Directory>
```

Finally, we need to change the authentication from `cookie` to `http`:

```
$ sudo nano /etc/phpMyAdmin/config.inc.php
```

And change this line to look like this:

```
$cfg['Servers'][$i]['auth_type']      = 'http';
```

So that the change can take effect, we need to restart Apache:

```
$ sudo systemctl restart httpd.service
```

To test whether it worked, we only need to type in any web browser located on the same network as the web server `http://Server_IP_Address/phpmyadmin`. Then we need to provide the database root user and its password to log in. We can secure `phpMyAdmin` by editing its configuration file such as restricting the source IP address that can access the service.

To be able to install a **Content Management System (CMS)** such as Wordpress, Joomla, or Drupal, we need to install some PHP modules:

```
$ sudo yum -y install php-gd php-ldap php-odbc php-pear php-xml php-
xmlrpc php-mbstring php-snmp php-soap curl curl-devel
```

After installing those modules, we can proceed with our CMS installation. In our case, we will be installing Joomla. First, we need to go to the Joomla website and download the latest version into /var/www or any Virtual Host folder. Using Wget we will download the Joomla package:

```
$ cd /var/www/packt2.co.uk/home/
$ get -c https://github.com/joomla/joomla-cms/releases/download/3.4.3/
Joomla_3.4.3-Stable-Full_Package.zip
```

Then we need to extract the package using the unzip command:

```
$ unzip Joomla_3.4.3-Stable-Full_Package.zip
```

 We need to make sure that the folder where we are going to extract the package is empty to have a safe installation with no errors.

After that we can go and open, in any client web browser, the domain where we extracted the CMS package:

```
http://packt2.co.uk
```

Then we need to follow the steps of the installation provided on the website. Here is a brief description of what we should provide to finish the installation:

1. We need to provide the website name and some of the site administrator information (mail, name, password):

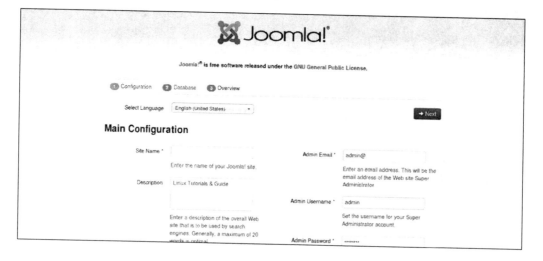

2. In the database part, we need to provide which database we are using (MySQL), then the server host name (localhost), and the user and password of the database (root), and finally a name of the database in which to store the site information:

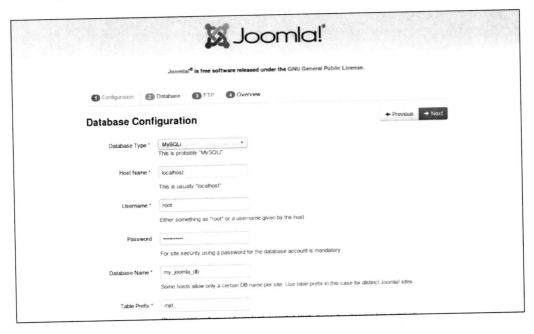

3. If needed, we can enable the FTP server by providing the FTP user and its password, and verify the service to check whether it is running.

4. Then we will have an overview where we can check the configuration that we have entered and we can have it sent to the administrator via e-mail.

5. Finally, we click install to have the website installed and configured.

As this screenshot shows, we can determine the status of the pre-requirement of our CMS:

Pre-Installation Check

PHP Version >= 5.3.1	Yes
Magic Quotes GPC Off	Yes
Register Globals Off	Yes
Zlib Compression Support	Yes
XML Support	Yes
Database Support: (postgresql, mysql, sqlite, pdo, mysqli)	Yes
MB Language is Default	Yes
MB String Overload Off	Yes
INI Parser Support	Yes
JSON Support	Yes
configuration.php Writeable	Yes

Recommended settings:

These settings are recommended for PHP in order to ensure full compatibility with Joomla.
However, Joomla! will still operate if your settings do not quite match the recommended configuration.

Directive	Recommended	Actual
Safe Mode	Off	Off
Display Errors	Off	On
File Uploads	On	On
Magic Quotes Runtime	Off	Off
Output Buffering	Off	Off
Session Auto Start	Off	Off
Native ZIP support	On	On

6. The installation site will remind us to remove the installation folder since it can present a vulnerability to the website. So to reinforce the security we need to remove it manually:

```
$ sudo rm -rf installation/
```

7. Then we need to copy the configuration provided on the site and put it inside a file that we create in the site folder and then save it:

```
$ sudo nano configuration.php
```

We can access the site and navigate to it or we can open the administration panel to make some tweaks to the site or manage the settings:

```
http://packt2.co.uk/administator
```

Now we can say that we have installed and secured our web server and it is ready for use.

Setting up an FTP server

As we know, multiple clients need a file exchange, and one of the common services that allows an easy and fast file exchange is the FTP technologies. In this section, we will talk about how to set up an FTP server to help transfer data between two machines in the same network or from different networks.

First, we need to install an FTP server using the default package manager:

```
$ sudo yum install vsftpd ftp
```

After having the server installed, we can start the configuration by editing the VSFTPD configuration file:

```
$ sudo nano /etc/vsftpd/vsftpd.conf
```

We need to find the following lines and change them as shown:

```
anonymous_enable=NO  # Disable anonymous login
ftpd_banner=Welcome to The Packt FTP Service.  # Banner message
use_localtime=YES  # Make the server use the local machine time
local_enable=YES  # Allow local users to login
write_enable=YES  # Allow Local users to write to directory
```

Then we should restart the service and add it to the system startup to auto-start at the next boot:

```
$ sudo systemctl enable vsftpd
$ sudo systemctl start vsftpd
```

Basically, most of the errors that won't let the service start are related to typos in the configuration file. If we ever get any, we should first check that file for any miswritten options.

After that, to make sure that the service is accessible from other machines other than the machine itself, we need to open the FTP port in the firewall:

```
$ sudo firewall-cmd --permanent --add-port=21/tcp
$ sudo firewall-cmd --permanent --add-port=20/tcp
$ sudo firewall-cmd --permanent --add-service=ftp
$ sudo firewall-cmd --reload
```

Then update the SELinux Boolean values for FTP service:

```
$ sudo setsebool -P ftp_home_dir on
```

And, finally, we should make some FTP users so clients can use them to log in:

```
$ sudo useradd packt
$ sudo passwd packt
```

Now we can start testing the service by going to one of the clients either on the same network or outside, and do as follows:

```
$ ftp Server_IP_Address
```

Or:

```
$ ftp domain_name
```

And then we type in the user and its password which we have already defined. If we get access to the FTP service that means that our FTP server is successfully set up.

Securing Apache and FTP with OpenSSL

Most services provided around the world are very attractive to hackers to attack and steal valuable information or to block its activity. In this section we are going to present a solution that helps secure two of the most commonly used services (HTTPFTP). This solution is OpenSSL as an open source toolkit implementing the **Secure Sockets Layer (SSL)** and **Transport Layer Security (TLS)** protocols as well as a robust cryptography library.

We will start with the implementation of OpenSSL for FTP file transfer to make it more secure. First, we need to ensure OpenSSL is installed on our system:

```
$ sudo yum install openssl
```

Then we start configuring the service to work with our FTP server VSFTPD. So we need to create an SSL certificate to use with TLS since it the latest most secure technology created. To do so we need to create a folder to store the files to be generated using SSL:

```
$ sudo mkdir /etc/ssl/private
```

Then we create the certificate with the keys:

```
$ sudo openssl req -x509 -nodes -days 365 -newkey rsa:2048 -keyout /etc/ssl/private/vsftpd.pem -out /etc/ssl/private/vsftpd.pem  -sha256
```

We need to fill in the details required during the execution of the command:

- openssl: The basic SSL command to manage SSL certificates and keys
- req -x509: To specify the public key infrastructure standards for SSL and TLS
- -node: To tell OpenSSL to skip the passphrase security option
- -days 365: To set the time of the validity of this certificate
- -newkey rsa:1024: To create a new RSA key 1024 bits long

- -keyout: To tell OpenSSL where to generate the private key file
- -out: To tell OpenSSL where to generate the certificate file

Then we add the SSL details to our FTP server main configuration file:

```
$ sudo nano /etc/vsftpd/vsftpd.conf
```

We specify the location of the certificate and the key files:

```
rsa_cert_file=/etc/ssl/private/vsftpd.pem
rsa_private_key_file=/etc/ssl/private/vsftpd.pem
```

Then we enable the use of SSL:

```
ssl_enable=YES
allow_anon_ssl=NO
force_local_data_ssl=YES
force_local_logins_ssl=YES
```

Then we restrict the connections to TLS:

```
ssl_tlsv1=YES
ssl_sslv2=NO
ssl_sslv3=NO
```

Then we add some optional configuration to reinforce the site security:

```
require_ssl_reuse=NO
ssl_ciphers=HIGH
```

Then we restart the FTP service to enable the change:

```
$ sudo systemctl restart vsftpd
```

Then we can test it via an FTP client (Filezilla) that has the capacity to connect via FTPS to see that the connection/transfer is now secured.

We now move on to the second part of this section where we are going to secure our web server Apache. We will be installing the OpenSSL module for Apache then we will configure it to secure Apache.

First, we need to make sure that Apache is successfully installed and the same thing can also be started for OpenSSL. Then we can start the installation of the module Mod_ssl:

```
$ sudo yum install mod_ssl
```

After installing it, we move to the configuration part. We need to create a folder in which we are going to store our keys and certificate files:

```
$ sudo mkdir /etc/httpd/ssl
```

Then we create our keys and certificates using OpenSSL:

```
$ sudo sudo openssl req -x509 -nodes -days 365 -newkey rsa:2048 -keyout /
etc/httpd/ssl/apache.key -out /etc/httpd/ssl/apache.crt -sha256
```

We need to fill in all the required details to finish the files' creation.

 The SSL key in Apache must be without password less to not cause a manual reconfiguration every time the server restart.

After creating all our files, we need to set up a virtual host to use with the new certificate. To do so we need to start by editing Apache's SSL configuration file:

```
$ sudo nano /etc/httpd/conf.d/ssl.conf
```

We need to find the section that begins with `<VirtualHost _default_:443>`, to make some changes to it to make sure that the SSL certificate is correctly set.

First, we need to uncomment the `DocumentRoot` line and change the location to the desired site that we need to secure:

```
DocumentRoot "/var/www/packt.co.uk/home"
```

We do the same thing for the line `ServerName` and we need to change the domain to the desired one:

```
ServerName packt.co.uk:443
```

And finally, we need to find the `SSLCertificateFile` and the `SSLCertificateKeyFile` lines and change them to point to where we have created the SSL certificate and key:

```
SSLCertificateFile /etc/httpd/ssl/apache.crt
SSLCertificateKeyFile /etc/httpd/ssl/apache.key
SSLEngine on
SSLProtocol all -SSLv2 -SSLv3
SSLCipherSuite HIGH:MEDIUM:!aNULL:!MD5
```

Then we save the file and restart Apache to enable the change:

```
$ sudo systemctl restart httpd
```

To test this configuration, we need to use a web browser of a client machine and type in `https://packt.co.uk`. Then accept the certificate and access the site.

References

Now that we have gone through the chapter, let's take a look at the references used:

- Firewalld configuration guide: `https://www.digitalocean.com/community/tutorials/how-to-set-up-a-firewall-using-firewalld-on-centos-7`
- OpenVPN server overview: `https://openvpn.net/index.php/access-server/overview.html`
- BIND DNS server page: `https://www.isc.org/downloads/bind/`
- Web server (LAMP) wiki page: `https://en.wikipedia.org/wiki/LAMP_(software_bundle)`
- FTP server Wiki page: `https://en.wikipedia.org/wiki/File_Transfer_Protocol`
- FTPS vs SFTP: `https://www.eldos.com/security/articles/4672.php?page=all`
- `Mod_SSL` for Apache documentation: `http://www.modssl.org/docs/`
- OpenSSL webpage: `https://www.openssl.org/`

Summary

This chapter is a description of a list of services that the CentOS Linux system offers to its users. This description is a step-by-step explanation of how those services can be installed on CentOS 7 and how to configure them for best practice. We have talked about implementing a Gateway server, using Firewalld, inside a local network. Then we have established a VPN server, using OpenVPN, to have clients access the network from all around the world. After that, we have set up a DNS server using the BIND service. Then we have installed the essential packages to set up a fully running web server that can support a dynamic website with some tweaking to make it more secure, easy to manage, and extensible, using Apache and its modules, MariaDB and PHP. We moved to set up an FTP server to have clients access it to transfer data. And we have finished with securing both our web server and our FTP server using the OpenSSL self-signed certificates and keys.

We are not done yet with what CentOS 7 can offer. Check out our next *Chapter 4, Mail server using PostFix*, which explores in depth how to set up, configure, and secure a mail server using Postfix.

Mail Server with Postfix

Nowadays, many people are already using configured and reliable web-based mail services such as Gmail, Yahoo, and so on. Most of those people are questioning the need for a local e-mail server installed inside their server environment. Well, servers also need to send e-mails, not only humans; and it is useful for many other needs, especially when notifying an administrator if a server is in a critical state.

Postfix is a high-performance open source **Mail Transfer Agent (MTA)** for Linux systems. It is fast, easy to administrate, and secure. It helps to route and deliver electronic mail. Postfix supports encryption and virtual domains, and its configuration files are clear, and easy to understand, and edit.

The installation of Postfix will be divided into multiple sections. Since this chapter is all about setting up an e-mail server using Postfix and adding some tools to make it fully qualified and then securing it, we will do the installation step by step, where we are going to stretch it into the different chapter sections every time we add a new tool or a new tweak.

During this chapter, we are going to learn the following things:

- Set up and configure the Postfix e-mail server using CentOS 7 Linux
- Configure it to store users and virtual domains on a MySQL database
- Set up a mail tool (Dovecot) to get e-mail
- Configure the OpenLDAP active directory
- Secure both mail services using SSL/TLS

Setting up and configuring of Postfix mail server

As we all know, Postfix as an MTA acts, as an SMTP server. It accepts incoming mail and passes it to the service responsible for retrieving mails. Then it forwards outgoing mails to the next responsible SMTP server. For the SMTP service, we need to have the port 25/TCP open in the system's firewall. Postfix is very easy to set up and configure. We only need to make sure that some pre-installation steps have been done in order to have a clean setup.

First, we need to open the required port at the firewall for all the needed services for a mail server, using `Firewalld`. The ports we are going to open are from the following services:

- **Simple Mail Transfer Protocol (SMTP)**: 25 on TCP
- **Secure SMTP (SMTPS)**: 465 on TCP
- **Mail Submission Agent (MSA)**: 587 on TCP
- **Post Office Protocol 3 (POP3)**: 110 on TCP
- **Secure POP3**: 995 on TCP
- **Internet Message Access Protocol (IMAP)**: 143 on TCP
- **Secure IMAP (IMAP SSL)**: 993 on TCP

  This is how to apply the change in the system local firewall using Firewalld:

  ```
  $ sudo firewall-cmd --permanent --add-port=25/tcp
  $ sudo firewall-cmd --permanent --add-port=465/tcp
  $ sudo firewall-cmd --permanent --add-port=587/tcp
  $ sudo firewall-cmd --permanent --add-port=995/tcp
  $ sudo firewall-cmd --permanent --add-port=993/tcp
  $ sudo firewall-cmd --permanent --add-port=143/tcp
  $ sudo firewall-cmd --permanent --add-port=110/tcp
  $ sudo firewall-cmd --reload
  ```

After that, we need to have an accurate time for the server, so we need to install an **NTP** client to synchronize the machine time with one of many worldwide available NTP servers. We need to install the NTP client service using the `yum` package manager:

```
$ sudo yum install ntpd
```

Usually, an NTP client, when installed, already has some default NTP servers configured to synchronize its time with them. But if we have a local NTP server and we want to use it, we can always go to the configuration file of NTP and add it. As a best practice, it is advised to always have at least three NTP servers:

```
$ sudo nano /etc/ntp.conf
```

We look for the lines that start with `server` and we comment the unneeded servers and add those that we want (shown as LOCAL_NTP_SERVER_IP_ADDRESS in the following snippet):

```
#server 0.centos.pool.ntp.org iburst

server LOCAL_NTP_SERVER_IP_ADDRESS iburst
```

We need to start the NTP service and add it to the system startup services:

```
$ sudo systemctl start ntpd
$ sudo systemctl enable ntpd
```

To verify whether the NTP client is synchronizing with the defined servers, we need to use the command `ntpq -p`. Let's have a look at the following output:

remote	refid	st	t	when	poll	reach	delay	offset	jitter
ns2.atlax.com	193.190.230.65	2	u	13	64	1	9.206	-0.940	0.000
ns1.atlax.com	193.190.230.65	2	u	13	64	1	9.532	0.904	0.000
ns3.atlax.com	131.188.3.221	2	u	12	64	1	3.131	-0.385	0.000
juniperberry.ca	140.203.204.77	2	u	11	64	1	47.422	-3.041	0.000

After making our server time accurate, we need to make sure that our server's hostname is well configured, since a foreign mail server may not accept mail from our server due to its suspicious name. We can verify this using the following command:

```
$ hostname -f
```

If we receive a fully-qualified domain name `server.domain` we can proceed, where `server` is the host name of our server and `domain` is where it belongs. Otherwise, we need to set one by editing the hostname configuration files:

```
$ sudo nano /etc/hosts
$ sudo nano /etc/hostname
```

Or you can also use the following command:

```
$ sudo hostnamectl set-hostname
```

We should ensure we write a well-written domain address. Then we save the files.

And, finally, we need to check our DNS resolution. Our server should be using a fully-qualified DNS, which means that it can resolve addresses from all around the Web. We need to check the `/etc/resov.conf` file:

```
$ sudo cat /etc/resolv.conf
```

If we are not sure that the configured DNS server is well updated to handle all our queries, we can edit the file and add some DNS servers that we are sure are qualified (Google DNS: `8.8.8.8`, `8.8.4.4`). We can test our DNS server using the `nslookup` command:

```
$ sudo nano /etc/resolv.conf
```

We are now ready to install Postfix on our server. As we have mentioned before, the installation and the configuration will keep adding and configuring to the same server for each section.

In this section, we will start by installing and configuring our Postfix as an SMTP server. First, we need to install the `postfix` package using `yum`. We need to plan for the coming sections. Since the default version of Postfix in the `yum` package manager doesn't support **MariaDB** (the drop-in replacement for MySQL), we need to install Postfix from the **CentOSPlus repository**. Just before starting the installation, we need to add an exclusion to some repositories to prevent overwriting the Postfix packages update:

```
$ sudo nano /etc/yum.repos.d/CentOS-Base.repo
```

Then we need to make sure to add the line `exclude=postfix` to the end of the [base] and the [updates] repository source to look like this:

```
[base]
name=CentOS-$releasever - Base
exclude=postfix

#released updates
[updates]
name=CentOS-$releasever - Updates
exclude=postfix
```

After saving the file, we can start the package installation. We will do the installation of the essential packages to have a fully-functioning mail server: Postfix as an MTA mail server for the SMTP, Dovecot serves for IMAP, and POP daemons and some supporting packages for the authentication service:

```
$ sudo yum --enablerepo=centosplus install postfix
$ sudo yum install dovecot mariadb-server dovecot-mysql
```

Here, we will merge the installation of the tools but the configuration will be separated into each section of this chapter.

After having the Postfix mail server installed, we can start with the configuration. Postfix has almost all of its options as either commented or not fully applicable. So to have Postfix fully configured we need to go to its main configuration file and make some changes. First, we open the file using any text editor:

```
$ sudo nano /etc/postfix/main.cf
```

Then we start changing uncommented lines and adding information about the desired mail server. Since we are going to make many separate changes in a big file, we should not add any unnecessary lines because we will be pointing to which line we should change at a time. At any point if we are using **nano** as a text editor we can always use the search option to look up the desired line using the combination of *Ctrl + W* and typing in the first part of the line.

Next, we need to define our mail server hostname. We go to the line of the option myhostname and we uncomment the line and change it with the desired information, such as in the following example:

```
myhostname = server.packt.co.uk
```

Then, we need to set up the domain name at the line of the option mydomain, as shown in the following example:

```
mydomain = packt.co.uk
```

This is followed by the origin, which has the same value as the domain, at the line of the option myorigin:

```
myorigin = $mydomain
```

Then we define which network interfaces our server will be providing its services (listening) to. In our case we will just use all of them. To set up that, we either comment line 116 and uncomment line 113, or just change line 116 to the following code:

```
inet_interfaces = all
```

Then we move to the line of the option mydestination to add the domain address to the end of the destination domain's line:

```
mydestination = $myhostname, localhost.$mydomain, localhost, $mydomain
```

Then we make a big jump to the line of the option mynetworks to uncomment it and add the other networks that we will be using for the network related to the server:

```
mynetworks = 127.0.0.0/8, 192.168.8.0/24, 10.0.1.0/24
```

Then we jump to the line of the option `home_mailbox` to uncomment the mailbox folder location option and change it to whatever suits our needs:

```
home_mailbox = maildir/
```

We end the line counting by going to the line of the option `smtpd_banner` and uncomment it and changing it to look like the following code:

```
smtpd_banner = $myhostname ESMTP
```

Then we go to the end of the file and add the following lines and limit the e-mail size for the server to handle (10 mega bytes= 10485760):

```
message_size_limit = 10485760
```

Also, we need to limit the mailbox folder size (1 giga bytes= 1073741824):

```
mailbox_size_limit = 1073741824
```

And, finally, we set up the SMTP server authentication configuration option lines:

```
smtpd_sasl_type = dovecot
smtpd_sasl_path = private/auth
smtpd_sasl_auth_enable = yes
smtpd_sasl_security_options = noanonymous
broken_sasl_auth_clients = yes
smtpd_sasl_local_domain = $myhostname
smtpd_recipient_restrictions = permit_mynetworks,permit_auth_
destination,permit_sasl_authenticated,reject
```

This configuration is considered as the initial one. After having it set, we can always use the command `postconf -e` to change an option or set a new one. If we ever needed to change the server hostname, we need to write it as follows:

```
$ sudo postconf -e 'myhostname = mailserver.packt.co.uk'
```

After making sure that all configurations are well set, we can start our Postfix service and add it to the system startup services:

```
$ sudo systemctl restart postfix
$ sudo systemctl enable postfix
```

Just to verify that everything is ok, we need to do a small test to the Postfix services. There are many ways to do this test. We will go with the traditional way of sending a mail using the command `mail` and then verifying the mail log file located at `/var/log/maillog`:

```
$ echo "Testing the Postfix mail service" | mail -s "This is a test mail"
user2@server.packt.co.uk && tail -f /var/log/maillog
```

Then we should see the following message in the mail log file, which tells us the following message to know that the mail has been sent ok and the Postfix services are working fine:

```
server postfix/local[28480]: 98E2F61B6365: to=<user2@server.packt.co.uk>,
relay=local, delay=0.02, delays=0.01/0/0/0, dsn=2.0.0, status=sent
(delivered to maildir)
```

With this step, we can say that we have successfully configured Postfix as an MTA. But this may not be a well set up mail server. We need to add and configure a few tools to help make it well qualified and secure. We will start adding and configuring the necessary tools during the next sections. This is how our mail server will look like after having all it components installed and running:

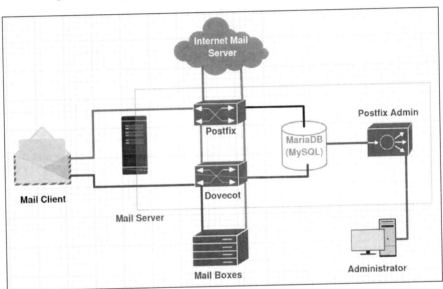

Setting up MariaDB for virtual domains and users

Since we have already installed **MariaDB** (the drop-in replacement for MySQL) during the postfix installation, we can proceed to the configuration. But if we ever needed to reinstall the package again, we can always use yum:

```
$ sudo yum install mariadb-server
```

The first thing to do to start the MariaDB configuration is to start the service. Also, we need to add it to the system startup services:

```
$ sudo systemctl enable mariadb.service
$ sudo systemctl start mariadb.service
```

Then we start the configuration by setting up the secure installation mode where we can set up or change the MariaDB root password, remove anonymous user accounts, disable root logins outside of the local host, and so on:

```
$ sudo mysql_secure_installation
```

We should make sure to answer yes at the end to finish the configuration.

Now we have the MariaDB service well configured and ready to be used. We will start setting up the new database to use it with Postfix. To add the new database, we need to open the MariaDB shell:

```
$ sudo mysql -u root -p
```

Then we create a new database:

```
> CREATE DATABASE mail;
```

Next, we switch to that database to start making changes in it:

```
> USE mail;
```

Then we create a database user to be the mail administrator by granting them permissions on the mail database:

```
> GRANT SELECT, INSERT, UPDATE, DELETE ON mail.* TO 'mail_
admin'@'localhost' IDENTIFIED BY 'mail_admin_password';
> GRANT SELECT, INSERT, UPDATE, DELETE ON mail.* TO 'mail_
admin'@'localhost.localdomain' IDENTIFIED BY 'mail_admin_password';
```

The administrator password `mail_admin_password` should be a very strong password to better secure the mail server database.

Then we submit the change:

```
> FLUSH PRIVILEGES;
```

Now we start creating the necessary tables inside our database. First, we create the virtual domains table:

```
> CREATE TABLE domains (domain varchar(50) NOT NULL, PRIMARY KEY (domain)
);
```

Then we create the table that handles mail forwarding:

```
> CREATE TABLE forwardings (source varchar(80) NOT NULL, destination TEXT
NOT NULL, PRIMARY KEY (source) );
```

Next, we create the table in which we are going to store the mail server users:

```
> CREATE TABLE users (email varchar(80) NOT NULL, password varchar(20)
NOT NULL, PRIMARY KEY (email) );
```

Finally, we create the transports table:

```
> CREATE TABLE transport ( domain varchar(128) NOT NULL default '',
transport varchar(128) NOT NULL default '', UNIQUE KEY domain (domain) );
```

We have set up our mail server database table's initial configuration successfully. We can now leave the MariaDB shell:

```
> quit
```

To enable Postfix to communicate with the MariaDB server, we need to set up MariaDB to listen to the localhost at IP address 127.0.0.1. To set this configuration, we need to edit /etc/my.cnf and add the following section [mysql]:

```
bind-address=127.0.0.1
```

Then we restart the MariaDB service:

```
$ sudo systemctl restart mariadb.service
```

We are not yet finished with our mail server database configuration. Now we go back to the Postfix configuration to set up communication with the database earlier created code within MariaDB. So we need tell Postfix which table of which database it should use to store specific information (users, virtual domains, and so on).

We start by creating configuration files for each table. For the virtual domains configuration, we are creating a file called /etc/postfix/mysql-virtual_domains.cf:

```
$ sudo nano /etc/postfix/mysql-virtual_domains.cf
```

Then we put the following code inside it and save it:

```
user = mail_admin
password = mail_admin_password
dbname = mail
query = SELECT domain AS virtual FROM domains WHERE domain='%s'
hosts = 127.0.0.1
```

Again, the `mail_admin_password` should be replaced with the strong one that we created earlier. This goes for all of the following files that we are going to create.

Then we create the configuration file for the virtual forwarding at `/etc/postfix/mysql-virtual_forwardings.cf`:

```
$ sudo nano /etc/postfix/mysql-virtual_forwardings.cf
```

We add the following code inside it:

```
user = mail_admin
password = mail_admin_password
dbname = mail
query = SELECT destination FROM forwardings WHERE source='%s'
hosts = 127.0.0.1
```

We create another configuration file for the virtual mailbox called `/etc/postfix/mysql-virtual_mailboxes.cf`:

```
$ sudo nano /etc/postfix/mysql-virtual_mailboxes.cf
```

And we insert the following code:

```
user = mail_admin
password = mail_admin_password
dbname = mail
query = SELECT CONCAT(SUBSTRING_INDEX(email,'@',-1),'/',SUBSTRING_
INDEX(email,'@',1),'/') FROM users WHERE email='%s'
hosts = 127.0.0.1
```

And, finally, we do the same for the virtual e-mail mapping by creating the file `/etc/postfix/mysql-virtual_email2email.cf`:

```
$ sudo nano /etc/postfix/ mysql-virtual_email2email.cf
```

Then add the following code inside it and save it:

```
user = mail_admin
password = mail_admin_password
dbname = mail
query = SELECT email FROM users WHERE email='%s'
hosts = 127.0.0.1
```

Now we set the files' permissions and ownership to make Postfix able to handle the new configuration files:

```
$ sudo chmod o= /etc/postfix/mysql-virtual_*.cf
$ sudo chgrp postfix /etc/postfix/mysql-virtual_*.cf
```

Then we create a user and group for mail handling. The virtual mailboxes will be all stored under this user home directory. We are choosing the group 5000 to keep our distance from the ones created by the system for the regular users:

```
$ sudo groupadd -g 5000 vmail
$ sudo useradd -g vmail -u 5000 vmail -d /home/vmail -m
```

To complete the configuration, we need to make some minor changes to the Postfix configuration. We will not open the configuration file and edit it, we will only add them using the command postconf -e.

We start by locating the new configuration file created to address the database tables:

```
$ sudo postconf -e 'virtual_alias_domains ='
$ sudo postconf -e 'virtual_alias_maps = proxy:mysql:/etc/postfix/mysql-virtual_forwardings.cf, mysql:/etc/postfix/mysql-virtual_email2email.cf'
$ sudo postconf -e 'virtual_mailbox_domains = proxy:mysql:/etc/postfix/mysql-virtual_domains.cf'
$ sudo postconf -e 'virtual_mailbox_maps = proxy:mysql:/etc/postfix/mysql-virtual_mailboxes.cf'
```

Then we set the location where the mailbox folder will be created:

```
$ sudo postconf -e 'virtual_mailbox_base = /home/vmail'
```

Finally, we see the user UID who will take control of the configuration files and add the mailbox folder:

```
$ sudo postconf -e 'virtual_uid_maps = static:5000'
$ sudo postconf -e 'virtual_gid_maps = static:5000'
```

To finish the mail server database configuration, we need to restart the Postfix service to submit the change:

```
$ sudo systemctl restart postfix.service
```

We can say that we have finished our mail server database service. Still, if we need to configure Postfix with the virtual domain to use them to send e-mail with a domain name different from the system's default domain name, we need to make some minor modifications to the Postfix main configuration file. Also, we can always use the command postconf -e to make quick changes:

```
$ sudo nano /etc/postfix/main.cf
```

Then we add the following code at the end of the file:

```
virtual_alias_domains = packtmail2.co.uk
virtual_alias_maps = hash:/etc/postfix/virtual
```

Then we need to add the new domain to the virtual domain file, `/etc/postfix/virtual`:

```
$ sudo nano /etc/postfix/virtual
```

Then we add the following snippet anywhere:

```
user1@mail.packtmail2.co.uk user1
```

Then we apply the change by refreshing the Postfix map and restarting the service:

```
$ sudo postmap /etc/postfix/virtual
$ sudo systemctl reload postfix
```

Setting up a mail tool (Dovecot) to retrieve mails

As we have said earlier, **Dovecot** is an open source **IMAP** and **POP3** server. It is fast, easy to set up and configure, and it uses very little RAM memory. For this section, we are going to install it to work with Postfix as **MDA** (POP/IMAP service) and sieve for sorting mail at the mail server POP/IMAP service. As this image shows, Dovocot is positioned between the user mailbox and Postfix:

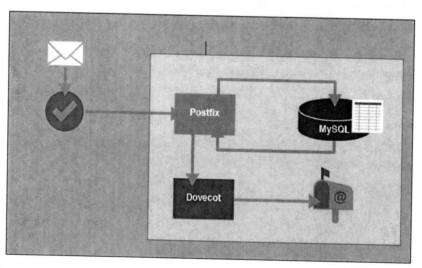

Since we have already installed Dovecot, we now only need to configure it to work alongside Postfix. If we ever miss the installation, we can always use the yum package manager to reinstall it:

```
$ sudo yum install dovecot
```

Then, we need to add Dovecot support to the Postfix configuration file. Again, we will not go and edit the file; we will only use the command `postconf -e`. First, we need to enable Dovecot to use the SMTP and enable the service authentication:

```
$ sudo postconf -e 'smtpd_sasl_type = dovecot'
$ sudo postconf -e 'smtpd_sasl_path = private/auth'
$ sudo postconf -e 'smtpd_sasl_auth_enable = yes'
$ sudo postconf -e 'broken_sasl_auth_clients = yes'
$ sudo postconf -e 'smtpd_sasl_authenticated_header = yes'
```

Then we enable Postfix to create and extend the mail directory if needed:

```
$ sudo postconf -e 'virtual_create_maildirsize = yes'
$ sudo postconf -e 'virtual_maildir_extended = yes'
```

Finally, we set the mail transport parameters:

```
$ sudo postconf -e 'proxy_read_maps = $local_recipient_maps
$mydestination $virtual_alias_maps $virtual_alias_domains $virtual_
mailbox_maps $virtual_mailbox_domains $relay_recipient_maps $relay_
domains $canonical_maps $sender_canonical_maps $recipient_canonical_maps
$relocated_maps $transport_maps $mynetworks $virtual_mailbox_limit_maps'
$ sudo postconf -e 'virtual_transport = dovecot'
$ sudo postconf -e 'dovecot_destination_recipient_limit = 1'
```

For this section, we will use the default security option provided by Dovecot so we need to tell Postfix to use the SSL certificate and key provided by Dovecot:

```
$ sudo postconf -e 'smtpd_use_tls = yes'
$ sudo postconf -e 'smtpd_tls_cert_file = /etc/pki/dovecot/certs/dovecot.
pem'
$ sudo postconf -e 'smtpd_tls_key_file = /etc/pki/dovecot/private/
dovecot.pem'
```

Then we move to the service configuration file of Postfix, `/etc/postfix/master.cf`:

```
$ sudo nano /etc/postfix/master.cf
```

Add the Dovecot service to the bottom of the file, then save it and exit:

```
dovecot    unix    -       n      n       -       -       pipe
    flags=DRhu user=vmail:vmail argv=/usr/libexec/dovecot/deliver -f
${sender} -d ${recipient}
```

Then we move to the Dovecot service configuration. Before we start the configuration, we need to have a copy of the initial configuration file backed up:

```
$ sudo cp /etc/dovecot/dovecot.conf /etc/dovecot/dovecot.conf-backup
```

For this example, we are going to create our own new configuration file where we will specify every single parameter one by one. We will create a new file with the same name as the original configuration file:

```
$ sudo nano /etc/dovecot/dovecot.conf
```

Then we add the following code without the description:

```
# We define the protocols that we want to be serving
protocols = imap pop3
# Enable Dovecot to listen to all domains
listen = *
# Define the time format to be shown at the log file
log_timestamp = "%Y-%m-%d %H:%M:%S "
# Define the location of the received mails
mail_location = maildir:/home/vmail/%d/%n/Maildir
# Locate the files to be used for the SSL authentication
ssl_cert = /etc/pki/dovecot/certs/dovecot.pem
ssl_key = /etc/pki/dovecot/private/dovecot.pem

# Define Mailbox main domain setting
namespace {
    type = private
    separator = .
    prefix = INBOX.
    inbox = yes
}

# Define the service users option
service auth {
    unix_listener auth-master {
        mode = 0600
        user = vmail
    }

    unix_listener /var/spool/postfix/private/auth {
        mode = 0666
        user = postfix
        group = postfix
    }

user = root
}

service auth-worker {
    user = root
}
```

```
# Configure the protocol LDA
protocol lda {
    log_path = /home/vmail/dovecot-deliver.log
    auth_socket_path = /var/run/dovecot/auth-master
    postmaster_address = postmaster@packt.co.uk
}
# Configure the protocol POP3
protocol pop3 {
    pop3_uidl_format = %08Xu%08Xv
}
# Database configuration
passdb {
    driver = sql
    args = /etc/dovecot/dovecot-sql.conf.ext
}

userdb {
    driver = static
    args = uid=5000 gid=5000 home=/home/vmail/%d/%n allow_all_
users=yes
}
```

We save the file to have the configuration stored. Then we need to create the database files already assigned to the Dovecot configuration file:

`$ sudo nano /etc/dovecot/dovecot-sql.conf.ext`

Then we add the following code, changing the mail administrator password `mail_admin_password` for the one already set in an earlier section where we have setup the MariaDB database:

```
driver = mysql
connect = host=127.0.0.1 dbname=mail user=mail_admin password=mail_
admin_password
default_pass_scheme = CRYPT
password_query = SELECT email as user, password FROM users WHERE
email='%u';
```

Then we arrange the files permission and ownership to restrict access to the files:

`$ sudo chgrp dovecot /etc/dovecot/dovecot-sql.conf.ext`

`$ sudo chmod o= /etc/dovecot/dovecot-sql.conf.ext`

Then we move to configure the Dovecot authentication parameters located in its configuration folder, /etc/dovecot/conf.d/. We start with the authentication process configuration file:

`$ sudo nano /etc/dovecot/conf.d/10-auth.conf`

We need to locate the following lines and change them:

```
# Line 10: needs to uncommented and changed
disable_plaintext_auth = no

# Line 100: We need to add it login at the end
auth_mechanisms = plain login
```

Then we move to the mailbox configuration file:

```
$ sudo nano /etc/dovecot/conf.d/10-mail.conf
```

Then uncomment the following line and change its end to match with the following code:

```
# Line 30: Define the mailbox directory location
mail_location = maildir:~/maildir
```

Similarly, we need to edit the master configuration file to define the Postfix user who will use the SMTP authentication:

```
$ sudo nano /etc/dovecot/conf.d/10-master.conf
```

Then uncomment the `unix_listener /var/spool/postfix/private/auth` section, and add it to the user and group lines:

```
# Line 96-100: Set the user and group for the Unix listener section
unix_listener /var/spool/postfix/private/auth {
    mode = 0666
    user = postfix
    group = postfix
}
```

Finally, we configure the SSL authentication configuration file:

```
$ sudo nano /etc/dovecot/conf.d/10-ssl.conf
```

And we change the SSL option from no to yes:

```
# Line 8: change it yes
ssl = yes
```

Before starting the test, we need to make sure that we have defined two variables in our /etc/aliases configuration file:

```
$ sudo nano /etc/aliases
```

Then we check the following code:

```
postmaster: root
root: postmaster@packt.co.uk
```

Then we update the aliases list:

```
$ sudo newaliases
```

And to finish the Dovecot configuration, we need to restart both the Postfix and Dovecot services. Also, we need to add Dovecot to the system startup services:

```
$ sudo systemctl restart postfix.service
$ sudo systemctl restart dovecot.service
$ sudo systemctl enable dovecot.service
```

To verify that the services are running well and there is no problem with the configuration files we need to check the mail log file:

```
$ sudo tail /var/log/maillog
```

We should see something like the following code to know that Dovecot is running well:

```
dovecot: master: Dovecot v2.2.10 starting up for imap, pop3 (core dumps
disabled)
```

 Sometimes, SELinux prevents Dovecot from using the system resource so we need to grant Dovecot access to the system resource, or if we have an alternative way to secure the server we can either disable SELinux or set it as permissive.

At this point, our mail server is fully qualified to work as a sender and receiver with a well-organized database and a medium security level. We can start testing our mail server.

First, we will use the **Telnet** service to check that **Postfix SMTP-AUTH** and **TLS** are working fine. We need to install Telnet and if it doesn't exist on the system, run the following command:

```
$ sudo yum install telnet
```

Then we run the test:

```
$ telnet localhost 25
```

Telnet will connect and we will see the Telnet shell, inside which we type inside the following command:

```
> ehlo localhost
```

To know that our test is positive, we need to see the following message:

```
250-server.packt.co.uk
250-PIPELINING
250-SIZE 10485760
250-VRFY
250-ETRN
250-STARTTLS
250-AUTH PLAIN
250-AUTH=PLAIN
250-ENHANCEDSTATUSCODES
250-8BITMIME
250 DSN
```

Then we exit the Telnet shell:

```
> quit
```

Now we will test the mail service. To do that, we need to first populate our database with a test domain and user. First, we enter the MariaDB database shell:

```
$ sudo mysql -u root -p
```

Then we switch to our mail database:

```
> USE mail;
```

Then we create a new domain at the domains table:

```
> INSERT INTO domains (domain) VALUES ('packtmail.co.uk');
```

We add a new user to that domain. We need to enter a good password for the real users later:

```
> INSERT INTO users (email, password) VALUES ('user1@packtmail.co.uk',
ENCRYPT('user_password'));
```

Then we exit the MariaDB shell.

Now we need to send a test mail to our newly created user. We need to use **Mailx**, so if we don't have it installed we need to do so before the test:

```
$ sudo yum install mailx
```

Then we send our test mail:

```
$ mailx user1@packtmail.co.uk
```

We need to put the `Subject` and then press *Enter*. If we ever need to insert a copied address, we need to write `Cc:` then add the copied address. Then we type in the message and press *Enter*, then to send it we need to put . at the end and press *Enter*.

To check whether the mail has been sent, we go to the mail log file;

```
$ sudo tail /var/log/maillog
```

Then we should see something like the following code to know that it is ok:

```
to=<user1@packtmail.co.uk>, relay=dovecot, delay=0.11,
delays=0.07/0.01/0/0.03, dsn=2.0.0, status=sent (delivered via dovecot
service)
```

Now we check the Dovecot delivery by visualizing the Dovecot delivery log:

```
$ sudo tail /home/vmail/dovecot-deliver.log
```

And we should see something like the following line to make sure that it is working:

```
lda(user1@packtmail.co.uk): Info: msgid=<20150822073408.6537761B3936@
server.packt.co.uk>: saved mail to INBOX
```

Now we can test our mailbox via the mail client. For this example, we are going to use **Mutt**, which is a simple mail client. But before using it, we need to install it first:

```
$ sudo yum install mutt
```

Then we need to go to the location where the new user mailbox is stored and run Mutt:

```
$ sudo cd /home/vmail/packtmail.co.uk/user1/Maildir/
```

And now we run Mutt:

```
$ sudo mutt -f .
```

The message showing that we need to create a root mailbox is not required, so we can skip it. And to exit Mutt type `q`.

Then we will have a pretty clear interface where we can navigate using keyboard direction and press *Enter* to see what is inside the mail. To confirm that our mail server is well configured and running, we should see the test mail that we have sent using Mailx:

Configuring the OpenLDAP Active Directory with Postfix

For this section, we are going to use OpenLDAP as a backend to both our Postfix (as an MTA) and Dovecot (as an POP3/IMAP server) users, in order for them to be connected to each other, and help with address lookup and aliases.

> OpenLDAP is an open source implementation of the **Lightweight Directory Access Protocol (LDAP)**. This section doesn't cover how to install an OpenLDAP server. We will assume that we have one already configured inside our network.

Our OpenLDAP server has the following information as follows:

```
dn: uid=user,ou=people,dc=packtldap,dc=co,dc=uk
objectClass: posixAccount
objectClass: inetOrgPerson
uid: user1
homeDirectory: /home/user1
userPassword: <passwordhash>
```

For the configuration of the LDAP settings for both of our services, we need to edit and add some options to their configuration files. We will start with Dovecot. We will first open the Dovecot main configuration file with a text editor, then make the necessary changes:

```
$ sudo nano /etc/dovecot/dovecot.conf
```

Then we check the following options if any change is needed or, if they don't exist, we need to add them:

```
# Define the mail user and group UID and GID
mail_uid = 5000
mail_gid = 5000
# Define the default Authentication method
auth default {
  mechanisms = plain
  # Define the LDAP database password file
  passdb ldap {
        args = /etc/dovecot/dovecot-ldap.pass
  }
  # Define the LDAP database user file
  userdb ldap {
        args = /etc/dovecot/dovecot-ldap.user
  }

  # Define the socket Listening parameters
  socket listen {
        client {
            path = /var/spool/postfix/private/auth
            mode = 0660
            user = postfix
            group = postfix
        }
  }
}
```

Then we need to create the LDAP database files and populate them:

```
$ sudo nano /etc/dovecot/dovecot-ldap.user
```

Next, we add the following code with the necessary change, then we save:

```
hosts = packtldap.co.uk:389
sasl_bind = no
auth_bind = yes
ldap_version = 3
deref = never
```

```
base = uid=%n,ou=people,dc=packtldap,dc=co,dc=uk
scope = base
user_attrs = homeDirectory=home
dn = uid=manager,dc=packtldap,dc=co,dc=uk
dnpass = password
```

The following image shows, OpenLDAP serves both inbox and outbox mail services:

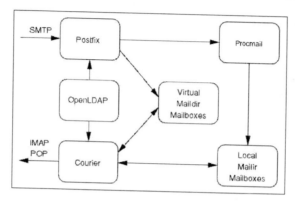

We do the same thing for the second LDAP database file:

```
$ sudo nano /etc/dovecot/dovecot-ldap.pass
```

Then we add the following code with the necessary change, save the file, and exit:

```
hosts = packtldap.co.uk:389
sasl_bind = no
auth_bind = yes
ldap_version = 3
deref = never
base = uid=%n,ou=people,dc=packtldap,dc=co,dc=uk
scope = base
dn = uid=manager,dc=packtldap,dc=co,dc=uk
dnpass = password
```

With this step, we can say that Dovecote is successfully configured to use our LDAP server. We proceed to the Postfix configuration. As usual we can edit the main configuration file, /etc/postfix/main.cf using a text editor or we can just use the fast configuration setup command:

```
$ sudo postconf -e 'accounts_server_host = packtldap.co.uk'
$ sudo postconf -e 'accounts_search_base = ou=people,dc=packtldap,dc=co,d
c=uk'
```

```
$ sudo postconf -e 'accounts_query_filter = (&(objectClass=inetOrgPerson)
(mail=%s))'
$ sudo postconf -e 'accounts_result_attribute = homeDirectory'
$ sudo postconf -e 'accounts_result_format = %s/Mailbox'
$ sudo postconf -e 'accounts_scope = sub'
$ sudo postconf -e 'accounts_cache = yes'
$ sudo postconf -e 'accounts_bind = yes'
$ sudo postconf -e 'accounts_bind_dn = uid=manager,dc=packtldap,dc=co,dc=
uk'
$ sudo postconf -e 'accounts_bind_pw = password'
$ sudo postconf -e 'accounts_version = 3'
$ sudo postconf -e 'virtual_transport = virtual'
$ sudo postconf -e 'virtual_uid_maps = static:5000'
$ sudo postconf -e 'virtual_gid_maps = static:5000'
$ sudo postconf -e 'virtual_mailbox_base = /'
$ sudo postconf -e 'virtual_mailbox_maps = ldap:accounts'
$ sudo postconf -e 'virtual_mailbox_domains = packtldap.co.uk'
```

Then to submit the change, we need to restart both services:

```
$ sudo systemctl restart postfix.service
$ sudo systemctl restart dovecot.service
```

Securing the mail server using SSL/TLS

SSL/TLS encryption for Postfix gives our mail server the capacity to not only authenticate remote SMTP servers but also to encrypt the e-mails that we send between our server and the receiver's server.

To configure SSL to encrypt connections, we first need to create our own personalized and specific SSL certificates.

We need to go the TLS certificates directory to create our new certificate there:

```
$ cd /etc/pki/tls/certs/
```

Then we create our first key file:

```
$ sudo openssl genrsa -des3 -out mailserver.key 2048
```

Then the tool will ask for a passphrase. We should give something strong and retype it when the tool asks us to do so.

After that we need to start using the OpenSSL tool; so if it is not installed we need to install it first:

```
$ sudo yum install openssl
```

Then we use OpenSSL to write the RSA key:

```
$ sudo openssl rsa -in server.key -out server.key
```

Then write in the passphrase that has already defined and carry on to have the key generated.

Now we move on to certificate creation. In the same folder, we run the following command:

```
$ sudo make mailserver.csr
```

Then we fill in the information as each filed asked: **Country Name**, **State or Province Name**, **Locality Name**, **Organization Name**, **Organizational Unit Name**, **Common Name**, and **Email Address** and for the final two entries (A challenge password, and an optional company name) we can skip them.

Then we create a private key using OpenSSL:

```
$ sudo openssl x509 -in mailserver.csr -out server.crt -req -signkey
mailserver.key -days 3650 -sha256
```

Then we move to the configuring Postfix and Dovecot to use the SSL/TLS encryption.

First, we are going to start by setting up Postfix to use SSL/TLS by making some modifications at its main configuration file, /etc/postfix/main.cf. We can always use a text editor to edit the file and change the parameters, or we can just use the command postconf -e to set them up in a faster way.

We will add some lines to the Postfix configuration file to protect it from some recent attacks against OpenSSL:

```
$ sudo nano "/etc/postfix/main.cf
smtpd_tls_exclude_ciphers = aNULL, eNULL, EXPORT, DES, RC4, MD5, PSK,
aECDH, EDH-DSS-DES-CBC3-SHA, EDH-RSA-DES-CDC3-SHA, KRB5-DE5, CBC3-SHA
smtpd_tls_dh1024_param_file = /etc/ssl/private/dhparams.pem

smtpd_tls_mandatory_protocols = !SSLv2, !SSLv3
smtpd_tls_protocols = !SSLv2, !SSLv3
smtp_tls_mandatory_protocols = !SSLv2, !SSLv3
smtp_tls_protocols = !SSLv2, !SSLv3
```

We create the cert file:

```
$ cd /etc/ssl/private/
$ sudo openssl dhparam -out dhparams.pem 2048
$ sudo chmod 600 dhparams.pem
```

Then we need to make sure that the TLS is enabled to be used with SMTP:

```
$ sudo postconf -e 'smtpd_use_tls = yes'
```

Then we need to redefine the certificate and key files position:

```
$ sudo postconf -e 'smtpd_tls_cert_file = /etc/pki/tls/certs/mailserver.crt'
$ sudo postconf -e 'smtpd_tls_key_file = /etc/pki/tls/certs/mailserver.key'
```

Then we set the location of the TLS session database cache:

```
$ sudo postconf -e 'smtpd_tls_session_cache_database = btree:/etc/postfix/smtpd_scache'
```

That is all for the main configuration file. We will now configure /etc/postfix/master.cf:

```
$ sudo nano /etc/postfix/master.cf
```

We need to uncomment some options of Submission and SMTPS between lines 16 to 35 of the original file, to look like the following uncommented:

```
    submission      inet  n        -        n        -        -        smtpd
      -o syslog_name=postfix/submission
      -o smtpd_sasl_auth_enable=yes
      -o smtpd_recipient_restrictions=permit_sasl_authenticated,reject
      -o milter_macro_daemon_name=ORIGINATING

    smtps           inet  n        -        n        -        -        smtpd
      -o syslog_name=postfix/smtps
      -o smtpd_tls_wrappermode=yes
      -o smtpd_sasl_auth_enable=yes
      -o smtpd_recipient_restrictions=permit_sasl_authenticated,reject
      -o milter_macro_daemon_name=ORIGINATING
```

We have finished with the Postfix configuration to use SSL. We can now configure SSL for Dovecot. We only need to make a few changes at the /etc/dovecot/conf.d/10-ssl.conf file:

```
$ sudo nano /etc/dovecot/conf.d/10-ssl.conf
```

First, we need to make sure that the SSL option is activated:

```
# Line8: change it to yes
ssl = yes
```

Then we change the SSL certificate and key location:

```
# Line 14, 15: change the files location to the new one
ssl_cert = </etc/pki/tls/certs/mailserver.crt
ssl_key = </etc/pki/tls/certs/mailserver.key
```

And, finally, we need to restart the services to submit the change:

```
$ sudo systemctl restart postfix.service
$ sudo systemctl restart dovecot.service
```

References

Now that we have gone through the chapter, let's take a look at the references used:

- Postfix home page: www.postfix.org
- Postfix MySQL support: http://www.postfix.org/MYSQL_README.html
- Dovecot home page overview: http://www.dovecot.org
- Postfix virtual hosts overview: http://www.akadia.com/services/postfix_separate_mailboxes.html
- Dovecot configuration file: http://wiki.dovecot.org/MainConfig
- LDAP support in Postfix: http://www.postfix.org/LDAP_README.html
- Postfix TLS support: http://www.postfix.org/TLS_README.html

Summary

This chapter describes in a step-by-step tutorial how to set up a fully-qualified mail server starting from sending a service SMTP using Postfix. We then started organizing the mail server, focusing on sending/receiving mail and virtual domains management via a secure database service MariaDB. Next, we learned about the mail reception service using POP3/IMAP using the MDA Dovecot with a medium level of security provided by the service itself. Then to start the extension part, which shows when the server can connect to an LDAP server and can gather useful information about the users and use them to send and receive mail. Finally, we finished off with a customized security level using OpenSSL to generate new certificate and keys to secure the service's authentication and encryption of the e-mails to be sent.

In the next chapter, we will learn how to set up and configure tools such as Nagios and syslog-ng on CentOS to monitor different services, and collect and process logs.

5
Monitoring and Logging

In a large computer infrastructure, system administrators cannot easily handle the monitoring of all system services and hardware issues for every machine. There should be a tool that helps gather the statuses of every machine in the infrastructure and presents them in a comprehensive way to the system administrators. Therefore, monitoring systems have been developed to satisfy the needs of monitoring a wide variety of computer infrastructure and help prevent system or hardware damage.

This chapter is an exploration of the world of monitoring and logging tools and the methodologies needed to better implement the right tools and configure them with the right parameters to guard and supervise a personalized computer infrastructure.

Through this chapter, you are going to learn these topics:

- The most common open source monitoring tools available
- How to set up Nagios as a monitoring server with some clients to monitor
- The variety of tools used as a logging server
- How to set up and configure syslog-ng as a logging server

Open source monitoring tools

Monitoring tools can show real-time information about the system, service, and hardware status. Through this information, a system administrator can tell whether there is something acting weirdly or showing weakness. Then, they can act and try to resolve the issue before it gets worse.

This section presents the most common open source monitoring tools. A monitoring tool is usually chosen depending on what its main need is. Some monitoring tools are specialized in monitoring the characteristics of a set of machines. Others help store and generate a graph of the history to be used for future system analysis.

Many organizations rely on their monitoring tools to output, in order to not only maintain their system and prevent potential problems, but also to determine their system's rush hours and when the system is more idle status This helps them rather reinforce their system capacities and save power and resources.

Ganglia

We will start by talking about one of the most common monitoring system tools. Ganglia is a scalable distributed monitoring system for high-performance computing infrastructures. It is widely used with clusters and grid architectures. It is a web-based tool that allows its users to visualize the history of a machine's statistics, such as CPU load averages, network usage, and so on. It has been developed to achieve a low per-node overhead and high concurrency. It is currently used by thousands of clusters worldwide.

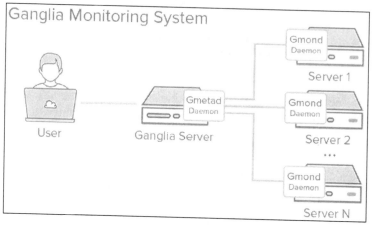

Source: http://assets.digitalocean.com/

Ganglia is based on two basic services, one installed on the client machine and one on the server. On the client-side, the service is called **gmond**. gmond is a multithreaded daemon that runs on the client machines that we want to monitor. Its services are basically related to:

- Monitoring a machine's status change
- Announcing the relevant changes
- Listening to the state of other Ganglia nodes
- Responding to requests for the XML descriptions of the machines it is running on

Then, we have the Ganglia PHP web frontend, which is installed on the monitoring server. It provides a view of the gathered information via real-time, dynamic web pages. These pages are the dashboards provided by Ganglia to its users (including system administrators). They are well organized in a meaningful way to present the machine's status to the system administrators to make the diagnostics part much more easier for them. The Ganglia web frontend stores data about machines for up to 1 year, and it has a lot of customizable parameters for viewing a machine's status history.

Ganglia is a very useful tool for monitoring machines' statuses and has a very reliable dashboard for history management and all types of troubleshooting related issues. Still, it is not a tool that can easily monitor every single service, especially when working in a server environment in which system administrators prioritize service administration over the machine itself.

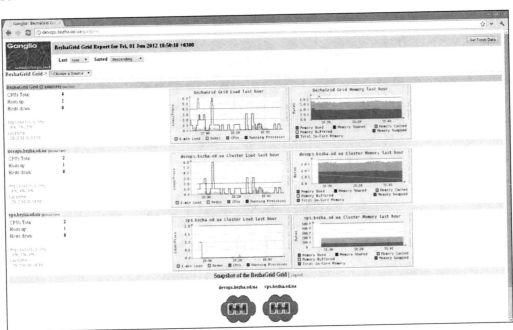

Source: http://bezha.od.ua

OpenNMS

OpenNMS is an open source, enterprise-grade network monitoring and management platform. It is a distributed and scalable management application for all aspects of network management. It is designed to be highly customizable to create a unique and integrated management solution.

OpenNMS supports four main functional areas:

- Event management and notification
- Discovery and provisioning
- Service monitoring
- Data collection

OpenNMS is accessible via a web-based interface that is smart and well organized to create high-level reports from the databases and the collected performance data. It is well used for its monitoring using the SNMP protocol, alerts/notifications, reporting, escalations, and its well-organized and clear dashboard. Still, it is pretty difficult to learn how to use it and personalize it by making personalized scripts. Also, most of the advanced features are paid and other costs are included. It could take a lot of time to set up and configure to work perfectly, but the result is always more than satisfying.

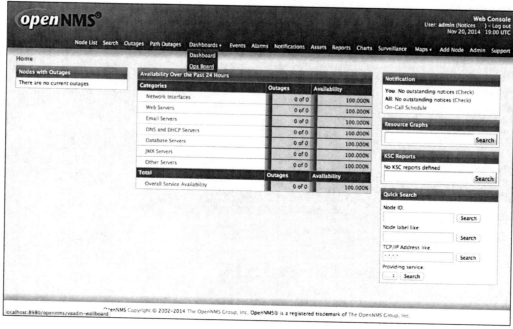

Source: http://docs.opennms.org

Zabbix

Zabbix is a piece of open source enterprise-level software used for the real-time monitoring of networks and applications. It has been designed to monitor and track the status of various network services, servers, and other pieces of network hardware. It has the capacity to monitor the main protocols (HTTP, FTP, SSH, POP3, SMTP, SNMP, MySQL, and so on).

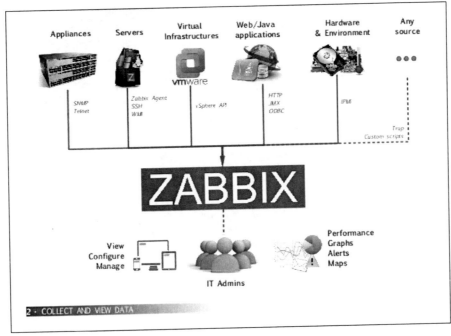

Source: http://image.slidesharecdn.com

Zabbix features a high-performance capacity for handling hundreds of thousands of devices. Also, it has the capacity of auto-discovery to identify machines within the same network. Zabbix comes with a web-based interface meant to show the monitoring dashboard. This interface is accessible via a secure user's authentication, and it has distributed monitoring with a centralized web administration that can visualize and compare any value it monitors. This dashboard can be customized to the needs of its user.

Zabbix has the capability to monitor just about any event on your network, from network traffic to how many papers are left in your printer.

However, Zabbix is more complex to set up and configure compared to other monitoring tools and it requires a good documentation to install it with best practices.

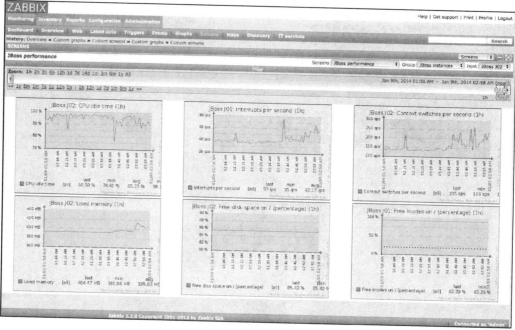

Source: http://dist.alternativeto.net/

Zenoss

Zenoss, sometimes called **Zenoss Core**, is a free open source application, server, and network management platform based on the Zope application server. It provides system administrators with a web-based interface that offers the capacity to monitor availability, inventory/configuration, performance, and events.

Zenoss features the following aspects:

- Monitoring a remote location worldwide through a nice-looking map, such as Google Maps
- A beautiful web interface that is very user friendly
- Automatic discovery of client system parameters
- Work with simple and plain SNMP

Zenoss looks very advanced and fancy, but still it has a slightly slow web interface. It doesn't support real-time notification. We should always wait for it to process the information to have a clear view on what is happening on the environment. It has a single dashboard, which makes monitoring a little difficult for many system administrators. Also, it is a limited open source solution; for more advanced features, we need to pay more. However, for those willing to pay and invest in it, we would say that it is a very good choice.

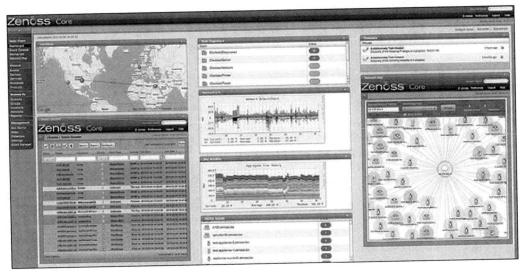

Source: `http://socializedsoftware.com/`

Nagios

Nagios is an open source application for monitoring systems, networks, and infrastructure. It offers monitoring and alerting services for servers, network equipment, applications, and services on large computer infrastructures. It has two types of alerts, one for notifying the issue and the other for notifying whether the issue has been resolved.

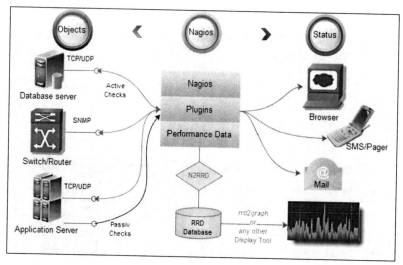

Source: http://n2rrd-wiki.diglinks.com

Nagios monitors network services, host resources, and probes via network plugins and via remotely run scripts. It has a large community, which has allowed the development of some really powerful plugins. It is considered one of the easiest monitoring tools to set up and use via its web interface. Still, it has some downsides related to the quality of third-party plugins and some complex writing and configuring of self-created plugins. Finally, it triggers a lot of notifications and alerts, so we might need to configure it with the proper plugins to help monitor everything in the infrastructure.

Icinga

Icinga is an open source system and network-monitoring tool. It was originally created as a fork of the Nagios monitoring system. It is well developed in terms of its web interface, to provide something more beautiful and more interactive than Nagios.

Icinga's efficacy lies in its capacity to implement really powerful plugins. It implements many famous preferment graphical tools, such as PNP4Nagios, inGraph, and Graphite. Icinga's most famous feature is its lightness, where it doesn't overload the system when running and it generates an information graph in real time. For extremely big infrastructures, Icinga is designed to run on multithreads to run thousands of checks every second without any overload on the system's resources.

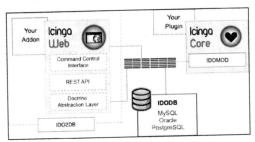

Source: `https://www.icinga.org/`

Icinga has a pretty large community, and they help integrate patches very quickly. There are two official versions of **Icinga**: one for the **Web 1 Icinga** and one for the **Web 2 Icinga2**. But it is still on the way to being well developed.

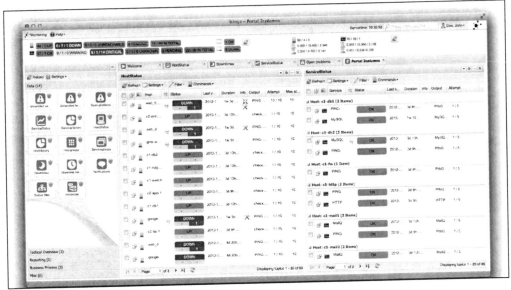

Source: `https://www.icinga.org/`

Setting up Nagios as a monitoring server

For this chapter, we are going to work with Nagios as our best choice, considering the performance and the simplicity of its setup and configuration. As we have already mentioned, Nagios is open source software that can be installed on multiple Linux distributions. In our case, we will be installing it on CentOS 7. It is a network, infrastructure, and server-monitoring tool. It will be monitoring switches, applications, and services. It has an alerting feature that helps inform users about all issues that occur while the infrastructure is being monitored. It also alerts the user if the issues have been fixed. Other than monitoring, Nagios also has the ability to identify system or network issues that could cause problems, with real-time problem notification. Furthermore, it has some security features, by virtue of which it can identify security breaches in the infrastructure.

In this section, we are going to install Nagios on a machine. It will act as our monitoring server. We need a test client to have it monitored. The client will have some common services; we will try to mess with them a little to test the Nagios notification service.

Let's talk a bit about the things we need before we start our monitoring server installation.

First, we need to have the **Linux Apache MySQL PHP (LAMP)** services installed on our machine. Since Nagios will be accessible via the web interface, having a web server installed is something obvious. For a more detailed and secure web server installation, you can go back and check out *Chapter 3, Linux for Different Purposes*.

Nagios won't be installed from the CentOS 7 package manager. We have to download it and then compile it, so we need basic compiling tools and a downloading tool to download the Nagios source code archive. We will install these using Yum, the CentOS package manager:

```
$ sudo yum install gcc cpp glibc glibc-common glibc-devel glibc-headers
gd gd-devel kernel-headers libgomp libmpc mpfr make net-snmp openssl-
devel xinetd
```

We wait until the installation is done and then proceed to the next step of the preparation.

In order to run the Nagios process, we need to create a Nagios user and give it a password:

```
$ sudo useradd nagios
$ sudo passwd Really_Secure_Password
```

We need to make sure that we are using well-secured passwords while creating any.

Next, we create a new group called `nagcmd` to allow external commands to be submitted through the web interface once it's up-and-running . Then, we need to add both Nagios and Apache to this group:

```
$ sudo groupadd nagcmd
$ sudo usermod -a -G nagcmd nagios
$ sudo usermod -a -G nagcmd apache
```

We move on to the final step, which is downloading the source archive for the latest version of Nagios. To do the downloading, we will be using **Wget**, a tool that we have already installed.

During this tutorial, we will be using Nagios 4:

```
$ wget http://prdownloads.sourceforge.net/sourceforge/nagios/nagios-
4.1.1.tar.gz
```

After downloading the latest Nagios stable version, we need to extract it. Well, since Nagios will be installed at the position where we are going to extract its source, we are going to put it in an appropriate location. We have a choice between /usr/local and /opt, so we need to copy the source package file there and then extract it. For this example, we will just go with /usr/local:

```
$ sudo cp nagios-4.1.1.tar.gz /usr/local/
$ cd /usr/local/
$ sudo tar xzvf nagios-4.1.1.tar.gz
```

After extracting the archive, there will be a new folder created, holding the named Nagios and including the corresponding version. We need to go inside the folder to start compiling it:

```
$ cd nagios-4.1.1/
```

Just before we start the compiling process, we need to run the configuration script that will help run the compiling process with no error by configuring it to use the available compiling tools that we have installed previously:

```
$ sudo ./configure --with-command-group=nagcmd
```

This configuration process has the option to set up the latest created group as the one that will be running the internal commands.

Now, we are actually able to start the compiling process:

```
$ sudo make all
```

This command can take a lot of time depending on the machine's processing power.

After doing this, we proceed to the installation phase. We need to install Nagios, its initialization scripts, some sample configuration files, and the Nagios web interface:

```
$ sudo make install
$ sudo make install-commandmode
$ sudo make install-init
$ sudo make install-config
$ sudo make install-webconf
```

Before moving on the next step, we need to set up our Nagios administrator user and password to access the web interface:

```
$ sudo htpasswd -c /usr/local/nagios/etc/htpasswd.users nagiosadmin
```

Then, we type in the password twice to have our web interface administrator well created and configured.

After Nagios has been installed, we can add some useful plugins. First, we need to download the latest stable source version of those plugins. We need to go to the /usr/local folder and download the plugin's source archive there. This step installs everything there well organized for future diagnostics:

```
$ cd /usr/local
```

Then, we start the download using **Wget**:

```
$ sudo wget http://nagios-plugins.org/download/nagios-plugins-2.1.1.tar.
gz
```

 We used the `sudo` command because during the download, the file is written in a folder with no user access to write on it.

After completing the download, we can start extracting the archive using the same command:

```
$ sudo tar xzvf nagios-plugins-2.1.1.tar.gz
```

Then, we enter the directory we just created:

```
$ cd nagios-plugins-2.1.1/
```

Again, we need to compile the source files. Just before compiling, we need to run the configuration script with some useful options, as follows:

```
$ sudo ./configure --with-nagios-user=nagios --with-nagios-group=nagios
--with-openssl
```

For the configuration option, we set the user and group Nagios as the default to access and use the plugins. Also, we use OpenSSL to secure the plugin usage.

Then, we start compiling the plugins:

```
$ sudo make
```

After that, we can start the installation:

```
$ sudo make install
```

Once this command is executed with no errors, we can say that our Nagios Plugins are well installed. We can move on to set up the **Nagios Remote Plugin Executor** (**NRPE**). This is a Nagios agent that simplifies remote system monitoring using scripts that are hosted on remote systems. We need to download, configure, compile, and install it in the same way. We first need to find the latest stable version of the source package, and then we download it to /usr/local:

```
$ cd /usr/local/
$ sudo wget http://downloads.sourceforge.net/project/nagios/nrpe-2.x/
nrpe-2.15/nrpe-2.15.tar.gz
```

Next, we extract it at the same location, and go inside the folder to start the compilation:

```
$ sudo tar xzvf nrpe-2.15.tar.gz
$ cd  nrpe-2.15/
```

We start by running the NRPE configuration script. We define the user and the group using the Nagios process and the security tools:

```
$ sudo ./configure --enable-command-args --with-nagios-user=nagios
--with-nagios-group=nagios --with-ssl=/usr/bin/openssl --with-ssl-lib=/
usr/lib/x86_64-linux-gnu
```

Then, we run the compiling command, followed by the installation commands:

```
$ sudo make all
$ sudo make install
$ sudo make install-xinetd
$ sudo make install-plugin
```

```
$ sudo make install-daemon
$ sudo make install-daemon-config
```

Next, we configure the `xinetd` startup script:

```
$ sudo nano /etc/xinetd.d/nrpe
```

We need to look for the line that starts with `only_from` and then, add the IP address of the monitoring server. It can be a public or a private address depending on where we want to make the server accessible from:

```
only_from = 127.0.0.1 10.0.2.1
```

Then, we save the file to give only our Nagios server the capacity to communicate with NRPE. After that, we add the following line to define the port number for the NRPE service:

```
$ sudo echo "nrpe 5666/tcp # NRPE" >> /etc/services
```

To have this configuration active and running, we need to restart `xinetd` to launch **NRPE**:

```
$ sudo service xinetd restart
```

Now, we have our Nagios monitoring server officially installed. We can proceed with the configuration steps. We go to the Nagios main configuration file and activate the folder that will store all the configuration files:

```
$ sudo nano /usr/local/nagios/etc/nagios.cfg
```

Then, we uncomment the following line, save the file, and exit:

```
cfg_dir=/usr/local/nagios/etc/servers
```

This is just an example of a server. It can also be done for network equipments or workstations or any other type of network-connected machine.

We create the configuration folder that will store the configuration file for each machine that will be monitored:

```
$ sudo mkdir /usr/local/nagios/etc/servers
```

Then, we move on to configure the Nagios contacts file to set the e-mail address associated with the Nagios administrator. Usually, it is used to receive alerts:

```
$ sudo nano /usr/local/nagios/etc/objects/contacts.cfg
```

Now, we need to change the administrator e-mail address. To do so, we need to type in the right one after the `email` option:

```
email                        packtadmin@packt.co.uk            ; <<*****
CHANGE THIS TO YOUR EMAIL ADDRESS ******
```

Then, we save the file and exit it.

Now, we proceed to the `check_nrpe` command configuration. We start by adding a new command to our Nagios server:

```
$ sudo nano /usr/local/nagios/etc/objects/commands.cfg
```

We add the following lines at the end:

```
define command{
        command_name check_nrpe
        command_line $USER1$/check_nrpe -H $HOSTADDRESS$ -c $ARG1$
}
```

We save the file and exit to allow the new command to become usable.

Now, we go ahead and configure the access restriction to IP addresses that can access the Nagios web interface:

```
$ sudo nano /etc/httpd/conf.d/nagios.conf
```

We need to comment these two lines:

```
Order allow,deny
Allow from all
```

Next, we uncomment the following three lines:

```
#   Order deny,allow
#   Deny from all
#   Allow from 127.0.0.1
```

 These lines appear twice in the configuration file, so we need to do the same thing twice in the same file. This step is only for reinforcing Nagios security.

We can always add any network or address to allow it to have access to the monitoring server:

```
Allow from 127.0.0.1 10.0.2.0/24
```

We can always check whether there is any configuration error in the Nagios configuration file using the following command:

```
$ /usr/local/nagios/bin/nagios -v /usr/local/nagios/etc/nagios.cfg
```

Just before starting Nagios, we need to make the Nagios CGI accessible by changing SELinux actions from enforcing mode to permissive:

```
$ sudo nano /etc/selinux/config
```

Then, we change this line to look like the following:

```
SELINUX=permissive
```

Now, we can restart the Nagios service and add it to the startup menu. We also need to restart the Apache service:

```
$ sudo systemctl start nagios.service
$ sudo systemctl enable nagios.service
$ sudo systemctl restart httpd.service
```

We can now access the Nagios server, but still we need to be allowed to try accessing it from the server itself, or from a machine that is connected to the network that is allowed to access the server. So, we go to the web browser and type http://Nagios_server_IP_Address/nagios. Then, we type the admin username, nagiosadmin, and its password, which has already been defined earlier, to get access to the Nagios interface.

Now, we move on to our client server — the one that we want to monitor using Nagios. First, we need to install the required packages. For CentOS 7, we need to have the EPEL repository installed in order to get the required packages:

```
$ sudo yum install epel-release
```

Now, we can install the Nagios plugins and NRPE:

```
$ sudo yum install nrpe nagios-plugins-all openssl
```

Let's start by updating the NRPE configuration file:

```
$ sudo nano /etc/nagios/nrpe.cfg
```

We have to find the line that starts with allowed_hosts and add the IP address of our monitoring server:

```
allowed_hosts=127.0.0.1,10.0.2.1
```

Then, we save and exit the file. To complete the configuration, we need to start the **NRPE** service and add it to the startup menu:

```
$ sudo systemctl start nrpe.service
$ sudo systemctl enable nrpe.service
```

Once we are done configuring the host that we want to monitor, we go to the Nagios server to add it to the configuration folder.

On the Nagios server, we need to create a file with the name of the machine. We can take the machine hostname or put something that indicates the role of the machine or any other indication:

```
$ sudo nano /usr/local/nagios/etc/servers/packtserver1.cfg
```

Then, we add the following lines, replacing host_name with the client hostname replacing the alias value with a short description of the server's main job, and finally replacing address with the server IP address:

```
define host {
        use                     linux-server
        host_name               packtserver1
        alias                   Packt Apache server
        address                 10.0.2.12
        max_check_attempts      5
        check_period            24x7
        notification_interval   30
        notification_period     24x7
}
```

With this configuration saved, Nagios will only monitor whether the host is up or down. To make it do more, we need to add some services to monitor, such as HTTP and SSH. Also, we are adding the option to check whether the server is active. We need to open the same file and define a service block for each service that we want to monitor:

```
$ sudo nano /usr/local/nagios/etc/servers/packtserver1.cfg
```

```
define service {
        use                     generic-service
        host_name               packtserver1
        service_description     SSH
        check_command           check_ssh
```

```
        command_line   $USER1$/check_ssh $ARG1$ $HOSTADDRESS$
        notifications_enabled           0
}


define service {
        use                             generic-service
        host_name                       packtserver1
        service_description             HTTP
        check_command                   check_http
     command_line   $USER1$/check_http -I $HOSTADDRESS$ $ARG1$
        notifications_enabled           0
}


define service {
        use                             generic-service
        host_name                       packtserver1
        service_description             PING
        check_command                   check_ping!100.0,20%!500.0,60%
}
```

Then, we save the file and reload the Nagios service:

```
$ sudo systemctl reload nagios.service
```

We will see the new server on the host list and its services on the services list. To test whether Nagios is doing its job, we disable the SSH service:

```
$ sudo systemctl stop sshd.service
```

Then, on the web interface, we can see how the service will go down from green to red. The red signal means that the test for that service has failed or has returned nothing, which means that the service is rather disabled or inaccessible. An error notification e-mail will be received by the Nagios administrator.

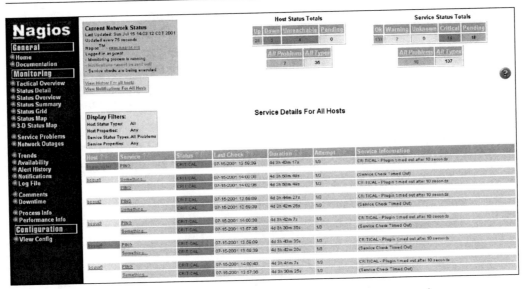

Source: https://thenullterminator.wordpress.com/

After that, we try the second test, to start the service:

```
$ sudo systemctl start sshd.service
```

To indicate that the service is back, another e-mail is received with the new status, where all its information will turn to green, as shown in the following screenshot:

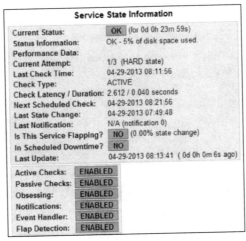

Source: https://www.digitalocean.com/

Now, after setting up the first server, we can go ahead and add all the machines, including the switches, printers, and workstations that we need to monitor. Also, to be more practical, we should add only those services that we care about. So, if we have a server that runs a number of services and we will be using only two of them, it is pointless to add all of them and overload the server dashboard and the mailbox of the administrator with things that we don't care about, which are later treated as spam.

Now, we will configure the NRPE daemon to receive information from the clients about their status. First, at the Nagios server, we edit the Xinetd NRPE configuration file to add which IP address the server should listen from:

```
$ sudo nano /etc/xinetd.d/nrpe
```

We need to add the IP address after the only_from option:

```
only_from        = 127.0.0.1 10.0.2.1
```

Then, we need to add the NRPE service to the system services:

```
$ sudo nano /etc/services
```

We add the following line at the end of the file:

```
nrpe 5666/tcp # NRPE
```

To have it submitted, we restart the Xinetd service:

```
$ sudo systemctl restart Xinetd
```

Then, we go to the client and make these modifications:

```
$ sudo /usr/lib/nagios/plugins/check_users -w 5 -c 10
$ sudo /usr/lib/nagios/plugins/ check_load -w 15,10,5 -c 30,25,20
$ sudo /usr/lib/nagios/plugins/check_disk -w 20% -c 10% -p /dev/sda1
```

These three commands are used to activate the Nagios agent to send information about server load and disk storage. In our case, our disk is defined as sda1. We can check the naming of the disk using the lsblk command.

Tools to set up a logging server

Logging means collecting system and service output information. It can be simple information, a warning, or an error for telling the status of the concerned daemon. For a system administrator, the daily work load can be really heavy. Thus, they have always been adopting the best logging tools to monitor their infrastructure's behavior. Also, the relevant information should be readable and quickly understandable.

Many system administrators mainly use either of two open source solutions:
Syslog-ng and **Rsyslog**.

Rsyslog

Rsyslog is a rocket-fast system for log processing. It offers high performance, great security, and a modular design. It has developed quickly and has evolved to be considered as a Swiss Army Knife in the logging field. It has a strong enterprise focus and also scales down to smaller systems. It supports MySQL, PostgreSQL, failover log destinations, syslog/tcp transport, fine-grained output format control, high-precision timestamps, queued operations, and the ability to filter parts of any message.

Rsyslog has the ability to listen to TCP/UDP connections, but with a downside due to its limitation to the log rate, where it can lose some of the log information during an overload. It can load a decent number of modules. It can also discriminate log filtering by program, source, message, PID, and so on.

Syslog-ng

Syslog-ng is an open source implementation of the syslog protocol for Linux and Unix-like systems. It features content-based filtering, rich filtering compatibilities, and flexible configuration. It also adds some important features to syslog, such as these:

- Using TCP for transporting logging information
- The ability to format log messages using the Unix-shell-like (bash) variable expansion
- The ability to send log messages to local applications
- The ability to save logging information directly to a database
- Classifying incoming log messages and, at the same time, extracting structured information from unstructured syslog messages
- Processing structured message formats transmitted over syslog
- The ability to correlate multiple incoming messages to form a more complex, correlated event

Syslog-ng is the next generation successor of syslog. It is one of the best tools for managing logs; it treats the log entities as an object (source, destination, filter, and so on), and its syntax is easily understandable. It is a highly portable application and is available for many more platforms, which makes it very suitable for sites with diversity in platforms. It has the capacity to compare the contents of log messages to a database of predefined message patterns. Thus, Syslog-ng is able to identify the exact type of messages and sort them into message classes. Then, it can be used to classify the type of event described in the log messages.

Here, we are going to install and configure Syslog-ng in CentOS 7 to be our logging server.

Setting up and configuring Syslog-ng

By default, with the installation of CentOS 7, there will be `Rsyslog` installed for storing the log of the system and its applications. Luckily, we will have all our system log files stored and organized the way syslog wants. We will be using these log files with the installation of `Syslog-ng`, and we will have them organized in a more suitable way:

First, before starting the installation, we need to set up the EPEL repository:

```
$ sudo yum install epel-release
```

All of the upcoming package repository checking and application availability is optional. We can always proceed with the installation of Syslog-ng.

To verify that the EPEL repository has been added, we can use the following command:

```
$ sudo yum repolist
```

This command shows the list of repositories available for the YUM package manager to download and install the packages from. Now, after having the EPEL repository, we need to check whether any change needs to be made after adding it. So, we need to type in this command:

```
$ sudo yum check-update
```

This command is not necessary; we wanted to use it for additional knowledge on how to check the Yum repository update.

Finally, to check the availability of the `syslog-ng` application in the newly added EPEL repository, we need to type the following:

```
$ sudo yum list *syslog-ng*
```

Now, we go back to the installation phase. We will be using yum since we have properly verified the existence of the application package:

```
$ sudo yum install syslog-ng syslog-ng-libdbi
```

We need to confirm the installation of these packages. Then, we wait until it is done.

To activate `syslog-ng` and make it the default logging tool, we need to start by disabling rsyslog:

```
$ sudo systemctl stop rsyslog
$ sudo systemctl disable rsyslog
```

Then, we go to its configuration file to have it working in a proper way. We open the file using any text editor:

```
$ sudo nano /etc/syslog-ng/syslog-ng.conf
```

Next, we make the required change to make it look like the following:

```
@version:3.5
@include "scl.conf"
#-----------------------------------------------------------------
--------
# /etc/syslog-ng/syslog-ng.conf: configuration file
# $Revision: 0.3-r5 (CentOS Edition by Wakko Warner) $
# $Comment: Any comments please send to wakko@acmelabs.spb.ru $
#-----------------------------------------------------------------
--------

# Note: it also sources additional configuration files (*.conf)
#       located in /etc/syslog-ng/conf.d/

# Global Options
options {
  # Enable or disable the chained hostname format
  chain_hostnames (off);
  # The number of lines buffered before written to file
  flush_lines (0);
  log_fifo_size (1000);
  # The default action of syslog-ng is to log a STATS line
```

```
    # to the file every 10 minutes.  That's pretty ugly after a
      while.
    # Change it to every 12 hours so you get a nice daily update of
    # how many messages syslog-ng missed (0).
    stats_freq (43200);
    time_reopen (10);
    # The default action of syslog-ng is to log a MARK line
    # to the file every 20 minutes.  That's seems high for most
    # people so turn it down to once an hour.  Set it to zero
    # if you don't want the functionality at all.
    mark_freq(3600);
    # Enable or disable hostname rewriting
    keep_hostname (yes);
    # Enable or disable directory creation for destination files
    create_dirs (yes);
    # userid/groupid/permission value for files
    owner ("root");
    group ("adm");
    perm (0640);
    # userid/groupid/permission value for directories
    dir_owner ("root");
    dir_group ("adm");
    dir_perm (0750);
    # Enable or disable DNS usage
    use_dns (no);
    # Add Fully Qualified Domain Name instead of short hostname
    use_fqdn (no);
    long_hostnames (off);
};

source s_sys {
    system();
    internal();
    # udp(ip(0.0.0.0) port(514));
};


# Sources of syslog messages (both local and remote messages on the
server)
source s_local {
  system();
  internal();
};
source s_tcp { tcp (ip ("127.0.0.1") port (514) max-connections (1) );
};
```

```
source s_udp { udp (ip ("0.0.0.0") port (514)); };

# By default messages are logged to tty12...
#destination d_console_all { file("/dev/tty12"); };
# ...if you intend to use /dev/console for programs like xconsole
# you can comment out the destination line above that references /dev/
tty12
# and uncomment the line below.
#destination d_console_all { file("/dev/console"); };
#destination d_console_all { file("/dev/null"); };
destination d_console_all { program("/bin/cat >/dev/null"); };

# Destinations
destination d_usertty { usertty("*"); };
destination d_everything {
  file("/var/log/syslog-$HOST/$YEAR-$MONTH/$FACILITY.$PRIORITY.log"
    template("$FULLDATE $MSGHDR$MSG\n")
    template_escape(no)
  );
};

# Filters
filter f_emergency { level(emerg); };
filter f_fetchmail_warnings {
  not(match("fetchmail" value("PROGRAM"))
  and match("Warning: the connection is insecure, continuing anyways."
value("MESSAGE")));
};

log {
  source(s_local);
  filter(f_emergency);
  destination(d_usertty);
};
log {
  source(s_local);
  filter(f_fetchmail_warnings);
  destination(d_everything);
};
log {
  source(s_local);
  filter(f_fetchmail_warnings);
  destination(d_console_all);
};
```

```
log {
    source(s_tcp);
    destination(d_everything);
};
log {
    source(s_tcp);
    destination(d_console_all);
};

log {
    source(s_udp);
    destination(d_everything);
};
log {
    source(s_udp);
    destination(d_console_all);
};

# Source additional configuration files (.conf extension only)
@include "/etc/syslog-ng/conf.d/*.conf"

# vim:ft=syslog-ng:ai:si:ts=4:sw=4:et:
```

At this point, we can start the `syslog-ng` service and enable it to start during system startup:

```
$ sudo systemctl start syslog-ng.service
$ sudo systemctl enable syslog-ng.service
```

With this step, we have configured our logging server using `syslog-ng` to perform well-organized and useful logging.

References

Now, let's look at the references used throughout the chapter:

- The Ganglia home page, `http://ganglia.sourceforge.net/`
- The OpenNMS home page, `http://www.opennms.org/`
- The Zabbix home page, `http://www.zabbix.com/`
- The Zenoss home page, `http://zenoss.com/`

- The Icinga home page, `https://www.icinga.org/`
- The Nagios home page, `https://www.nagios.org/`
- The Rsyslog home page, `http://www.rsyslog.com/doc/master/index.html`
- The Syslog-ng home page, `https://syslog-ng.org/`

Summary

Over the course of this chapter, we introduced a variety of choices of open source monitoring and logging tools for CentOS 7 servers. Then, we discussed a step-by-step tutorial on how to set up and configure Nagios and Syslog-ng logging as our logging server. We also talked about some of these tools' major features that help simplify our choice.

In the next chapter, we will have a brief introduction to a variety of virtualization technologies. Also, we will take this opportunity to give you a step-by-step tutorial on establishing a small virtual machine.

6

Virtualization

These days, computer infrastructures have changed in many ways. We no longer see a room full of servers, each responsible for providing several services depending on how powerful they are. In these times, we only see a few big servers composed of several units so as to reinforce their capacities. This type of server hosts several virtual servers that serve the same old purposes as per the infrastructure requirements.

In our days, being a system administrator for bare-metal machines is just not enough. Virtual machines are on the rise; we should admit this. Big companies are no longer using old architectures; it is no longer a good option. A lot of money and huge management effort is required to sustain them.

In this chapter, we are going to explain virtualization as a concept, where we will see how to set up several virtualization technologies, and then give an example of how to create some virtual machines for each one of those technologies. Finally, we will explain, in brief, what Docker is and how to add an image and access the Docker container.

Through this chapter, you are going to learn the following topics:

- Basics of virtualization
- Concept of full virtualization
- Concept of paravirtualization
- Understanding Xen and how to use it
- Using KVM to set up some Linux virtual machines
- Creating a virtual machine using OpenVZ
- Setting up and configuring virtual machines on VirtualBox
- Understanding Docker and how to create a container and access it
- Establishing services' high availability using HAProxy

The basics of virtualization on Linux

Virtualization is the capacity to create a machine-like program that simulates, the physical behavior of a real machine running through virtual hardware including CPU, RAM, Hard disk, Network card, and so on, where those resources are all being taken from the physical machine running the virtual one.

Earlier, the way of managing services was to deploy a new server or upgrade the old one to meet the requirements of the new services to perform long and complex migrations in the event of a hardware failure. All the time, there would be too little RAM, too few disks, or low processing power. Managers got tired of trying to fix the existent system while paying a lot of money to help maintain an old server that was no longer supported. However, they did not have too many options, since the services running on those machines were very important and essential. Companies were deploying servers that would not work on their peak capacity, and there was no better way of controlling every server's capacity for the right services with the right hardware equipment. All of these reasons made the newborn solution of virtualization grow so fast. Just after a while from its first deployment, virtualization has been integrated in many fields, specially in the field of computer science. Virtualization allows an abstraction of the physical hardware, to run multiple virtual machines on a single shared resource (CPU, Memory, Networking, and Storage):

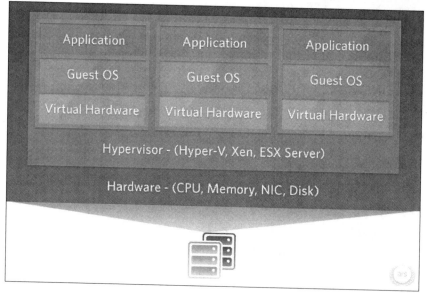

Source: http://cdn.arstechnica.net

Now, this new technology is booming. We are witnessing a new virtualization service being born each day. Virtualization has been divided into many types:

- We have network virtualization, which is related to virtual network creation and management to separate groups of machines from each other. They are connected to the same switch and group of switches.

- We also have application virtualization, wherein we put an application or an ensemble of applications inside a container, and then we make the application believe that it is running on its original supported system. So, it believes that it can access the resource that it needs.

- Finally, we have full machine virtualization. This is a kind of virtualization that creates a full virtual machine (desktop, server) with its virtual hardware and the dedicated services on demand. This virtualization involves abstraction of the server-based workload (the work load demanded by the virtual machine user) from the underlying hardware. The virtual machine won't notice if it is running on a physical or a virtual hardware as long as the hardware answering its service's demands for resources (store data, network access to other machines, and so on).

In this chapter, we will focus on both application virtualization and desktop virtualization.

A piece of software called hypervisor is executed on the physical machine to help with the virtualization of the data center, with a goal of a platform for the virtual machines. The hypervisor's main job is to organize dynamically the physical resources between the different virtual machines running under its control. This gives them the capacity to run independently of the physical machine where a system administrator can relocate a virtual machine from a host to another without affecting it. A hypervisor, also called a virtual machine manager, is a program that allows multiple operating systems to share a single hardware host.

While using a virtual machine or a container, we are expecting to provide the applications or services with an operating system that can host them and simplify their communication to the hardware. Since those machines are not really running on the physical hardware, virtualization allows them to access dynamically and flexibly the CPU, memory, storage, and networking resources as necessary.

Virtualization can increase flexibility and management and offers a better scalability with an enormous saving in costs. The service's workload gets deployed faster, with a visible increase in performance-on-demand availability, while getting the scalability function automated, to simplify the infrastructure management for the IT support guys.

Let's enumerate some of the major advantages of having a virtualization solution installed on a server infrastructure:

- Reduction in the number of hardware and operating costs
- Delivery of high availability of applications and services
- Minimization or elimination of downtime (with best practice methods)
- Increase in the IT team's productivity, efficiency, agility, and responsiveness
- Increase in speed and simplification of application and resource provisioning
- Support for business continuity and disaster recovery as an increase in the system's security
- Enabling centralized management
- Building a true software-defined data center
- Exploiting the full advantages of multicore processor machines

The following figure shows an example of three Linux virtual machines running on one Linux server. These machines are controlled and managed by a type of hypervisor depending on the virtualization chosen:

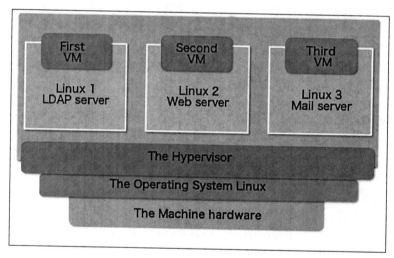

A virtual machine really is just some files in some format stored at a specific location on the host machine. For some technologies, it can also be an LVM logical volume or a direct device. The virtual disk used by a virtual machine is just another file encapsulated within it. Inside a virtual machine, managing the OS and applications can be simplified (in some ways; it is complicated in others).

But the good thing is that having the virtual machine as just a folder full of files that can be copied and moved makes it easier to backup in the event of a hardware failure on the physical machine. In such cases, the manager should simply buy a new server, load the backed-up virtual machines on it, and run the entire environment again as if nothing ever happened.

Using the CentOS repository, we have a choice between two virtualization technologies: **Xen** and **KVM**. To understand these virtualization technologies, you need to understand the two different approaches to virtualization: full virtualization and paravirtualization.

A combination of paravirtualization and full virtualization has been created, called **hybrid virtualization**. In it, some parts of the guest operating system use paravirtualization for certain hardware drivers, and the host uses full virtualization for other features. This often produces superior performance on the guest without the need for the guest to be completely paravirtualized.

Full virtualization

Full virtualization is a virtualization technology that completely simulates virtual hardware underneath the virtual machines, with no interaction with the physical hardware. It requires that the entire hardware underneath the virtual machine to become unnoticeable. This technology can simulate any kind of physical hardware on demand to answer the need of the system running on the virtual machine, which answers any service or application demand for specific baremetal hardware. In other words, full virtualization is a virtualization capacity to fully run the guest machine without letting it become aware that it is running on a virtual environment. The virtual machine, in this case, has a fully virtualized hardware to run its services on. They don't have any interaction with the physical hardware.

The following diagram shows how, during full virtualization, the underlying platform runs the guest OS without being modified or being aware that it is running on a virtualization:

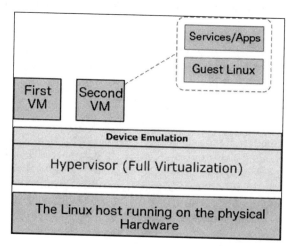

There is a specific type of full virtualization called hardware-assisted virtualization. In this, the CPU architecture helps with the execution of hardware virtualization through some special instructions that might allow the guest machine to execute privileged instructions directly on the CPU, even though it is a virtualization.

Using the CentOS 7 server, we can conduct full virtualization or hardware-assisted full virtualization by using either Xen or KVM. We will see how to do so in the *Setting up Xen for CentOS 7* section.

On a larger scale, solutions that can implement full virtualization include VMware's family of hypervisors, Xen and XenServer, VirtualBox, QEMU, and KVM.

Paravirtualization

Paravirtualization is a new kind of enhancement to the virtualization technology. It has the capacity of making the guest OS recompile before being installed on the vertical machine that serves the virtual machines to identify between virtual and physical hardware. With the use of this virtualization, we have a better optimization in system performance via conserving computing resources. It is due to this technology that we don't need to dedicate resources for the virtual machines and will be used only as necessary. Differing from the full virtualization where we need to create the virtual resources and dedicate them to the virtual machine, it is rather being used or not.

In paravirtualization, the guest operating system is managed by the hypervisor—as a layer lying between the physical machine and the virtual machines—to efficiently enable and share physical device access. While it normally doesn't require full device emulation or dynamic recompiling to perform privileged instructions, paravirtualization often performs at a near-native speed.

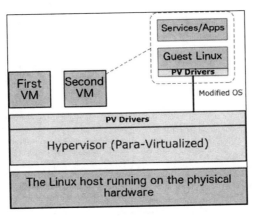

This preceding architecture shows how the paravirtualization virtual machines interact with the physical hardware through the special hypervisor that communicates directly with the modifier OS to optimize the communication.

Paravirtualization is an expansion of a technology invented by IBM. Xen is an open source software project that incorporates paravirtualization. The Xen hypervisor is what brought about the term *paravirtualization*. Today, most virtualization solutions support paravirtualization as a norm. A number of Linux development vendors have collaborated on a new form of paravirtualization, initially developed by the Xen group, and it provides a hypervisor-agnostic interface between the hypervisor and guest OS kernels.

Setting up Xen on CentOS 7

Xen is an open source solution used to run multiple virtual systems on one machine. It supports both paravirtualization and hardware-assisted full-virtualization. Xen is a very powerful virtualization solution. It offers the capacity to use both virtualization technologies at the same time to always answer the user's demands.

To create our virtualization environment using Xen, we need to make sure that the Xen Hypervisor will boot just before the machine's own kernel to have access to as much physical hardware as possible, so it can be used to serve our environment's virtual machines.

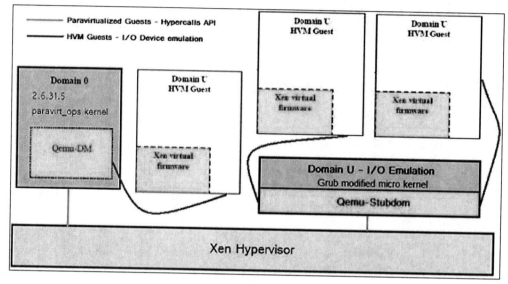

Source: http://www.2virt.com

In this section, we are going to set up Xen4 for CentOS 7. Xen4 is not supported by the default CentOS 7 repository, so we need to add the CentOS Xen repository. But first, we need to make sure that we have some packages installed. These will be needed later during the installation of Xen:

```
$ sudo yum install bridge-utils SDL net-tools
```

Then we add the latest Xen repository using YUM:

```
$ sudo yum install centos-release-xen
```

In this tutorial, we will be installing Xen Version 4.5, so we need to run the installation command as follows:

```
$ sudo yum install xen
```

To verify that the installation is done, we need to list the Xen kernel archive, which is in the /boot folder:

```
$ ls -l /boot/xen.gz
```

We should see the following code:

```
lrwxrwxrwx. 1 root root         12 Aug 23 02:10 /boot/xen.gz -> xen-
4.5.1.gz
```

Now, we move on to the installation of the `kernel-xen` package. This installation should be executed separately from the Xen installation and after it so that the system boot loader grub can detect the new kernel and get configured correctly:

```
$ sudo yum install kernel-xen
```

After having the new kernel installed, we should resolve the SELinux issue. We can try to resolve the issues by determining which modules the SELinux is blocking and resolve that, or if we have a better method to secure our server, we can just disable it. To disable SELinux, we just need to go to its configuration file and disable it:

```
$ sudo nano /etc/sysconfig/selinux
```

Then, consider this line:

```
SELINUX=enforcing
```

Change it to the following:

```
SELINUX=disabled
```

Otherwise, if we need to check the issues, we can follow this. First, we check the log file for the cause of the issue:

```
$ sudo cat /var/log/messages
```

Then, we activate the blockage:

```
$ sudo grep xend /var/log/audit/audit.log | audit2allow -M custom_xen
$ sudo semodule -i custom_xen.pp
```

And this should resolve the issue. Finally, we can restart the system and boot the new Xen kernel. After the restart, we need to check whether the Xen kernel is correctly installed:

```
$ sudo xl info
```

To use Xen, we need to install some tools and packages to make the virtual machines run well. First, we need to make sure that the basic usage packages are installed:

```
$ sudo yum install bridge-utils tunctl wget vim-enhanced rsync openssh-
clients libvirt python-virtinst libvirt-daemon-xen
```

Then, we need to configure the network. But before that, we must create the bridge interface:

```
$ sudo nano /etc/sysconfig/network-scripts/ifcfg-brid0
```

Next, we add the following lines inside the file that we have just opened using nano and save it:

```
DEVICE=brid0
TYPE=Bridge
BOOTPROTO=dhcp
ONBOOT=yes
```

Then, we make minor changes to the default network interface configuration file to use the bridged interface:

```
$ sudo nano /etc/sysconfig/network-scripts/ifcfg-eth0
DEVICE=eth0
HWADDR=XX:XX:XX:XX:XX:XX
ONBOOT=yes
TYPE=Ethernet
IPV6INIT=no
USERCTL=no
BRIDGE=brid0
```

 We need to change the MAC address with the Ethernet interface MAC address. We can check that using `ifconfig`.

After that, we reboot the system. With this, the bridge network is ready to be used. Then, we download any Linux system for the test. Next, we need to make it an IMG file using the dd command:

```
$ sudo dd if=/dev/zero of=Centos.img bs=4K count=0 seek=1024K
qemu-img create -f raw Centos.img 8G
```

Then, we download any Linux system for the test. Moreover, we must create a kick-start file and put it at the same location:

```
$ sudo nano ks.cfg
```

Then, we add the following code with the required modification:

```
kernel = "/boot/vmlinuz-xen-install"
ramdisk = "/boot/initrd-xen-install"
extra = "text"
name = "mailserver"
memory = "256"
disk = [ 'tap:aio:/srv/xen/mailserver.img,xvda,w', ]
vif = [ 'bridge=brid0', ]
vcpus=1
on_reboot = 'destroy'
on_crash = 'destroy'
```

Finally, we use `virt-install` to create the VM:

```
$ sudo virt-install -d -n CentOS7VM1 -r 1024 --vcpus=2 \
--bridge=brid0 --disk ./Centos.img \
--nographics -p -l "./Centos" \
--extra-args="text console=com1 utf8 console=hvc0 ks=./ks.cfg"
```

Now the virtual machine should start and be able to get an IP from the DHCP server; so we can continue tweaking it and adding the required service.

For Xen usage, we need to use the following commands (we are going to present the most common ones. For more, you can always follow this link `https://www.centos.org/docs/5/html/Virtualization-en-US/virt-task-xm-create-manage-doms.html`):

- To connect to the virtual machine:

  ```
  $ sudo xm console CentOS7VM1
  ```

- To shutdown or reboot a machine:

  ```
  $ sudo xm shutdown CentOS7VM1
  $ sudo xm reboot CentOS7VM1
  ```

- To remove (terminate) a machine:

  ```
  $ sudo xm destroy CentOS7VM1
  ```

- To suspend and resume a machine:

  ```
  $ sudo xm suspend CentOS7VM1
  $ sudo xm resume CentOS7VM1
  ```

- To rename a machine

```
$ sudo xm rename CentOS7VM1 CentOS7VM2
```

- To pause, and then unpause a machine:

```
$ sudo xm pause CentOS7VM1
$ sudo xm unpause CentOS7VM1
```

Setting up KVM for full virtualization on CentOS 7

KVM can only support hardware-assisted full virtualization. And there is still work going on in supporting paravirtualization. KVM is a kernel module that only works with the default Linux kernel (we should not install it on the Xen one). KVM creates virtual machines using a personalized version of Qemu for KVM called **Qemu-kvm**.

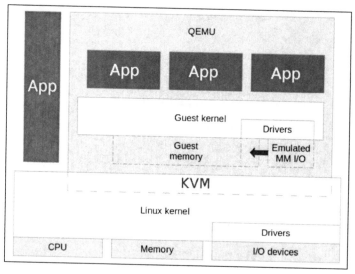

Source: http://www.virtualopensystems.com

KVM has many useful features and advantages supported by its hypervisor:

- **Thin provisioning**: This is the capacity to allocate flexible storage and manage the available space for the virtual machines
- **Overcommitting**: This is the capacity to allocate more CPU and memory power more that the available resource on the physical machine
- **Automatic NUMA balancing**: This is an improvement to the application running on the NUMA hardware

- **Disk I/O throttling**: This is the capacity to manage limits of the physical system disk input and output requests sent by the virtual machines
- **Virtual CPU hot add capability**: This is the capacity to adjust the processing power of the virtual machines without any downtime

Before starting the KVM installation, we need to check some pre-installation steps. First, we check whether the machine CPU can handle the virtualization technology:

```
$ sudo grep -e '(vmx|svm)' /proc/cpuinfo
```

To know whether that's true, we need to see the vmx or svm word highlighted in the command output:

Then, we make sure that the system packages are all updated:

```
$ sudo yum update
```

Next, we change the working mode of SELinux to permissive to make sure that it won't bother the execution of KVM:

```
$ sudo nano /etc/sysconfig/selinux
```

Then, consider this line:

```
SELINUX=enforcing
```

Change it to the following:

```
SELINUX=permissive
```

We can now start the installation. First, we will install the Qemu package to provide a user level for KVM and its disk image manager:

```
$ sudo yum install qemu-img qemu-kvm
```

Then, we need to install the GUI for the virtual machine's administration, the command-line tools to administrate the virtual environment, the tool that helps create virtual machines from the CLI, and the hypervisor library:

```
$ sudo yum install virt-manager libvirt libvirt-python libvirt-client
xauth dejavu-lgc-sans-fonts
```

Finally, for CentOS 7, we add the virtualization client, virtualization platform, and virtualization tools:

```
$ sudo yum groupinstall virtualization-client virtualization-tools
virtualization-platform
```

With this step done, we can say that we have finished installing the required tools and packages. Now, we go to the configuration part. First, we need to restart the virtualization daemon to make sure that the entire configuration is well set:

```
$ sudo systemctl restart libvirtd
```

Then, we check whether it is running well or not:

```
$ sudo systemctl status libvirtd
```

We should see this as the output:

```
libvirtd.service - Virtualization daemon
    Loaded: loaded (/usr/lib/systemd/system/libvirtd.service; enabled)
    Active: active (running) since Sat 2015-10-03 16:22:34 BST; 10s ago
      Docs: man:libvirtd(8)
            http://libvirt.org
 Main PID: 10696 (libvirtd)
   CGroup: /system.slice/libvirtd.service
           ├─10672 /sbin/dnsmasq --conf-file=/var/lib/libvirt/dnsmasq/default.conf --dhcp-script=/usr/libexec/libvirt_leaseshelper
           ├─10673 /sbin/dnsmasq --conf-file=/var/lib/libvirt/dnsmasq/default.conf --dhcp-script=/usr/libexec/libvirt_leaseshelper
           └─10696 /usr/sbin/libvirtd
```

Now, we move on to the network configuration. We need to create a bridge interface to allow the guest system to access an external network. To do so, we must enable IP forwarding:

```
$ sudo echo "net.ipv4.ip_forward = 1"|sudo tee /etc/sysctl.d/99-ipforward.conf
```

Then, we check whether it is well set:

```
$ sudo sysctl -p /etc/sysctl.d/99-ipforward.conf
```

After that, we need to change the network configuration by keeping the original interface as it is, but we will assign its IP address to the bridge:

```
$ sudo nano /etc/sysconfig/network-scripts/ifcfg-eth0
```

Next, we add the following line to the end of the file and save it:

```
BRIDGE=virbrid0
```

Then, we create the bridge interface configuration file:

```
$ sudo nano /etc/sysconfig/network-scripts/ifcfg-brid0
```

After that, we put the following code inside the file we just opened for editing, and save it:

```
DEVICE="brid0"
TYPE=BRIDGE
```

```
ONBOOT=yes
BOOTPROTO=static
IPADDR="10.0.0.2"
NETMASK="255.255.255.0"
GATEWAY="10.0.0.1"
DNS1="8.8.8.8"
```

After rebooting the system, we can say that the network configuration is well set.

After we complete the KVM installation and configuration, it's time to start using the host. The first thing we need to do is create a new domain or virtual machine. To do so, using the CLI, we will make use of the virt-install command. First, we need to see the list of templates known to our KVM installation:

```
$ sudo virt-install --os-variant=list
```

We need an ISO of the Linux OS to use it for the installation. Then, we can start the setup of a new virtual machine:

```
$ sudo virt-install --name=CentOS7guest --ram=1024 --vcpus=2
--cdrom=./CentOS-7.1-x86_64-minimal.iso --os-type=linux --os-
variant=rhel7 --network bridge=brid0 --graphics=spice --disk path=/var/
lib/libvirt/images/CentOS7.dsk,size=10
```

The options written in the preceding command are as follows:

- name: This is the name of the virtual machine
- ram: This is the memory size in MB
- vcpus: This is the number of virtual CPUs
- cdrom: This is the location of the ISO image
- os-type: This is the OS type, such as Linux, Windows, or Unix
- os-variant: This is the OS variant, such as rhel 6 or Solaris
- network: This is the network interface and connectivity
- graphics: This is the guest display settings
- disk path: This is the location of the disk with a size of 10 GB

Once we have issued the preceding command, virt-install will create a virtual machine and start the virt viewer console for the OS installation.

There is always a graphical mode perform the previous treatment. The graphical tools is called virt-manager found a the system tools.

The following commands are meant for better management of the KVM virtual machines after being deployed:

- To list the virtual machines running on KVM:

```
$ sudo virsh --connect qemu:///system list
```

- To get more information about a virtual machine:

```
$ sudo virsh dominfo CentOS7guest
```

- To stop a running guest machine:

```
$ sudo virsh --connect qemu:///system shutdown CentOS7guest
```

- To start a virtual machine:

```
$ sudo virsh --connect qemu:///system start CentOS7guest
```

- To delete a guest machine:

```
$ sudo virsh --connect qemu:///system destroy CentOS7guest
$ sudo virsh --connect qemu:///system undefineCentOS7guest
$ sudo rm -f /var/lib/libvirt/images/CentOS7guest.img
```

- Finally, the code used to automatically start a virtual machine with the host system startup:

```
$ sudo virsh --connect qemu:///system autostart CentOS7guest
$ sudo virsh --connect qemu:///system dominfo CentOS7guest | grep
Auto
```

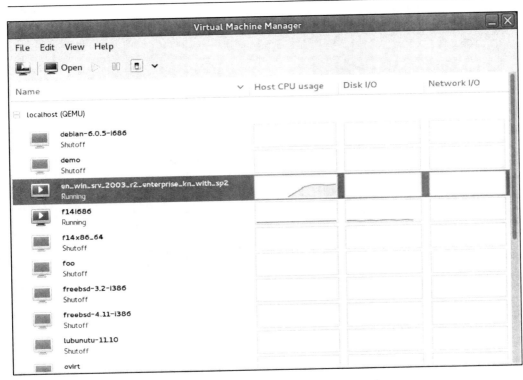

Source: `https://virt-manager.org/`

Setting up OpenVZ virtualization on CentOS 7

OpenVZ is a new form of virtualization technology that we call a container based one. It basically creates multiple secure and isolated Linux containers running on a single Linux server. This container technology allows better server utilization, since we are not installing a full virtual machine, just a container to hold some of it, and it eliminates application conflict. The virtual machine running on OpenVZ platform are on a standalone mode, where it is the capacity to run without falling in any type of conflict with any other virtual machine running on the same platform. Those machines are independent from each other.

The virtual machines running on OpenVZ have their own operating system, IP address, processes, memory or storage space, application and configuration files, and so on.

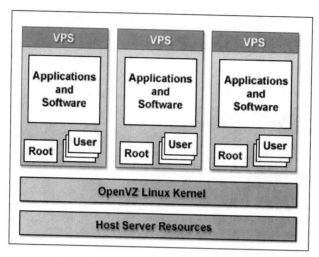

Source: http://www.quantact.com

While using OpenVZ, the virtualization is run through the system-level virtualization technology, where the guest system uses the same kernel as the physical machine system unlike KVM and VirtualBox and this helps with the usage effectiveness of the physical machine processing power and the storage power.

For a better usage for OpenVZ, we might need to use QEMU and Virtuozzo as management utilities. We really recommend the usage of the OpenVZ container and virtual machines on a Virtuozzo installation of images.

For CentOS 7, there is no working OpenVZ distribution as of now. So, we are going to install its forked project, Virtuozzo 7, which is capable of all OpenVZ options and more. Yet, we are going to use the OpenVZ tools only.

To install Virtuozzo 7, we need to install the RPM-based distribution package. First, we need to bring the meta information of the `virtuozzo-release` package into the YUM repository:

```
$ sudo yum localinstall http://download.openvz.org/virtuozzo/
releases/7.0/x86_64/os/Packages/v/virtuozzo-release-7.0.0-10.vz7.x86_64.
rpm
```

Then, we install the mandatory Virtuozzo RPM packages:

```
$ sudo yum install -y prlctl prl-disp-service vzkernel
```

Now, we have OpenVZ kernel installed. We move on to the kernel parameter configuration:

```
$ sudo nano /etc/sysctl.conf
```

Then, we add the following code:

```
# On Hardware Node we generally need
# packet forwarding enabled and proxy arp disabled
net.ipv4.ip_forward = 1
net.ipv6.conf.default.forwarding = 1
net.ipv6.conf.all.forwarding = 1
net.ipv4.conf.default.proxy_arp = 0


# Enables source route verification
net.ipv4.conf.all.rp_filter = 1


# Enables the magic-sysrq key
kernel.sysrq = 1


# We do not want all our interfaces to send redirects
net.ipv4.conf.default.send_redirects = 1
net.ipv4.conf.all.send_redirects = 0
```

After that, we make SELinux act permissive to ensure that OpenVZ works fine:

```
$ sudo nano /etc/sysconfig/selinux
```

Next, we need to have the configuration line to make it look like the following:

```
SELINUX=permissive
```

This part is optional. We can install the OpenVZ usage statistics tools if needed:

```
$ sudo yum install vzctl vzquota ploop
```

Now, since we have successfully installed OpenVZ, we can reboot the system and log in through the OpenVZ kernel. We need to edit the OpenVZ configuration file to set the same subnet for physical and virtual machines:

```
$ sudo nano /etc/vz/vz.conf
```

Then, we find and uncomment the following line and change its option to this:

```
NEIGHBOUR_DEVS=all
```

Now, we can set up a web-based interface for OpenVZ to help administrate it. We need to download the installation script and run it:

```
$ sudo wget -O - http://ovz-web-panel.googlecode.com/svn/installer/ai.sh
| sh
```

Then, add the port from where this web interface is going to serve using Firewalld:

```
$ sudo firewall-cmd --zone=public --permanent --add-port=3000/tcp
```

Then, reload Firewalld:

```
$ sudo firewall-cmd --reload
```

The web-based interface will be serving its web interface at the machine hostname or IP address followed by port number `3000`:

```
http://<the-hostname>:3000
```

Now, we are going to start using OpenVZ to download a container and start using it. First, we need to specify a folder to put our containers into:

```
$ mkdir OpenVZCont
$ cd OpenVZCont
```

Then, we download an example container:

```
$ wget http://download.openvz.org/template/precreated/centos-7-x86_64-
minimal.tar.gz
```

Next, we unpack the `tar` file:

```
$ tar -xzvf centos-7-x86_64-minimal.tar.gz
```

Then, we type this command to create our first virtual machine:

```
$ sudo vzctl create 101 --ostemplate centos-7-x86_64-minimal
```

Our container ID is `101`, since they typically start from `100`. Now, we set an IP address for our container:

```
$ sudo vzctl set 101 --ipadd 10.0.0.14 --save
```

Then comes a DNS server:

```
$ sudo vzctl set 101 --nameserver 8.8.8.8 --save
```

After having the network configuration ready, we can start our newly created container:

```
$ sudo vzctl start 101
```

We can verify that it is running by pinging its IP address:

```
$ ping 10.0.0.14
```

Now, we can log in to our container to explore it:

```
$ sudo vzctl enter 101
```

We are in the newly created container. We can do whatever we want with it. To exit the virtual machine, we can simply type exit in the terminal. Also, using the OpenVZ web interface, we can visualize its status and do some administrative management through it.

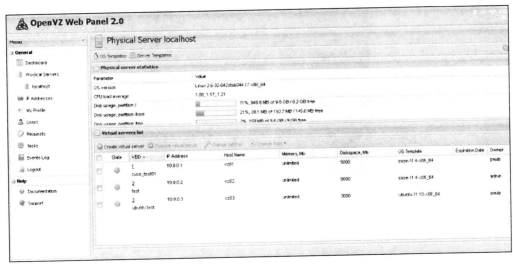

Source: `http://4.bp.blogspot.com/`

Setting up VirtualBox virtualization on CentOS 7

Oracle VirtualBox is a virtualization application that has the capacity to run on multiple computer architectures (Intel, AMD-based systems) and on almost every available OS (OSX, Linux, Windows, Solaris, and so on), where it allows its users to run multiple operating systems on the same physical machine. Basically, virtual box is a full virtualization technology.

Most people count on it while using multiple systems and need to export and import template virtual machines, where virtual box offers a variety of options to exchange virtual machines between all kinds of infrastructures.

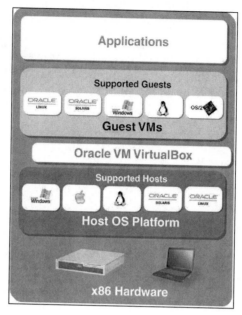

Source: http://www.oracle.com

This section will show you how to install Oracle VirtualBox 5.0.2 on CentOS 7. Firstly, we need to add the VirtualBox yum repository to our system. So, we need to create its repo file in the YUM repository directory:

```
$ sudo nano /etc/yum.repos.d/virtualbox.repo
```

Then, we need to put the following code into the file and save it:

```
[virtualbox]
name=Oracle Linux / RHEL / CentOS-$releasever / $basearch - VirtualBox
baseurl=http://download.virtualbox.org/virtualbox/rpm/
el/$releasever/$basearch
enabled=1
gpgcheck=1
gpgkey=http://download.virtualbox.org/virtualbox/debian/oracle_vbox.asc
```

We should also have the EPEL repository installed:

```
$ sudo rpm -ivh http://ftp.jaist.ac.jp/pub/Linux/Fedora/epel/7/x86_64/e/
epel-release-7-5.noarch.rpm
```

Before we start the installation, we need to install some necessary packages to make sure that VirtualBox works fine:

```
$ sudo yum install gcc make kernel-headers kernel-devel fontforge
binutils patch  dkms glibc-headers glibc-devel qt libgomp
```

Then, we set up an environment variable called KERN_DIR, from which VirtualBox will get the kernel source code:

```
$ export KERN_DIR=/usr/src/kernels/3.10.0-229.14.1.el7.x86_64
```

 My latest kernel version is stored in this directory: 3.10.0-229.14.1.el7.x86_64. It might change over time due to upgrades.

Then, we can start the installation of VirtualBox using YUM:

```
$ sudo yum install VirtualBox-5.0
```

After the installation, we need to rebuild the kernel modules using the following command:

```
$ sudo systemctl start vboxdrv
```

Now, we have VirtualBox installed and ready for use. Still, VirtualBox only supports graphical interfaces, so we need to have one installed and then we can start it and use it.

We need to have a graphical interface installed on our server and we have a long list to choose from. I would recommend Gnome, as it is one of the most used interfaces with its user-friendliness and its low resources consumption.

Using Gnome as the graphical interface, we can start VirtualBox:

```
$ sudo virtualbox &
```

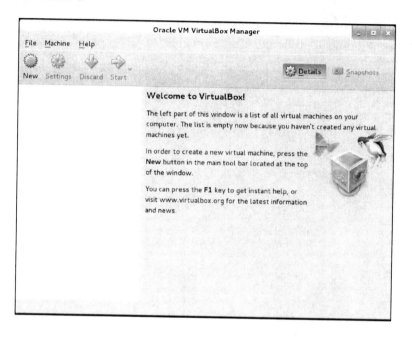

Then, we can go ahead and create a new virtual machine. We give it a name and a type, as shown here:

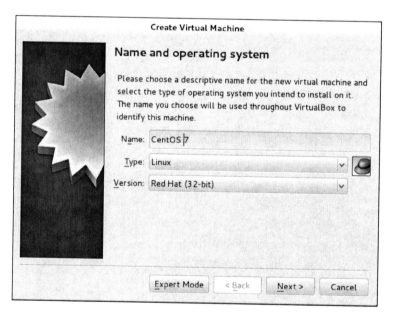

Next, we proceed to configure the amount of RAM to give it, as shown in the following screenshot:

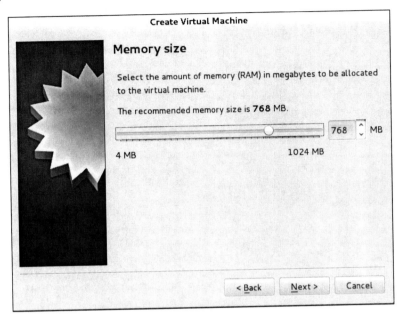

Then comes the amount of disk space, as follows:

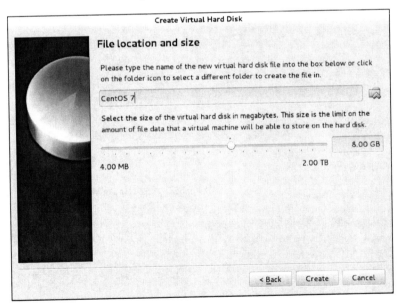

VirtualBox offers some extra services that allow the mouse and the keyboard of the original system to switch between the physical and the virtual machine. To install those tools, we can go to the VM menu, then the **Guest** option, and then install the virtual machine guest tools. It will take some time to get installed, then we need to restart the virtual machine so that those tools can start working.

To finish, we have our virtual machine ready to be executed, as shown in the following screenshot:

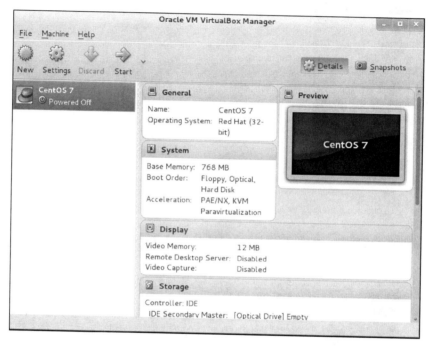

Setting up Docker on CentOS 7

Sharing the same technology as OpenVZ on using the container technology, Docker is another alternative for container-based software virtualization. Docker is famous due to its capacity to automatically deploy applications. Those templates or containers are divided between community containers presented as templates provided by the Docker community, or private containers provided by individual users. Some of the user-personalized containers can be publicly available, others can be stored in a private folder that can be accessed by their creator or some one he wants to share with. Docker containers are portable, lightweight, and encapsulated application modules.

According to the industry analyst firm, 451 Research:

"Docker is a tool that can package an application and its dependencies in a virtual container that can run on any Linux server. This helps enable flexibility and portability on where the application can run, whether on premises, public cloud, private cloud, bare metal, etc."

To install Docker, we are going to use the Docker installation script. Here, we have another way to install Docker via YUM — the traditional way:

1. First, we need to make sure that our system packages are updated:

    ```
    $ sudo yum update
    ```

2. Then, we run the Docker installation script:

    ```
    $ sudo curl -sSL https://get.docker.com/ | sh
    ```

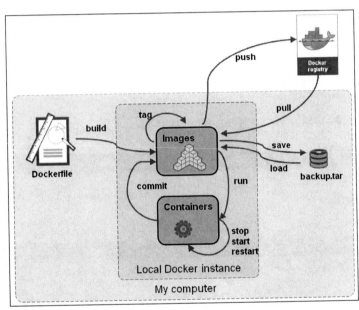

Source: `http://blog.ouseful.info/`

3. This script will add the Docker repository to the system repository and then install Docker.

4. If too many users are going to use Docker in our system, we need to add them to the Docker group:

    ```
    $ sudo usermod -aG docker packt
    ```

5. Then, we start the Docker daemon. Add it to the system startup script:

```
$ sudo systemctl docker start
$ sudo systemctl enable docker.service
```

6. To verify that Docker is correctly installed, we have a simple image container that we can test:

```
$ sudo docker run hello-world
```

7. To download a Docker container, we need to look for its name and then type in the following command:

```
$ sudo docker pull centos7
```

8. To run the container, we need to use the `docker run` command with the `-i` option to attach `stdin` and `stdout` to the container, and the `-t` option to allocate a `tty` interface:

```
$ sudo docker run -i -t centos7 /bin/bash
```

9. To leave the Docker container without losing the shell terminal, we need to follow the following sequence: `Ctrl-p` and `Ctrl-q` at the same time.

10. For more community containers that are publicly available on the Web, we can always use the following command:

```
$ sudo docker search centos7
```

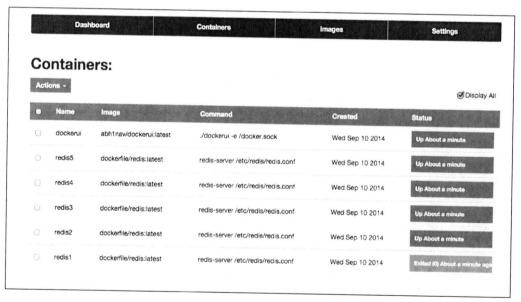

Source: `http://blog.ouseful.info/`

Establishing services' high availability using HAProxy

For this section, we are going to show in brief how to setup a high-availability/load balancer to control traffic over a specific service; in our case, we will use HTTP as for web server's traffic.

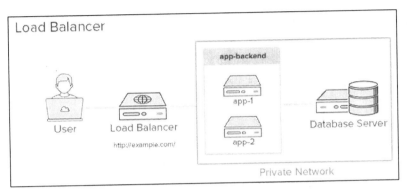

Source: `assets.digitalocean.com`

For this job, we are using HAProxy as an open source solution for load balancing and services' high availability through multiple servers. It is commonly used for a website's traffic load balancing. HAProxy distributes the workload over many servers that offer the same services (basically web servers, databases, and so on) to improve the overall performance of the service and its reliability.

As we said earlier, this section is going to install and configure a high availability load balancer to share the load between three web servers and a backup server in case of server or service failure to take over.

So, we will have an infrastructure that looks like this:

- HAProxy server:
    - **OS**: CentOS 7
    - **IP address**: 172.25.25.166 and 10.0.0.10
    - **Hostname**: haproxy.packt.co.uk

- Web server 1:
    - **OS**: CentOS 7
    - **IP address**: 10.0.0.11
    - **Hostname**: webserver1.packt.co.uk

- Web server 2:
    - ○ **OS**: CentOS 7
    - ○ **IP address**: 10.0.0.12
    - ○ **Hostname**: webserver2.packt.co.uk

- Web server 3:
    - ○ **OS**: CentOS 7
    - ○ **IP address**: 10.0.0.13
    - ○ **Hostname**: webserver3.packt.co.uk

- Backup web server:
    - ○ **OS**: CentOS 7
    - ○ **IP address**: 10.0.0.20
    - ○ **Hostname**: backupwebserver.packt.co.uk

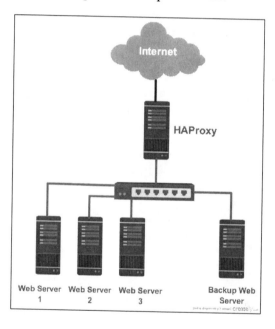

First, we will start by setting the web servers and to do so, we will be only using the default page generated by Apache after being installed. For more information on how to setup a web server, you can always refer to *Chapter 3, Linux for Different Purposes*. So, we will only need to have Apache installed and running and we need to configure the network and the machine's hostname.

First, we will use the default package manager for CentOS 7 YUM to install the Apache web server:

```
$ sudo yum install httpd
```

Then after that, we configure the hostname:

```
$ sudo nano /etc/hostname
```

And we make sure it looks like this:

```
Webserver1.packt.co.uk
```

After that, we go to each hosts file and we configure the domain to the default localhost while adding the list of all the servers with their IP addresses:

```
$ sudo nano /etc/hosts
```

 This part is only needed if there is no reliable DNS server inside the infrastructure that can resolve all the infrastructure servers.

We change the default localhost address `127.0.0.1` domain name:

```
127.0.0.1  webserver1  Webserver1.packt.co.uk
```

Then, we add the following lines:

```
10.0.0.10  haproxy  haproxy.packt.co.uk
10.0.0.11  Webserver1  Webserver1.packt.co.uk
10.0.0.12  Webserver2  Webserver2.packt.co.uk
10.0.0.13  Webserver3  Webserver3.packt.co.uk
10.0.0.20  backupWebserver    backupWebserver.packt.co.uk
```

Before finishing, we need to open the HTTPS and HTTPS ports at the webserver firewall to make the service accessible for the visitors:

```
$ sudo firewallcmd permanent zone=public addport=80/tcp
$ sudo firewallcmd permanent zone=public addport=443/tcp
$ sudo firewallcmd reload
```

By this step, we can say that we have all our web servers ready. We can now move to our HAProxy server installation. First, we need to open the needed ports for the web service and log reception used by HAProxy:

```
$ sudo firewallcmd permanent zone=public addport=80/tcp
$ sudo firewallcmd permanent zone=public addport=443/tcp
```

```
$ sudo firewallcmd permanent zone=public addport=514/udp
$ sudo firewallcmd reload
```

Then, we can start the installation:

```
$ sudo yum install haproxy
```

And now, we go to the configuration part. Before doing the main HAProxy configuration, we need to setup the HAProxy logging feature configuration for debugging:

```
$ sudo nano /etc/haproxy/haproxy.cfg
```

Under the **#Global settings** options, we need to make sure that the following line is not commented:

```
log          127.0.0.1 local2 info
```

Some minor modification needs to happen at the `Rsyslog` configuration file too:

```
$ sudo nano /etc/rsyslog.conf
```

That is where we need to uncomment the following two lines:

```
$ModLoad imudp
$UDPServerRun 514
```

Before finishing, we need to have a file that represents `HAProxy` at the `Rsyslog log` folder:

```
$ sudo nano /etc/rsyslog.d/haproxy.conf
```

And while creating it using Nano, we need to put the following line inside it:

```
local2.*   /var/log/haproxy.log
```

Save the file, then apply the changes and restart `Rsyslog service`:

```
$ sudo systemctl restart rsyslog.service
```

Now, we can go to the HAProxy Global settings configuration:

```
$ sudo nano /etc/haproxy/haproxy.cfg
```

First, at the default section, we need to setup the timeout for a more personalized solution. Since our server is just doing the load balancing, we can always use port 80. So, we need to take over that port, by removing its association to the `Httpd` service:

```
$ sudo nano /etc/httpd/conf/httpd.conf
```

Then, we change the listening port to anything other than 80. In our example, `8080`:

```
Listen 8080
```

Then, we go to the **Main Frontend** section to change the port on which the web interface is serving. So we need to change the whole section to look like the following:

```
Frontend  HAProxy
bind  *:80
reqadd X-Forwarded-Proto:\ http
default_backend  HAProxy
```

And we need to comment out the **Backend** section to replace it with the following:

```
# use_backend static  if url_static
backend HAProxy *:80
mode http
stats enable
stats hide-version
stats uri /stats
stats realm Haproxy\ Statistics
stats auth haproxy:password    # Change "password" with a well secured
password
balance roundrobin
option httpchk
option  httpclose
option forwardfor
cookie LB insert
   server webserver1 10.0.0.11:80 cookie webserver1 check
server webserver3 10.0.0.12:80 cookie webserver2 check
server webserver3 10.0.0.13:80 cookie webserver3 check
server backupwebserver 10.0.0.20:80 check backup
```

We need to make sure that the end of the file matches our infrastructure IP addresses and hostnames. Then, we can start the HAProxy server and add it to the startup system services:

```
$ sudo systemctl start haproxy.service
$ sudo systemctl enable haproxy.service
```

To verify that there is no error at the configuration file, we can always check the service status using the following command:

```
$ sudo systemctl status haproxy.service -l
```

Then, we get each web server and put a test page just to access it and collect the test results. Then, we open the web interface of HAProxy to visualize the status of the load balancing `http://10.0.0.10/stats` or `http://172.25.25.166/stats`.

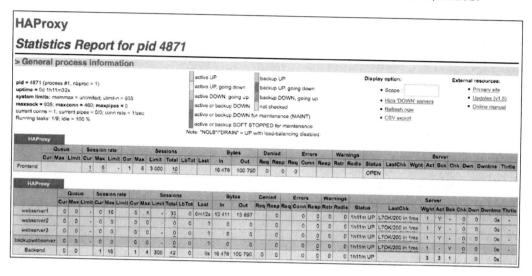

If we get to see the following interface, that means that our high availability server is running well. If we need to enable https to access the web interface of HAProxy using SSL, we can always install OpenSSL and configure our server to use it.

References

Now, let's look at the references used throughout the chapter:

- **VMware Documentation Center**: `http://pubs.vmware.com/vsphere-51/index.jsp`

- **VMware Virtualization**: `http://www.vmware.com/virtualization.html`

- **Full virtualization wiki**: `https://en.wikipedia.org/wiki/Full_virtualization`

- **Paravirtualization wiki**: `https://en.wikipedia.org/wiki/Paravirtualization`

- **Xen project wiki**: `http://wiki.xen.org/wiki/Xen_Project_Software_Overview`

- **KVM home page**: `http://www.linux-kvm.org/page/Main_Page`
- **OpenVZ home page**: `https://openvz.org/Main_Page`
- **VirtualBox home page**: `https://www.virtualbox.org`
- **Docker documentation**: `https://docs.docker.com/installation/centos/`
- **HAProxy web page**: `http://www.haproxy.org/`

Summary

This chapter started with a brief description of the basics of virtualization. Then, we defined full virtualization and paravirtualization. Next, to better explain all of that practically using a variety of open source virtualization tools, we started with Xen as a paravirtualization and full virtualization solution. We moved on to KVM as a full virtualization solution, container virtualization, OpenVZ, and the VirtualBox tool. This allows an easy setup through its beautiful graphical interface.

We concluded the chapter with Docker and its ways of using containers from the Web. By the end of this chapter, we can say that we have seen various virtualization technologies and how to create virtual machines using them.

In the next chapter, we will get a chance to explore the cloud computing technology and apply some examples using the open source solution, OpenStack.

7
Cloud Computing

The new generation of services provided via the Internet is known as cloud computing. In the computer industry, many organizations use cloud computing as they don't like to purchase the equipment that can resolve their resource solutions, or hire what is required to manage and maintain it. Cloud computing is like a third-party data source that offers various capabilities to store and process data.

Within the list of the best solutions for establishing a cloud-computing environment, we have chosen OpenStack. In this chapter, we will cover in brief what cloud computing is and how to set up a single node using OpenStack.

Over the course of this chapter, we will go through the following topics:

- Overview of cloud computing
- Cloud-computing services
- Introducing OpenStack
- Components of OpenStack
- Installing and setting up of OpenStack

An overview of cloud computing

Cloud computing is the capacity to perform computing outside the usual way of relying on local machines. Cloud computing relies on shared resources to handle the needed calculation or treatment. It shares the same aspects as Grid computing where both technologies have its processing power gathered to resolve or treat problems too heavy for a standalone machine (server or a personal computer).

The goal of cloud computing is to harness high supercomputing power to perform high-level computations in consumer-oriented applications, such as finance, personalized information delivery, data storage, and so on.

In order to perform this overwhelming task, cloud computing relies on a gigantic number of super powerful servers (blades...) connected through an extremely fast connection (InfiniBand (IB)) to share the workload across their computing units. This kind of infrastructure runs on specially configured systems, where they are linked together to simplify the task. Some infrastructures rely on virtualization technology to enhance their cloud computing.

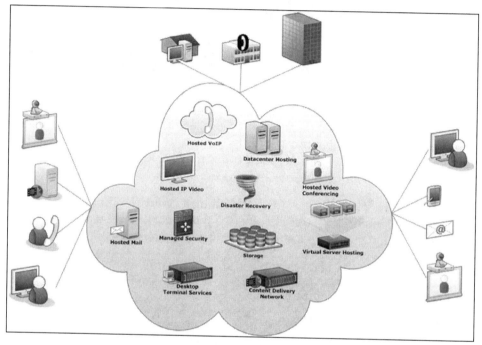

Source: http://networksolutionsintl.com

Briefly, the most precise reason for many companies to use cloud computing is that it enables them to make computer resources look like a utility, which they can pay for over time without having the real hardware on site and the burden of managing it and sustaining it within their team. Also, cloud computing offers many interesting features for enterprises, such as:

- **Elasticity**: The capacity to scale computing resources up and down as the need requires

- **Self-service provisioning**: The capacity to provide the required amount of resources for the job, on demand

- **Pay per use**: The capacity to measure the resources used by the users so they only get charged for the resources they have used

Cloud computing has hugely evolved over time. However, it has always kept the main three board services:

- **Software as a Service (SaaS)**
- **Platform as a Service (PaaS)**
- **Infrastructure as a Service (IaaS)**

Software as a Service

SaaS refers to every application running on a machine other than the current user machine, where the user has access to some or all of its services through their web browser, and sometimes through a thin client application that only works as a presentation interface. SaaS applications are generally accessible worldwide using any kind of device that can access the Internet (computer, mobile, and so on). The thing that makes an SaaS application work well is that it is a kind of scalable application where the user can process its treatment over as many virtual machines as needed to answer the load demand. Most cloud-computing infrastructures use a load-balancing system to organize the load between the virtual machines, where the application keeps running without any interruption and perform a better execution results.

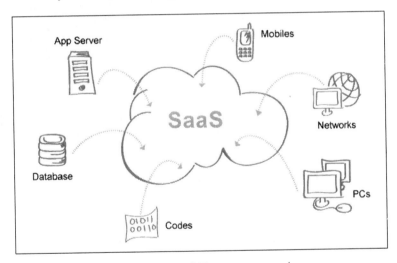

Source: `http://icorees.com/`

SaaS is characterized as follows:

- Its services are accessible for any connected device
- Easy-to-use application just after signing in
- Where everything is stored on the cloud over hundreds of machines well configured for disasters such as disk crash and so on, plus user data and services are always available
- Computing power for applications is always scalable when needed

We can distinguish some of the most famous SaaS that we use every day, such as e-mail services (Gmail, Yahoo...), social media and communication tools (Facebook, Skype...). All we need to use these daily services is an Internet connection and a device that has a web browser or a thin client application for mobile.

Platform as a Service (PaaS)

PaaS is a service that offers its clients the capacity to build and deploy applications on a cloud-based environment. PaaS acts like SaaS when providing scalability to its users. When deploying their applications, they have on-demand access to the needed resource to run their application, where it offers all those services without the pain of buying, maintaining and managing the hardware needed for the application to run, with all the logistics behind it. PaaS has been well developed to offer to its clients pre-prepared templates to simplify the initialization on the platform.

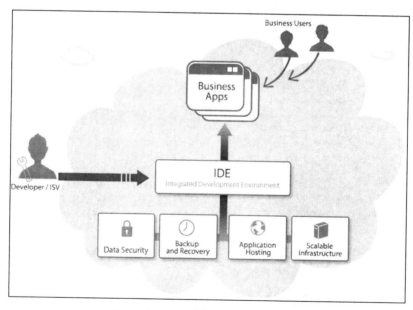

Source: https://www.zoho.com/

We can distinguish some major benefits of using PaaS from the traditional solution, as follows:

- Speeds up the development of applications where the environment is already there, and makes it ready for marketing where it is already hosted

- Removes the complexity of managing the middleware and simplifies the task of having it

- Simplifies the deployment of web applications

Infrastructure as a Service (IaaS)

The third service is IaaS, a kind of service that offers its users everything needed to establish a fully qualified infrastructure. IaaS provides servers with different characteristics, network equipment, and storage space on demand. The user of the infrastructure has all the rights to manage his infrastructure as desired, with all the rights of a system and network administrator. This service offers its users more than just the infrastructure but a pack-kind of resource (small, medium, and extra-large computing power and memory) to answer the workload requirements. As we said before, users act as system and network administrators so as to deploy their applications. They then need to establish their networks, install the desired OS, and set up their machines, where the users also maintain, manage and update their systems manually, as desired.

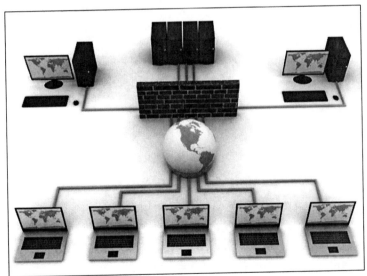

Source: http://cloudplus.com/

The benefits of IaaS can be summed up as follows:

- It removes the task of investing in hardware
- As with other cloud solutions, IaaS is scalable on demand to answer the user need for resources and equipment
- A variety of flexible and innovative services are provided as per user requirements

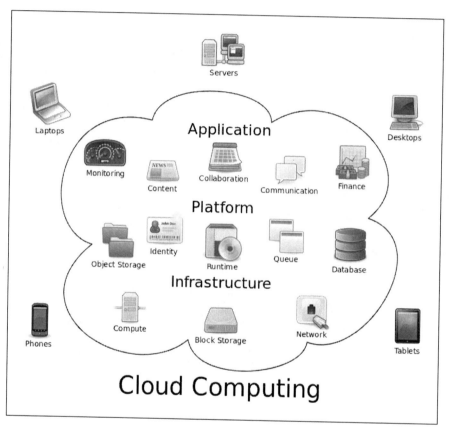

Cloud computing services

After explaining the different types of cloud computing, we should now have a look at how those services are provided. For that, we categorize them into three major types: public cloud, private cloud, and hybrid cloud.

Public cloud

We will start by introducing the public cloud. The public cloud, as its name suggests, is a publicly available cloud. Usually, a public cloud service is scalable on how much the user is willing to pay, either for resources or special services. Since it is on the cloud, users don't have to worry about hardware purchases, management, and maintenance. Most services provided as a public cloud are SaaS, with a small number as PaaS. Most of those services are available on demand. Usually, the users are charged for the resources they are using (CPU, memory, storage, Internet bandwidth) more than for the service itself.

Source: http://nextgenaccess.zserver.co.uk/

Resources sharing on a public cloud appear when multiple users access the same service where it is hosted on one or many servers, and also where those servers need to process the tasks sent by the clients. Some infrastructures are better than others whereby they can handle really heavy traffic; others may find it a bit more difficult. On this stage, clients may experience slowness in their application and that is what really affects the service in a bad way.

Private cloud

In contrast to the public cloud, the private cloud is a kind of dedicated service for one user or one organization. Being used by one customer does not make it different to any other cloud. It can still be managed and administrated by a third-party company or by an internal team.

Most organizations tend to use a private cloud due to its advantages of allocation and to be able to control the resources. This is different from the public cloud where it is shared between multiple users. Also the public cloud features a self-service interface that helps and simplifies the resources management and allocation for system administrators with a faster method on demand, more advanced security protocols for better security of the user data, and an advanced automated system that helps with the resource management to optimize the workload.

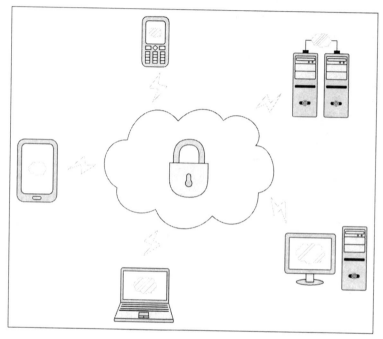

Source: http://blogs.dlt.com

Hybrid cloud

A hybrid cloud is a combination of the public cloud and the private cloud. To be more specific, the private cloud can sometimes be very expensive and hard to adjust, especially for little applications that do not require the advantages that the private cloud is offering. While a public cloud is not that much more expensive a solution, and has the advantage of fast deployment of its applications, organizations tend to mix the use of both services, depending on their needs, and that's what has made the hybrid cloud popular. The hybrid cloud allows organizations to keep important data on their private cloud and offer light services such as SaaS on a public cloud, with the capacity to switch to the desired service whenever needed.

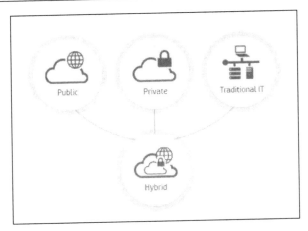

Source: `http://www8.hp.com`

Introducing OpenStack

We have now thoroughly described cloud computing, its services, and how a customer can utilize these services. Now, we need to talk about our role in this. Knowing how to use a cloud-computing service, such as an IaaS to deploy an infrastructure on it, is not really one of the hardest tasks for a system administrator. But the one that every system administrator should know is how to deploy one and how to offer those services to their clients. In this section, we are going to explore how to have a cloud running within our infrastructure and how to provide those services running on our CentOS 7 server. To perform this task we will be using one of the most famous open source cloud solutions for Linux, OpenStack, which is a free cloud-computing solution that helps initiate, manage, and sustain a huge pool of virtual machines with the required resources (CPU, memory, networking, and storage). This infrastructure is managed through a user-friendly web interface that helps present the status of the nodes to the system administrator, and gives them easy access to manage the infrastructure resources. OpenStack provides open source and enterprise services as per the user's demands, which make it well used by multiple organizations.

Today, OpenStack is used by hundreds of worldwide organizations to maintain their cloud infrastructure where they use it to have their cloud solutions up and running, and where it is used for both public or private cloud services. Most organizations providing cloud services, to either the public or private, use OpenStack to deliver an IaaS service.

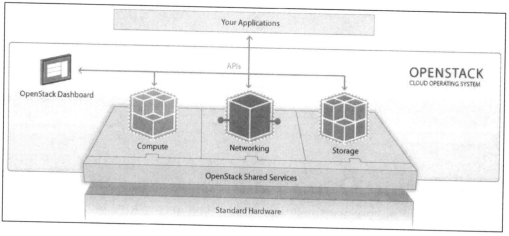

Source: https://www.openstack.org/software/

OpenStack manages three major sections under its API: compute, networking and storage. Through this API, OpenStack creates a sustainable environment for the infrastructures it manages.

OpenStack compute

OpenStack compute is the capacity to offer computing resources on demand for the customer while managing the resources that have been requested. OpenStack compute not only offers what the customers are running on their applications but also ensures that the service itself is running well by organizing the resources and the applications. OpenStack compute is accessible via both the web interface for administration and via the API for developing and building applications. This architecture enables economic usage of the physical hardware where it scales it horizontally. This technology also manages and automates a huge pool of computing resources, while it offers a compatibility with a variety of virtualization technologies.

OpenStack networking

OpenStack networking is the capacity to manage networking for the cloud resources managed by OpenStack. This technology ensures that the network resources connecting the cloud infrastructure are always available and do not contain any bottlenecks, other that just performing what a network administrator should do to maintain its infrastructure network.

OpenStack networking offers a flexible networking model to answer needs such as flat networks, VLAN configurations, GRE, and VXLAN. It provides the same services that the ordinary physical network hardware provides such as routing, NAT and DHCP, and static IP association. IT is also equipped with an intelligent system that helps redirect traffic in case of a failure or overload, to help maintain a better networking capacity. OpenStack networking not only supports automated network management but also offers its users the capacity to manage their network manually by adjusting their proper connections, and connect servers and terminals to each other as required. Users can also take advantage of **Software-defined networking (SDN)** technology for a multi-tenancy configuration and massive scale such as OpenFlow. It also offers support for advanced networking services architecture from multiple common vendors. Finally, it offers an advanced extension that integrates common network administration techniques such as VPN for private connection, IDS for reinforcing security, load balancing, firewalls for setting access rules, and so on.

OpenStack storage

OpenStack storage is the data storage services offered by OpenStack inside its architecture. Through its fully distributed API storage platform, cloud applications can access storage space through multiple technologies and architectures (archiving, backup, data retention). Storage with OpenStack is always scalable, to answer the user and application's demands, by allowing block devices to be added to each other and assuring a better performance. OpenStack storage has the capacity to be integrated with enterprise storage platforms such as SolidFire and NetApp.

Components of OpenStack

OpenStack is a very big platform that has many small components, assuring the full functionality of its services. Most of those components are made by the open source community to help meet the needs of its users. For this section, we are going to talk about the OpenStack community components as part of its core. What characterizes those components are that they are maintained by the OpenStack community, to be presented as part of the solution.

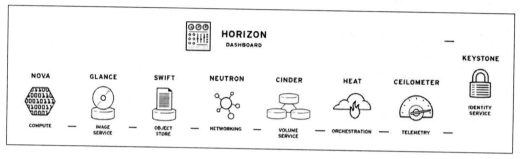

Source: http://redhatstackblog.redhat.com/

These components are described as follows:

- **Horizon**: This is the component responsible of setting up the OpenStack dashboard. It is from where the OpenStack administrator manages the infrastructure. It is the only graphical interface OpenStack has, so far. Horizon provides a look into what is happening in the cloud infrastructure and gives to the system administrators some functionality to manage it. On the other hand, the dashboard does not support developer's access. There is always an **application-programming interface (API)** where they can access resources and other aspects of the cloud.

- **Nova**: This is OpenStack's primary computing engine. It is the main component responsible for deploying and managing the virtual machines of the cloud infrastructure, rather than just being a small infrastructure or a grid of super computers. It also manages and organizes other instances such as handling cloud-computing tasks.

- **Neutron**: This is OpenStack's networking component. It is basically the one essential part to ensure networking between different components of the cloud infrastructure. It also supports multiple technologies to make sure that communication is reliable.

- **Keystone**: This is the service responsible for identifying management for OpenStack. It organizes the users using the cloud and also organizes their access permissions. It organizes the resources which they are using. It is also a great help for the developer for tracking user usage and access methods.

- **Swift**: This is the component responsible of the storage system for OpenStack. It stores the data in an advanced method where the developers only specify the file as a piece of information, and OpenStack decides where to store that, which helps with scaling and resolves storage capacity issues. It makes most of the common tasks, such as backup and security, the responsibility of the system more than the developer.

- **Cinder**: This is a smaller storage component that organizes block storage. It helps with the enhancement of data access in the disk drive and organizes in traditional ways the speed of data access depending on the need.

- **Heat**: This is the OpenStack orchestration component. It is a method to store information about cloud applications where it has defined the resources needed for that application for better organization of the cloud infrastructure.

- **Glance**: This is the component that organizes the virtual copies of the hard disks, what are known as images, to be used later as templates for deploying new virtual machines.

- **Ceilometer**: This is the component that helps with the billing services for cloud usage by individual users. It acts as a meter that reports the system usage during the period where the user starts using the cloud.

These components are very important where some of them depend on the other, and many basic cloud services won't be available if some of them become disabled or excluded. One of the components that is very important is the orchestration component where it helps organize a large number of machines and perform high-computer processing without any difficulty.

Installing and configuring OpenStack

After a brief explanation of cloud computing and OpenStack, we can now move on to OpenStack installation on a CentOS 7 Linux server. First of all, we are going to make a few basic environment configurations and then set it up.

For this installation, we will have our cloud infrastructure as follows:

- The Router/Gateway server as *e*th machine to provide Internet access to the external websites, with the IP address: `10.0.1.1`

- The cloud server to host OpenStack, with the IP address: `10.0.1.2`

- The hosts that will be used for the cloud computing, with their IP addresses as follows: `10.0.1.4, 10.0.1.5, 10.0.1.6`

To have OpenStack well secured, the community integrated many services to ensure that some of those services secure data access and user authentication with encrypted data transmission. For this action, we will need to have OpenSSL installed on our cloud server so that OpenStack can use it to run its services:

```
$ sudo yum install openssl
```

To have a safe installation without errors, we need to disable the firewall, if there is one, like this:

```
$ sudo systemctl stop firewalld.service
```

Then we need to make sure that the server is connected to the local network and has Internet access. To do so, we need to ping one machine at the local network and a nicely working web server (https://www.google.co.in/):

```
$ ping -c 5 10.0.1.1
PING 10.0.1.1 (10.0.1.1) 56(84) bytes of data.
64 bytes from 10.0.1.1: icmp_seq=1 ttl=255 time=1.21 ms
64 bytes from 10.0.1.1: icmp_seq=2 ttl=255 time=4.19 ms
64 bytes from 10.0.1.1: icmp_seq=3 ttl=255 time=4.32 ms
64 bytes from 10.0.1.1: icmp_seq=4 ttl=255 time=4.15 ms
64 bytes from 10.0.1.1: icmp_seq=5 ttl=255 time=4.01 ms
--- 10.0.1.1 ping statistics ---
5 packets transmitted, 5 received, 0% packet loss, time 4007ms
rtt min/avg/max/mdev = 1.214/3.580/4.324/1.186 ms
$ ping -c 5 www.google.com
```

The result of the test should look like the following:

```
PING www.google.com (173.194.45.81) 56(84) bytes of data.
64 bytes from par03s13-in-f17.1e100.net (173.194.45.81): icmp_seq=1 ttl=49 time=28.8 ms
64 bytes from par03s13-in-f17.1e100.net (173.194.45.81): icmp_seq=2 ttl=49 time=32.3 ms
64 bytes from par03s13-in-f17.1e100.net (173.194.45.81): icmp_seq=3 ttl=49 time=32.2 ms
64 bytes from par03s13-in-f17.1e100.net (173.194.45.81): icmp_seq=4 ttl=49 time=29.6 ms
64 bytes from par03s13-in-f17.1e100.net (173.194.45.81): icmp_seq=5 ttl=49 time=32.4 ms

--- www.google.com ping statistics ---
5 packets transmitted, 5 received, 0% packet loss, time 4008ms
rtt min/avg/max/mdev = 28.863/31.124/32.461/1.550 ms
```

Then we need to add all the nodes involved (controller node, network node, compute node, object storage node, and block storage node):

```
$ sudo nano /etc/hosts
```

Next, to have the nodes well synchronized among each other, we need to set up a time server to configure a time for all the servers. To do this, we will be using the NTP service. First, however, we need to install it:

```
$ sudo yum install ntp
```

Then we need to start it and make it run at system startup:

```
$ sudo systemctl enable ntpd.service
$ sudo systemctl start ntpd.service
```

To verify the installation, we need to use the following command:

```
$ sudo ntpq -c peers
```

To see the output of this command, have a look at the following:

remote	refid	st t when poll reach	delay	offset	jitter
*ns3.atlax.com	131.188.3.221	2 u 14 64 1	4.745	-0.914	0.695
ns2.atlax.com	131.188.3.221	2 u 13 64 1	10.065	-1.751	0.438

```
$ sudo ntpq -c assoc
```

To see the output of this command, refer to the following:

ind assid status	conf reach auth	condition	last_event cnt
1 56063 963a	yes yes none	sys.peer	sys_peer 3
2 56064 9024	yes yes none	reject	reachable 2

We need to see `sys.peer` in the condition column at any line.

 We need to do the same for all the involved nodes.

Now, we put SELinux into permissive mode:

```
$ sudo nano /etc/selinux/config
```

Then consider this line:

```
SELINUX=enforcing
```

Change it to the following line:

```
SELINUX= permissive
```

Then we should reboot the system so that the change can take effect.

After the system starts up, we can move on to the package source configuration. First, we need to make sure that our system packages are all updated:

```
$ sudo yum update -y
```

Then we install the `epel` repository:

```
$ sudo yum install epel-release
```

Next, we check whether the additional EPEL repository is enabled:

```
$ sudo nano /etc/yum.repos.d/epel.repo
```

We need to make sure that all modules (`[epel]` `[epel-debuginfo]` `[epel-source]`) are enabled:

```
enabled=1
```

Then we proceed to install the YUM plugin priorities to enable assignment of relative priorities within repositories:

```
$ sudo yum install yum-plugin-priorities
```

Finally, we can set up the OpenStack repository:

```
$ sudo yum install https://repos.fedorapeople.org/repos/openstack/
openstack-juno/rdo-release-juno-1.noarch.rpm
```

To make OpenStack automatically manage security policies for its services, we need to install the OpenStack-SELinux package:

```
$ sudo yum install openstack-selinux
```

Just before installing the official package for the OpenStack service, we will be installing some tools needed for the SELinux policies for OpenStack of our cloud-computing platform. We will first install the database server. For that, we will have the Python MySQL library and the MariaDB server:

```
$ sudo yum install mariadb mariadb-server MySQL-python
```

After having MariaDB installed, we need to go ahead and configure it. First, we need to start the database server and add it to the system startup:

```
$ sudo systemctl enable mariadb.service
$ sudo systemctl start mariadb.service
```

By default, OpenStack is installed with a no password policy for the root. We need to change that during the first use, while performing a secure setup.

At this point, we have properly set all the required tools and configurations. We can start the OpenStack package installation. We can install each OpenStack component individually, or make it faster by installing and configuring them all at the same time. To do so, we will be using the yum package manager:

```
$ sudo yum install -y openstack-packstack
```

For a single-node OpenStack deployment, we should use the following command to configure it:

```
$ sudo packstack --allinone
```

We should see a message that starts as follows to conclude that the installation is done correctly and the configuration has been started properly. This may take some time to finish.

```
Welcome to the Packstack setup utility

The installation log file is available at: /var/tmp/packstack/20151018-153237-b9EVDh/openstack-setup.log
Packstack changed given value  to required value /root/.ssh/id_rsa.pub


Installing:
Clean Up                                                    [ DONE ]
Setting up ssh keys                                         [ DONE ]
Discovering hosts' details                                  [ DONE ]
Adding pre install manifest entries                         [ DONE ]
Preparing servers                                           [ DONE ]
Adding AMQP manifest entries                                [ DONE ]
Adding MariaDB manifest entries                             [ DONE ]
Fixing Keystone LDAP config parameters to be undef if empty[ DONE ]
Adding Keystone manifest entries                            [ DONE ]
Adding Glance Keystone manifest entries                     [ DONE ]
Adding Glance manifest entries                              [ DONE ]
Adding Cinder Keystone manifest entries                     [ DONE ]
Checking if the Cinder server has a cinder-volumes vg       [ DONE ]
Adding Cinder manifest entries                              [ DONE ]
Adding Nova API manifest entries                            [ DONE ]
Adding Nova Keystone manifest entries                       [ DONE ]
Adding Nova Cert manifest entries                           [ DONE ]
Adding Nova Conductor manifest entries                      [ DONE ]
Creating ssh keys for Nova migration                        [ DONE ]
Gathering ssh host keys for Nova migration                  [ DONE ]
```

The following screen appears if the configuration is done properly:

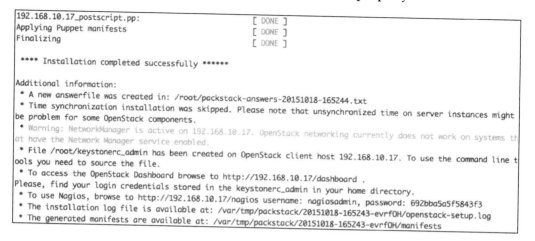

After getting the configuration done, there will be two authentication credentials generated to be used by the administrator. The first is for the Nagios Server. The login and the password will appear on the screen, so we need to save them to change the password later. The second one is for the OpenStack dashboard, which will be stored in a file at the `root` directory, called `keystonerc_admin`.

The first of the two web interfaces should look like this as a confirmation that the node is running:

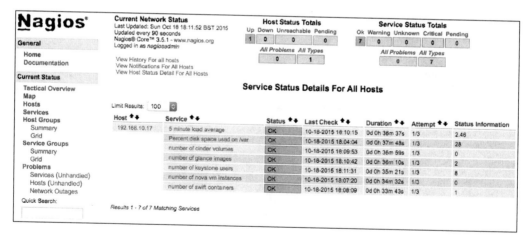

The second interface looks like what is shown in the following screenshot:

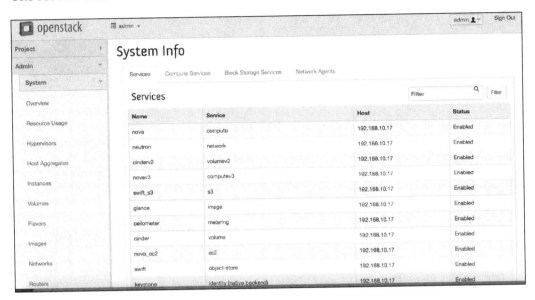

Now we can move on to the network-bridging configuration. We need to create a bridge interface:

```
$ sudo nano /etc/sysconfig/network-scripts/ifcfg-br-ex
```

After creating the file, we need to put the following code into it:

```
DEVICE=br-ex
DEVICETYPE=ovs
TYPE=OVSBridge
BOOTPROTO=static
IPADDR=10.0.1.2 # Old eth0 IP
NETMASK=255.255.255.0 # the netmask
GATEWAY=10.0.1.1 # the gateway
DNS1=8.8.8.8 # the nameserver
ONBOOT=yes
Now we've got to fix the eth0 configuration file to look like the
following:
BOOTPROTO="none"
IPV4_FAILURE_FATAL="no"
IPV6INIT="yes"
IPV6_AUTOCONF="yes"
```

```
IPV6_DEFROUTE="yes"
IPV6_FAILURE_FATAL="no"
NAME="eth0"
UUID="XXXXXXXXXX"
ONBOOT="yes"
HWADDR="XXXXXXXXXXXXX" # this is the Ethernet network Mac address
IPV6_PEERDNS="yes"
IPV6_PEERROUTES="yes"
TYPE=OVSPort
DEVICETYPE=ovs
OVS_BRIDGE=br-ex
ONBOOT=yes
```

Then we add the following lines to the Neutron configuration file to look like the following in the [ovs] module:

```
$ sudo nano /etc/neutron/plugin.ini
[ovs]
network_vlan_ranges = physnet1
bridge_mappings = physnet1:br-ex
```

Next, we restart the network:

```
$ sudo systemctl restart network.service
```

The following part is optional, wherein we are going to show in detail what happens if we run the manual way and not the automatic interactive way.

If we want to deploy other nodes manually, we should be using packstack with the --install-hosts option and then put the other host IP address:

```
$ sudo packstack --install-hosts=10.0.1.4
```

If there are many hosts, we can add a comma (,) between the IP addresses:

```
$ sudo packstack --install-hosts=10.0.1.4,10.0.1.5,10.0.1.6
```

While this command is executed, we will be asked to type the root password from each system individually to connect to the system, install OpenStack, and take control over it:

```
root@10.0.1.4's password:
```

We know that the installation is done when we see the following message:

```
**** Installation completed successfully ******
```

An answer file containing all the chosen configuration options is saved to the disk in the system from which we run `packstack`. This file can be used to automate future deployments:

```
* A new answerfile was created in: /root/packstack-answers-XXXXXXXX-XXXX.
txt
```

A file containing the authentication details of the OpenStack admin user is saved to the disk in the system on which the OpenStack client tools were deployed. We will need these details to manage the OpenStack environment:

```
* To use the command line tools you need to source the file /root/
keystonerc_admin created on 10.0.1.4
```

We can run `packstack` interactively to create both single-node and multiple-node OpenStack deployments:

```
$ sudo packstack
```

After running this command, we need to follow the list of steps to have the nodes deployed.

First, it will ask for the public key to be stored in the server to get automatic SSH access, so we need to have one generated already:

```
$ ssh-keygen -t rsa
```

Then we give its location, which is `~/.ssh/id_rsa.pub`:

```
Enter the path to your ssh Public key to install on servers:
```

Next, we select the services that we need to deploy. We can choose whatever we need:

```
Should Packstack install Glance image service [y|n] [y] :
Should Packstack install Cinder volume service [y|n] [y] :
Should Packstack install Nova compute service [y|n] [y] :
Should Packstack install Horizon dashboard [y|n] [y] :
Should Packstack install Swift object storage [y|n] [y] :
```

Each selected service can be deployed on either a local or a remote system. Where each service is deployed will be determined based on the IP addresses that we provide later in the deployment process.

OpenStack includes a number of client tools. Enter y to install the client tools. A file containing the authentication values of the administrative user will also be created:

```
Should Packstack install OpenStack client tools [y|n] [y] :
```

Optionally, the `packstack` script will configure all servers in the deployment to retrieve date and time information using the **Network Time Protocol (NTP)**. To use this facility, enter a comma-separated pool of NTP servers:

```
Enter a comma separated list of NTP server(s). Leave plain if Packstack
should not install ntpd on instances.:
```

Optionally, the `packstack` script will install and configure Nagios to provide advanced facilities for monitoring the nodes in the OpenStack environment:

```
Should Packstack install Nagios to monitor openstack hosts [y|n] [n] :
```

We now move on to the configuration of the MySQL Instance. OpenStack services require a MySQL database to store data in. To configure the database, we go through the following.

We type the IP address of the server to deploy the MySQL database server on:

```
Enter the IP address of the MySQL server [10.0.1.1] :
```

Enter the password to be used for the MySQL administrative user. If we do not enter a value, it will be generated randomly. The generated password will be available in both the `~/.my.cnf` file of the current user and the answer file:

```
Enter the password for the MySQL admin user :
```

OpenStack services use the Qpid messaging system to communicate. Enter the IP address of the server to deploy Qpid on:

```
Enter the IP address of the QPID service  [10.0.1.2] :
```

OpenStack uses keystone (openstack-keystone) for identity, token, catalog, and policy services. If the keystone installation has been selected, then enter the IP address of the server to deploy keystone on when prompted:

```
Enter the IP address of the Keystone server  [10.0.1.2] :
```

OpenStack uses glance (`openstack-glance-*`) to store, discover, and retrieve virtual machine images. If the glance installation has been selected, then enter the IP address of the server to deploy glance on when prompted:

```
Enter the IP address of the Glance server  [10.0.1.2] :
```

To provide volume storage services, OpenStack uses Cinder (`openstack-cinder-*`). Enter the IP address of the server to deploy Cinder on. If the installation of the volume services was selected, then these additional configuration prompts will be presented:

```
Enter the IP address of the Cinder server   [10.0.1.2] :
```

The `packstack` utility expects the storage for use with Cinder to be available in a volume group named cinder-volumes. If this volume group does not exist, then we will be asked whether we want it to be created automatically.

Answering `yes` means that `packstack` will create a raw disk image in `/var/lib/cinder` and mount it for use by Cinder using a loopback device:

```
Should Cinder's volumes group be createdi (for proof-of-concept
installation)? [y|n] [y]:
```

If we chose to have packstack create the cinder-volumes volume group, then we will be prompted to enter its size in **gigabytes (GB)**:

```
Enter Cinder's volume group size   [20G] :
```

OpenStack uses Nova to provide compute services. Nova is itself made up of a number of complementary services that must be deployed. If the installation of the compute services was selected, then these additional configuration prompts will be presented.

The Nova API service (`openstack-nova-api`) provides web service endpoints for authenticating and interacting with the OpenStack environment over HTTP or HTTPS. We type the IP address of the server to deploy the Nova API service on:

```
Enter the IP address of the Nova API service   [10.0.1.3] :
```

Nova includes a certificate management service (`openstack-nova-cert`). Enter the IP address of the server to deploy the Nova certificate management service on:

```
Enter the IP address of the Nova Cert service   [10.0.1.3] :
```

The Nova VNC proxy provides facilities to connect users of the Nova compute service to their instances running in the OpenStack cloud. Enter the IP address of the server to deploy the Nova VNC proxy on:

```
Enter the IP address of the Nova VNC proxy   [10.0.1.3] :
```

The `packstack` script is able to deploy one or more compute nodes. Enter a comma-separated list containing the IP addresses or hostnames of all the nodes that you wish to deploy compute services on:

```
Enter a comma separated list of IP addresses on which to install the Nova
Compute services  [10.0.1.3]  :
```

A private interface must be configured to provide DHCP services on the Nova compute nodes. Enter the name of the private interface to use:

```
Enter the Private interface for Flat DHCP on the Nova compute servers
[eth1]  :
```

The Nova network service (`openstack-nova-network`) provides network services for compute instances. Enter the IP address of the server to deploy the Nova network service on:

```
Enter the IP address of the Nova Network service  [10.0.1.3]  :
```

A public interface must be configured to allow connections from other nodes and clients. Enter the name of the public interface to use:

```
Enter the Public interface on the Nova network server  [eth0]  :
```

A private interface must be configured to provide DHCP services on the Nova network server. Enter the name of the private interface to use:

```
Enter the Private interface for Flat DHCP on the Nova network server
[eth1]  :
```

All compute instances are automatically assigned a private IP address. Enter the range within which these private IP addresses must be assigned:

```
Enter the IP Range for Flat DHCP [10.0.2.0/24]  :
```

Compute instances can optionally be assigned publicly accessible floating IP addresses. Enter the range within which floating IP addresses will be assigned:

```
Enter the IP Range for Floating IP's [10.0.1.0/24]  :
```

The Nova scheduler (`openstack-nova-scheduler`) is used to map compute requests to compute resources. Enter the IP address of the server on which you want to deploy the Nova scheduler:

```
Enter the IP address of the Nova Scheduler service  [10.0.1.4]  :
```

In the default configuration, Nova allows `overcommitment` of physical CPU and memory resources. This means that more of these resources can be made available for running instances than actually physically exist on the compute node.

The amount of `overcommitment` that is permitted is configurable.

The default level of CPU `overcommitment` allows 16 virtual CPUs to be allocated for each physical CPU socket or core that exists on the physical compute node. Press *Enter* to accept the default level or enter a different value if desired:

```
Enter the CPU overcommitment ratio. Set to 1.0 to disable CPU
overcommitment [16.0] :
```

The default level of memory over commitment allows up to 50% more virtual memory to be allocated than what exists on the physical compute node. Press *Enter* to accept the default or enter a different value if desired:

```
Enter the RAM overcommitment ratio. Set to 1.0 to disable RAM
overcommitment [1.5] :
```

If installation of the client tools was selected then enter the IP address of the server to install the client tools on when prompted:

```
Enter the IP address of the client server  [10.0.1.4] :
```

OpenStack uses Horizon (`openstack-dashboard`) to provide a web-based user interface or dashboard for access to OpenStack services, including Cinder, Nova, Swift, and Keystone. If the installation of the Horizon dashboard was selected then these additional configuration values will be requested.

Enter the IP address of the server to deploy Horizon on:

```
Enter the IP address of the Horizon server  [10.0.1.4] :
```

To enable HTTPS communication with the dashboard, we enter y when prompted. Enabling this option ensures that user access to the dashboard is encrypted:

```
Would you like to set up Horizon communication over https [y|n] [n] :
```

If we have already selected to install `swift` object storage, then these additional configuration values will be requested.

Enter the IP address of the server that is to act as the Swift proxy. This server will act as the public link between clients and the Swift object storage:

```
Enter the IP address of the Swift proxy service  [10.0.1.2] :
```

Enter a comma-separated list of devices that the Swift object storage will use to store objects. Each entry must be specified in HOST/DEVICE format, where the Host is replaced by the IP address of the host the device is attached to, and Device is replaced by the appropriate path to the device:

```
Enter the Swift Storage servers e.g. host/dev,host/dev  [10.0.1.2] :
```

The `Swift` object storage uses zones to ensure that each replica of a given object is stored separately. A zone might represent an individual disk drive or array, a server, all the servers in a rack, or even an entire data center.

When prompted, enter the number of Swift storage zones that must be defined. Note that the number provided must not be bigger than the number of individual devices specified, as follows:

```
Enter the number of swift storage zones, MUST be no bigger than the
number of storage devices configured  [1]  :
```

The Swift object storage relies on replication to maintain the state of objects, even in the event of a storage outage in one or more of the configured storage zones. Enter the number of replicas that Swift must keep of each object when prompted.

A minimum of three replicas is recommended to ensure a reasonable degree of fault tolerance in the object store. Note, however, that the number of replicas specified must not be greater than the number of storage zones, as it would result in one or more of the zones containing multiple replicas of the same object:

```
Enter the number of swift storage replicas, MUST be no bigger than the
number of storage zones configured  [1]  :
```

Currently, `packstack` supports the use of either `Ext4` or `XFS` file systems for object storage. The default and recommended choice is `ext4`. Enter the desired value when prompted:

```
Enter FileSystem type for storage nodes [xfs|ext4]   [ext4]  :
```

The `packstack` utility allows us to configure the target servers to retrieve software packages from a number of sources. We can leave this part blank to rely on the nodes' default package sources:

```
Enter a comma-separated list of URLs to any additional yum repositories
to install:
```

At this point, we will be asked to confirm the deployment details that we provided. Type yes and press *Enter* to continue with the deployment. Then, it will show us all the information already provided during the entire phase. After verifying that everything is set properly, we type yes for the following question:

```
Proceed with the configuration listed above? (yes|no): yes
```

Now, `packstack` will commence deployment. Note that when `packstack` is setting up SSH keys, it will prompt us to enter the root password to connect to machines that are not already configured to use key authentication.

Applying the Puppet manifests to all machines involved in the deployment takes a significant amount of time. The `packstack` utility provides continuous updates, indicating which manifests are being deployed as it progresses through the deployment process. Once the process completes, a confirmation message will be displayed:

```
**** Installation completed successfully ******

    (Please allow Installer a few moments to start up.....)

Additional information:
 * A new answerfile was created in: /root/packstack-answers-xxxxx-xxxxx.
txt
 * Time synchronization was skipped. Please note that unsynchronized time
on server instances might be a problem for some OpenStack components.
 * To use the command line tools source the file /root/keystonerc_admin
created on 10.0.1.2
 * To use the console, browse to http://10.0.0.2/dashboard
 * The installation log file is available at: /var/tmp/packstack/xxxx-
xxxx-TkY04B/openstack-setup.log
You have mail in /var/spool/mail/root
You have successfully deployed OpenStack using packstack.
```

The configuration details that we provided are also recorded in an answer file, which can be used to recreate the deployment in future. This answer file is stored in `~/answers.txt` by default.

With this step, we can say that we have nicely installed and configured OpenStack as a cloud-computing solution to be used inside a little infrastructure of CentOS 7 Linux servers.

The OpenStack dashboard will be our best way to have a better and clean way to visualize useful information about the status of the cloud infrastructure. It is extremely useful for system administrators to maintain the infrastructure and troubleshoot the system for any issues. Here are some screenshots that show some of the dashboard overview pages:

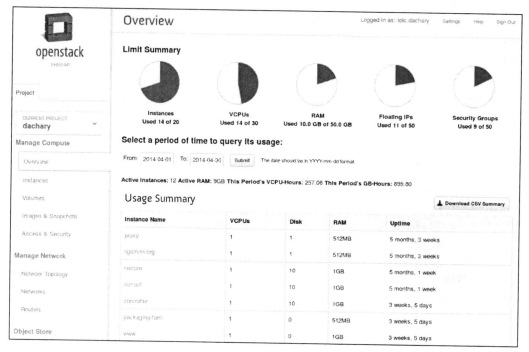

Source: http://3.bp.blogspot.com

The following page presents the list of the running machines (nodes) with some useful information about the nodes, and also gives us some options to manage them.

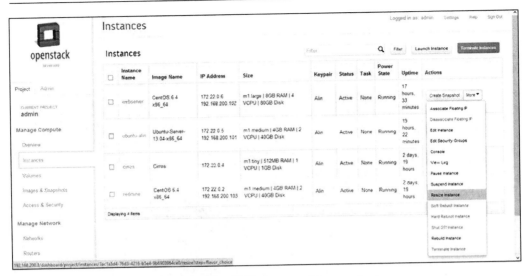

Source: http://assist-software.net

Then we shall see the network page that shows the topology of the network holding
the cloud nodes.

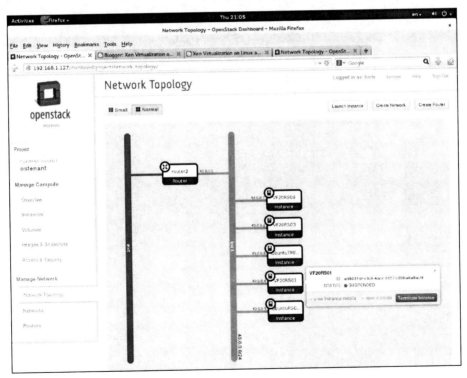

Source: http://4.bp.blogspot.com

There is another Nova API dashboard with a better-designed interface to be used for presentation and a gigantic dashboard screen used specially for monitoring big grid computer infrastructure. The first dashboard screen shows information about the API's in use:

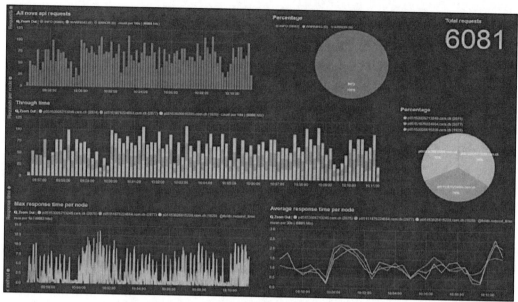

Source: `http://openstack-in-production.blogspot.com`

The second dashboard screen shows the history of execution of those API as well presented log:

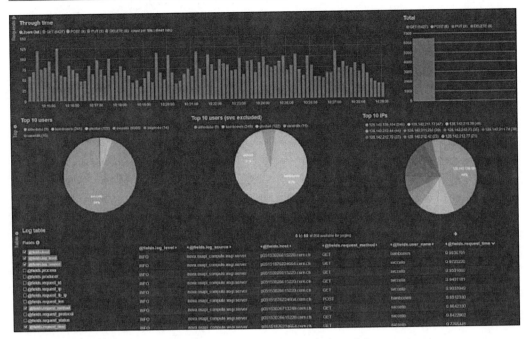

Source: `http://openstack-in-production.blogspot.com`

References

Now, let's have a look at the references used throughout the chapter:

- What is cloud computing?, IBM: `http://www.ibm.com/cloud-computing/what-is-cloud-computing.html`

- OpenStack home page: `https://www.openstack.org/`

- OpenStack platform for Redhat: `https://access.redhat.com/documentation/en/`

Summary

This chapter was a description of how to have an open source cloud-computing solution within a small or large computer infrastructure. We started by defining the concept of cloud computing, and then we introduced OpenStack and described its components in brief. We showed a practical way to set up and configure an OpenStack node using—by choice—all of its components.

In the next chapter, you are going to learn automatic system configuration using one of the most recent tools that does this in a well-organized way—Puppet.

8
Configuration Management

According to a study, most of the critical errors that occur in large IT systems are due to people and processes. Half of those errors are due to a lack of release synchronization, coordination between machines, and configuration management. Big machinery and infrastructure are way too hard to manage and maintain for any single team. Having an identical configuration set for every machine to make them all work in synchronization is a nightmare for management teams. For these reasons, we have a process called **Configuration Management (CM)**.

In this chapter, we are going to describe how to use the CM process to maintain and manage a CentOS 7 Linux server infrastructure. We are going to describe in brief some of the most common open source configuration management tools, with an example of setting up a management server with a client using Puppet.

Through this chapter, you are going to learn these topics:

- Operating system configuration management
- Open source configuration management tools
- Installation and configuration of a Puppet server and client

Introducing configuration management

Configuration management is a process that helps organize multiple machines/ systems so that they can coordinate with each other to perform one rather big process or run multiple redundant processes. It is widely used by military organizations to manage their systems, such as weapon systems, vehicles, and information systems. Outside the military, it is widely used in IT service management for big infrastructure handling.

There are still many IT organizations that work with old and traditional tools such as customized scripts (shell scripts, expect scripts, and so on) and manual process implementation to run repetitive tasks. We have well acknowledged the fact that those techniques are no longer effective, especially when used in large-scale infrastructures. Even for small infrastructures, it is hard to track and maintain them due to all-time configuration changes. All of this may have a direct impact on the reliability of the infrastructure itself, which may also affect the productivity of the organization.

Automated configuration management has put an end to manual scripting and configuration; it has also been used to perform other tasks that most system administrators do on a daily basis (system updates, firmware patch, release update and management, and so on).

For the new generation of system administrators, everything is automated. Most machines run on the same set of configurations, and a set of servers to manage them all. Everything is watched by monitoring tools. The job of a system administrator is to initialize their infrastructure's basic configuration to start their configuration management server, set up clients if needed on other machines, and then start sending configurations to the clients to apply it. The configuration management server will act as the master of the Puppets and send them direct orders to follow for whatever their architecture or type of OS is.

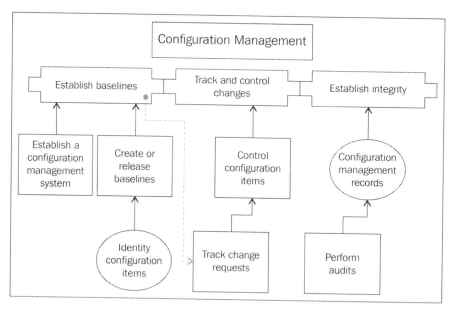

Source: http://flylib.com/

For our case, we will be setting up a CentOS 7 server to control a CentOS 7 client using configuration management, where we are going to show you how manual configuration is time consuming and unreliable. Before that, we will be showing you a list of famous open source tools used for configuration management:

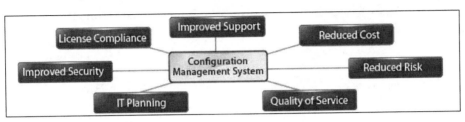

Source: `http://www.axiossystems.it`

Open source configuration management tools

In this section, we are going to enumerate the world's most famous open source configuration management tools, going through the description of each tool, the major focus, and where it can serve well.

Chef

Chef is a configuration management tool that helps us configure and maintain servers that provide a variety of services. Chef uses something called recipes, made to describe the desired management (configuration, installation, change) for the server's applications and utilities. It is widely used for infrastructure with cloud-computing-based platforms (such as Rackspace, Internap, Amazon, Google, OpenStack, SoftLayer, and Microsoft) because of its capacity to automatically provision and configure new machines on the go. The scalability of Chef allows it to be used for small and large infrastructures on demand.

Chef can be executed as a server or a client. The clients are executed on the servers/machines that we want to manage using our server. And the Chef server agent is installed in one centralized server, on which it manages the recipes depending on what the administrator has defined for each node (web server, cluster machine, storage server, and so on). Then the client executes the recipes sent to it by the server. By default, the client updates its recipe from the server every 30 minutes to see whether there is any change that needs to be done.

At the beginning of the project, Chef used to manage only Linux machines, but now it is capable of managing Windows machines as well. The Chef server is now supported by multiple Linux platforms (RHEL/CentOS, FreeBSD, OSX, Solaris, and so on).

This is what it looks like, architecture-wise, after having Chef installed. The first images shows the interaction between chef and a variety of nodes that can manage.

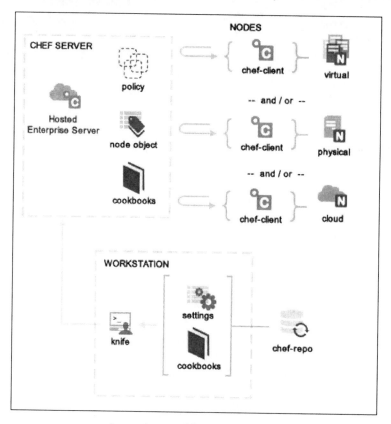

Source: http://www.yet.org

The following screenshot show the interaction between chef and the Amazon web services to be on use for advanced configuration

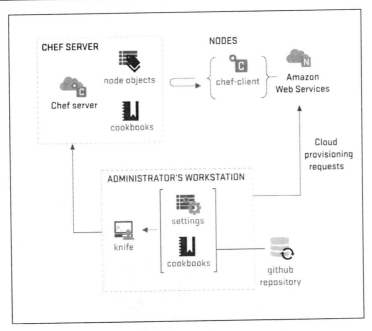

Source: https://www.chef.io/

For more detailed information on how to set up and master Chef, please have a look at some of Packt's other books on Chef at: https://www.packtpub.com/all/?search=chef

SaltStack (Salt)

SaltStack is a Python-based open source configuration management tool. It is also called a remote engine. In a way, it is a new approach to infrastructure management. It is easy to run, scalable, can handle thousands of nodes, and can establish very fast communication between its nodes (servers, terminals, and so on).

It is well known due to its dynamic communication inside the infrastructures it mages, where it benefit amazingly from that to organize, execute, and establish configuration management through its nodes, as well as much more.

It is available for a variety of operating systems (CentOS, Debian, RHEL, Ubuntu, and even Windows).

Salt is designed to be very extensible, wherein it has the capacity to use module management so as to be moldable to a variety of applications. Salt offers dynamic modules to manage the remote execution and administration of its components. They are categorized as follows: execution modules, state modules, grains, renderer modules, returners, and runners.

SaltStack has a paid product called SaltStack Enterprise. It is designed for big infrastructures in IT organizations, system administration, site reliability engineering, and development configuration and management for modern data center infrastructures, applications, and code. It is briefly depicted in the following figure, which shows how it covers a variety of fields to help the establishment, management, and maintenance of the following services shown in the two following figures:

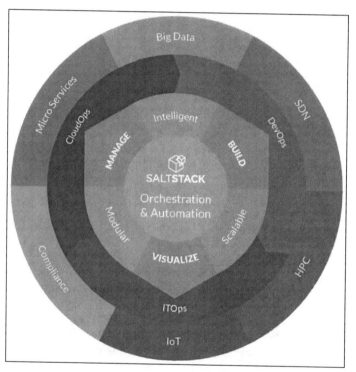

Source: http://www.saltstack.com

This figure shows the interaction between the three major services (ITOps, DevOps, CloudOps) and the capacity to use SaltStack to manage those all together.

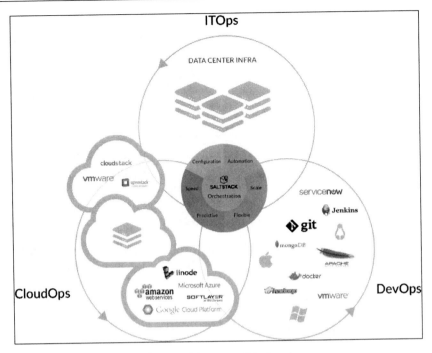

Source: http://www.saltstack.com

SaltStack services operate on several steps as shown in the following figure:

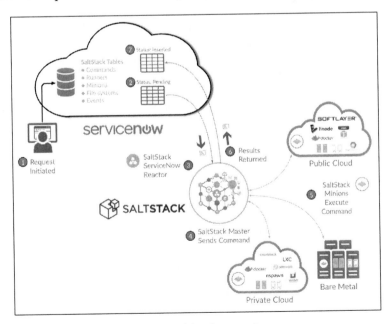

Source: http://saltstack.com

For more detailed information on how to set up and master SaltStack, please have a look at some of Packt's other books on SaltStack at: https://www.packtpub.com/all/?search=saltstack.

Ansible

Ansible is a free and simple solution for configuration management. It is well known for automated configuration management, whereby it relies on SSH to access nodes and configure them through Python-based solutions. It uses a minimal amount of dependencies and environment tools (such as client agents), and is secure. It is also very reliable and does not require very advanced learning lessons to start using it.

Its configuration requires the editing of some human-readable configuration files to ensure that everyone can understand them, if an update or reconfiguration is ever needed. It requires only the SSH password or an SSH key in order to access the nodes to be managed, without the need for the installation of an agent. So, there will definitely be no need to worry about not having the agent running due to an upgrade, patch, or daemon malfunction.

Ansible supports modules as well. Basically, most of them run on JSON and it has standard output support for all kinds of programming languages. It also includes more than 200 modules, which can be used to manage and automate services.

It is well supported by the RHEL community (Red Hat, Fedora, CentOS, and Scientific Linux). It is easily downloadable through the EPEL repository. It is also supported by other Linux distributions of the Debian family, and other Unix-like systems such as OS X, BSD, and recently by MS Windows.

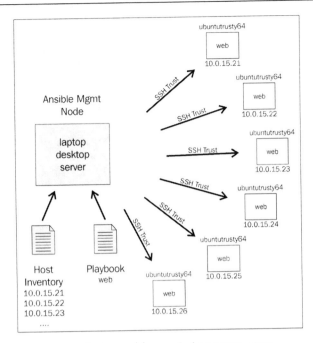

Source: `https://sysadmincasts.com`

 For more detailed information on how to set up and master Ansible, please have a look at some of Packt's other books on Ansible at: `https://www.packtpub.com/all/?search=ansible`

Puppet

Puppet is an open source configuration management tool designed to manage and configure machines within the same infrastructure, to simplify various system administration tasks where the user declares the machines' states and resources using different ways (Ruby DSL, Puppet declaration language, and others). It is published under the GPL and Apache licenses. It is mainly used to manage and configure Unix-based machines and Microsoft systems. To establish Puppet, as best practice, we require a Puppet server agent to do the role of a configuration management server and for the other nodes, the ones the server is going to manage, we require the client version. Puppet inspects each node's configuration, and then identifies the changes between the old and the new configurations specified at its configuration file, if there are any. Then it starts making the required changes to adjust the node to the specified state. This task is useful; not only for establishing a new configuration, but also for regaining it if anything goes wrong with the machines.

Basically, Puppet's major advantages are that it automates every step of the software delivery process, from the provisioning of physical and virtual machines to organization and reporting. Puppet is widely used by many organizations because it has the following features:

- It is designed to prevent duplication during the process of problem resolution
- It gives the capacity to make rapid and repeatable configurations automatically
- It simplifies the management of both physical and virtual devices
- It makes the task of system administration much easier

Puppet offers two services: one as an open source and free solution, and the other as a paid solution for enterprises. Both of them serve to help system administrators automate their infrastructure configuration management. Puppet Enterprise has much more to offer for big enterprises.

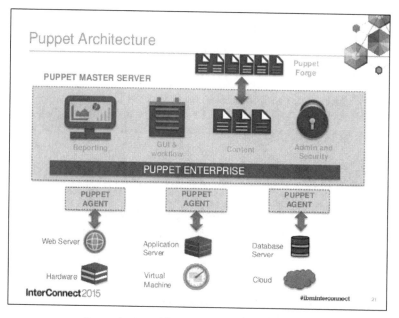

Source: http://www.slideshare.net/

Puppet is not just a simple configuration management tool. It is a streamlined node installation, management, and repair solution that simplifies the management of a grid of nodes.

As the following figure shows, to use Puppet to establish a new configuration, there are four important steps to be followed: Define, Simulate, Enforce, and Report. Herein, the system administrator first defines what kind of configuration needs to be set. Then, Puppet tests the deployment without harming the infrastructure and makes sure that it will work ok. After that, Puppet starts comparing what is new to what is already being used, and starts enforcing what needs to be done to meet the user's demands. Finally, it reports the status of each node on its dashboard.

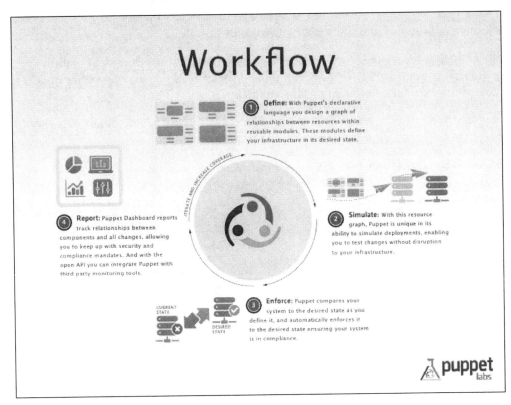

Source: http://www.slideshare.net

Installing and configuring Puppet

For our Puppet installation, we are going to install the free open source version of Puppet.

We have chosen Puppet to be our primary configuration management solution because Puppet is a more declarative solution. This has made it more attractive for damage repair than any other solution.

There are two possible architectures for Puppet: the Agent/Master architecture or the standalone architecture. The Agent/Master architecture is based on one or many Puppet master servers managing servers/nodes that has a Puppet client agent running as a background service. In the standalone architecture, the client nodes run Puppet as a master and slave agent at the same time. Which is used usually to schedule management tasks or jobs to that machine it is installed on.

In this chapter, we are going to use the Client/Master architecture, where we are going to use two CentOS 7 servers; one will be used as the master Puppet server and the other as the client that the Puppet agent will run on.

Before starting the installation, we need to make sure that some preinstallation tasks are done. We have already decided on the architecture, so we have a better idea of which software packages we are going to install.

Then we should define which machine will act as a Puppet server agent. We should always start by installing the server and then move on to the clients.

The following figure presents the interaction between the Puppet master and client when trying to establish a change requested by the manager from the Puppet master interface:

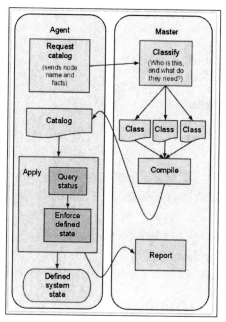

Source: http://elatov.github.io/2014/08/setting-up-puppet-master-on-centos-7/

Our infrastructure will consist of the following:

- Puppet master server:
    - **OS**: `CentOS 7`
    - **IP address**: `10.0.0.10`
    - **Hostname**: `masterpuppet.packt.co.uk`
- First client server:
    - **OS**: `CentOS 7`
    - **IP address**: `10.0.0.11`
    - **Hostname**: `webserver1.packt.co.uk`
- Second client server:
    - **OS**: `CentOS 7`
    - **IP address**: `10.0.0.12`
    - **Hostname**: `webserver2.packt.co.uk`

Usually, we should check which Linux version and family we are using for the clients and the servers of the infrastructure. In our case, we have already defined those to be CentOS 7 for all the machines of our environment.

After that, the Puppet architecture will be managed through the network, so we should make sure that all the nodes (servers and clients) are well configured to run the Puppet traffic. And we need to open the default Puppet access port 8140 for incoming connections at the server so that the client can access it:

```
$ sudo firewall-cmd --permanent --zone=public --add-port=8140/tcp
$ sudo firewall-cmd --reload
```

Finally, for the network, we should have all the nodes configured with a unique hostname, and each one of the machines needs to have in its `/etc/hosts` file all the other machines defined with their IP addresses:

```
$ sudo nano /etc/hosts
10.0.0.10  masterpuppet.packt.co.uk
10.0.0.11  webserver1.packt.co.uk
10.0.0.12  webserver2.packt.co.uk
```

To ensure that all the confirmations are synchronized between the nodes, we need to establish a network time-server (using NTP) connection to have all nodes synchronized with the same time:

```
[root@ntp ~]# ntpq -p
     remote           refid      st t when poll reach   delay   offset  jitter
==============================================================================
+dns1-ha.au.syra 218.100.43.70    2 u   65   64  377   53.674    5.641   1.264
+ns2.mel.0101.ne 47.187.174.51    2 u   55   64  377   36.441    8.223   1.209
-ntp01.lagoon.nc 203.14.0.250     3 u   60   64  373   66.174   11.053   1.141
*warrane.connect 203.35.83.242    2 u    2   64  377   48.200    8.326   1.310
```

We can now start the installation of our Puppet server:

1. The first step is to enable the Puppet open source repository that offers Puppet, PuppetDB, and other packages. We will be using RPM to add the Puppetlabs file to the system:

   ```
   $ sudo rpm -ivh https://yum.puppetlabs.com/puppetlabs-release-
   el-7.noarch.rpm
   ```

2. Then we install the Puppet server:

   ```
   $ sudo yum install puppet-server
   ```

3. We need to accept all that the installation manager may ask, for example, the RPM-GPG-Key verification, and whether we want to install the package or not.

4. Then we need to configure Puppet to understand that this node is the master Puppet server:

   ```
   $ sudo nano /etc/puppet/puppet.conf
   ```

5. Next, we need to add these two lines under the [main] section:

   ```
   dns_alt_names = masterpuppet,masterpuppet.packt.co.uk
   certname = masterpuppet.packt.co.uk
   ```

6. Since this is our Puppet server, we need to create its certificate. We need to start the Puppet server manually, for long enough until it creates the required certificate. After that, we need to stop it because we are still running the configuration:

   ```
   $ sudo puppet master --verbose --no-daemonize
   ```

7. After getting the following message, we need to hit Ctrl + C to stop the service:

   ```
   Notice: Starting Puppet master version 3.8.4
   ```

At this point, we can start Puppet. But we would like to integrate the Puppet service with Apache to make it one service that can serve both by installing a special module. To do this, we need to install some useful packages:

```
$ sudo yum install mod_passenger curl curl-devel make automake httpd
httpd-devel mod_ssl ruby-devel rubygems gcc gcc-c++ pygpgme zlib-devel
openssl-devel
```

Then we need to install Passenger, which is an open source tool that we will use to install some Apache plugins to help with the development of the Puppet web server. For the installation task, we will use GEM, a Ruby tool for installing Ruby-based packages:

```
$ sudo gem install rack passenger
```

From that point onward, we can install the Passenger Apache module.
For CentOS 7, we need to locate the executable file. It doesn't get its binary set in the BIN environment during the installation. So, we need to execute it from where it is installed:

```
$ sudo locate passenger-install-apache2-module
$ sudo /usr/local/share/gems/gems/passenger-5.0.21/bin/passenger-install-
apache2-module
```

After that, we follow the instructions provided by the last command as follows.

First, we need to write 1 to install the Apache 2 module:

```
1. The Apache 2 module will be installed for you.
```

Then we just type *Enter* whenever the program asks. We can ignore the warnings and hope for no errors. Otherwise, we need to make sure that we have installed all the required tools earlier. We know that it is done when we see the error and warning summary, and we get this message:

```
Phusion Passenger is a registered trademark of Hongli Lai & Ninh Bui.
```

Next, we create the two directories where Puppet is going to generate its public and temporary files, and set ownership to its configuration file:

```
$ sudo mkdir -p /usr/share/puppet/rack/puppetmasterd/public /usr/share/
puppet/rack/puppetmasterd/tmp

$ sudo cp /usr/share/puppet/ext/rack/config.ru /usr/share/puppet/rack/
puppetmasterd/

$ sudo chown puppet:puppet /usr/share/puppet/rack/puppetmasterd/config.ru
```

To finish, we create the Puppet virtual host file at the Apache2 configuration directory, as follows:

```
$ sudo nano /etc/httpd/conf.d/puppetmaster.conf
```

We fill it with the following configuration options, changing the red text depending on what we have configured on a different environment:

```
# CentOS 7:
# Set those as the Gems and Passenger version installed on your system
LoadModule passenger_module  /usr/local/share/gems/gems/passenger-5.0.21/
buildout/apache2/mod_passenger.so
PassengerRoot /usr/local/share/gems/gems/passenger-5.0.21/

PassengerRuby /usr/bin/ruby
# And the passenger performance tuning settings:
PassengerHighPerformance On
PassengerUseGlobalQueue On
# Passenger Max Pool should be configured as 3/2 the number of CPU cores
of the master machine:
PassengerMaxPoolSize 4
# Limit number of request before recycling
```

```
PassengerMaxRequests 1000

# Limit time for process to set as idle

PassengerPoolIdleTime 600

Listen 8140

<VirtualHost *:8140>

    SSLEngine On

    # Only allow high security cryptography. Alter if needed for
compatibility.

    SSLProtocol              All -SSLv3

    SSLCipherSuite           HIGH:!ADH:RC4+RSA:-MEDIUM:-LOW:-EXP

    SSLCertificateFile       /var/lib/puppet/ssl/certs/unixmen-centos7.
arnhem.chello.nl.pem

    SSLCertificateKeyFile    /var/lib/puppet/ssl/private_keys/unixmen-
centos7.arnhem.chello.nl.pem

    SSLCertificateChainFile  /var/lib/puppet/ssl/ca/ca_crt.pem

    SSLCACertificateFile     /var/lib/puppet/ssl/ca/ca_crt.pem

    SSLCARevocationFile      /var/lib/puppet/ssl/ca/ca_crl.pem

    SSLVerifyClient          optional

    SSLVerifyDepth           1

    SSLOptions               +StdEnvVars +ExportCertData

    # These request headers are used to pass the client certificate

    # authentication information on to the puppet master process

    RequestHeader set X-SSL-Subject %{SSL_CLIENT_S_DN}e

    RequestHeader set X-Client-DN %{SSL_CLIENT_S_DN}e

    RequestHeader set X-Client-Verify %{SSL_CLIENT_VERIFY}e

    #RackAutoDetect On

    DocumentRoot /usr/share/puppet/rack/puppetmasterd/public/

    <Directory /usr/share/puppet/rack/puppetmasterd/>

        Options None

        AllowOverride None

        Order Allow,Deny

        Allow from All

    </Directory>

</VirtualHost>
```

We set SELinux to permissive to let the new modules use the resources:

```
$ sudo nano /etc/selinux/config
```

Next, we change the SELINUX option to look like this:

```
SELINUX=permissive
```

Then we need to restart the Apache service and add it to the system startup services, while disabling the Puppet service:

```
$ sudo systemctl restart httpd.service
$ sudo systemctl enable httpd.service
$ sudo systemctl disable puppetmaster.service
```

With this step done, we can say that we are done configuring the server. We can now proceed to setting up and configuring the clients.

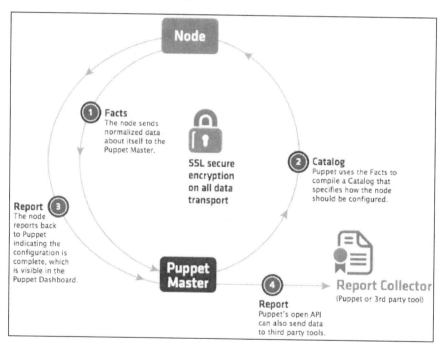

Source: http://www.aosabook.org

As we said earlier, we need to make sure that the /etc/hosts file is well configured and has all the nodes (whether client or server) on it. Plus, we need to make sure that the NTP service is running and loading the time for the same time-server as our server. Usually, we can just go with the default set by the system and that works fine:

```
$ sudo yum install ntp ntpdate
$ sudo systemctl start ntpd
$ sudo systemctl enable ntpd
```

As with the server, we do the same thing to configure the Puppet repository for the clients:

```
$ sudo rpm -ivh https://yum.puppetlabs.com/puppetlabs-release-el-7.
noarch.rpm
```

Then we install the Puppet client agent:

```
$ sudo yum install puppet
```

Next, just before starting the service, we need to add the Puppet master server id to the client agent configuration file. So, we go ahead and edit the Puppet configuration file. We add the server address under the agent option:

```
$ sudo nano /etc/puppet/puppet.conf
[agnet]
server = masterpuppet.packt.co.uk
report = true
pluginsync = true
```

Then we save the file, start the service, and enable it for the system startup services:

```
$ sudo systemctl enable puppet.service
$ sudo systemctl start puppet.service
```

We need to do the same for all client servers.

After that, we go back to our Puppet server and check whether the certificate has been sent:

```
$ sudo puppet cert list
```

We should see something like this:

```
"webserver1.packt.co.uk" (SHA256) 04:55:E0:82:4E:AD:7F:3C:9C:C7:52:79:98:
ED:5E:A6:B0:B5:85:08:DC:81:E5:2D:A6:32:ED:8B:5C:F4:3B:DA
```

This means that we have a client asking the server to approve a certificate request. We can sign each server certificate using this command:

```
$ sudo puppet cert sign webserver1.packt.co.uk
```

We can now go back to the client to check whether the certificate is successfully set using the following command:

```
$ sudo puppet agent -t
```

We know that it is well configured if we get the following output:

```
Info: Caching certificate for webserver1.packt.co.uk
Info: Caching certificate_revocation_list for ca
Info: Caching certificate for webserver1.packt.co.uk
Info: Retrieving pluginfacts
Info: Retrieving plugin
Info: Caching catalog for webserver1.packt.co.uk
Info: Applying configuration version '1449418854'
Info: Creating state file /var/lib/puppet/state/state.yaml
Notice: Finished catalog run in 0.01 seconds
```

At this point, our puppet Master and Client infrastructure is working fine. Let's try and create a configuration from the Puppet server and send it to the client to apply it.

We need to create a manifest file called `site.pp` in the `/etc/puppet/manifest` folder, as follows:

```
$ sudo nano /etc/puppet/manifests/site.pp
```

Then we test the service by making the client nodes (`webserver1` and `webserver2`) and install some tools. We need to add the following code to the last opened file for editing:

```
node 'webserver1', 'webserver2 {
        package { 'php' :
        ensure => installed,
                }
}
```

To verify that Puppet is running well we can always go to the client and type in the following:

```
$ sudo puppet agent --test
```

```
Info: Retrieving pluginfacts
Info: Retrieving plugin
Info: Loading facts
Info: Caching catalog for webserver2
Info: Applying configuration version '1449441137'
Notice: /Stage[main]/Main/Node[webserver2]/Package[php]/ensure: created
Notice: Finished catalog run in 4.04 seconds
```

By default, the Puppet agent will check the Puppet server every 30 minutes to see whether there is any change that has happened so that it can apply it. Therefore, during the test, we can always force a manual update, as we did earlier. The update time can be changed, by changing it in the Puppet configuration file under the [main] section, as follows:

```
$ sudo nano /etc/puppet/puppet.conf
runinterval = 900 # To make change every 15 minutes (60 x time in
minutes)
```

Then we can change it to have a service installed and ensure that it is running:

```
node 'webserver1', 'webserver2 {

            package { 'httpd' :
            ensure => installed,
                         } ->  # this to ensure that the order before it
is executed before going to the order after it
            service {'httpd':
            ensure => running,
            enable => true,
                     }

}
```

```
Info: Retrieving pluginfacts
Info: Retrieving plugin
Info: Loading facts
Info: Caching catalog for webserver2
Info: Applying configuration version '1449440438'
Notice: /Stage[main]/Main/Node[webserver2]/Package[httpd]/ensure: created
Notice: /Stage[main]/Main/Node[webserver2]/Service[httpd]/ensure: ensure changed '
stopped' to 'running'
Info: /Stage[main]/Main/Node[webserver2]/Service[httpd]: Unscheduling refresh on S
ervice[httpd]
Notice: Finished catalog run in 4.83 seconds
```

We can also install a program that is located only at the EPEL repository by forcing the installation of the EPEL repository before the program:

```
node 'webserver1', 'webserver2 {
package { 'epel-release' :
            ensure => installed,
                    } ->
```

```
        package { 'iperf' :
        ensure => installed,
                      }
    }
```

```
Info: Retrieving pluginfacts
Info: Retrieving plugin
Info: Loading facts
Info: Caching catalog for webserver2
Info: Applying configuration version '1449440825'
Notice: /Stage[main]/Main/Node[webserver2]/Package[epel-release]/ensure: created
Notice: /Stage[main]/Main/Node[webserver2]/Package[iperf]/ensure: created
Notice: Finished catalog run in 9.70 seconds
```

Then we can perform some user manipulation where we can create a user on all the client servers. First, we need to create it at the same machine to get its password with the hashing. Then we edit the site.pp file to give some information about the user:

```
node 'webserver1' {

        user { "usertest":
        ensure => "present",
        shell => '/bin/bash',
        home => '/home/usertest',
        managehome => true,
        password => '#############################', }
    }
```

Before finishing the chapter, we would like to explore what the Puppet Labs offer as extra modules, which we can use without the need to create our own, to perform simple, daily tasks. To search for the modules, we use the following command:

$ sudo puppet module search ftp

Then, to install the desired one, we use the install option:

$ sudo puppet module install puppetlabs-apache

Then, to check what is installed, we go to the /etc/puppet/module folder, and there we will have all the modules with their configuration files. We can always change them depending on our needs.

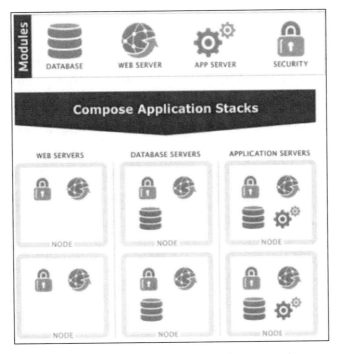

Source: http://static.virtualizationpractice.com

 We believe that we have presented some decent information about how to use Puppet for CentOS 7 but still Puppet has a lot to offer. To explore more about it, please check some of Packt's other books on mastering Puppet at: https://www.packtpub.com/all/?search=puppet

References

Now, let's have a look at the references used throughout the chapter:

- Configuration management on Wikipedia: https://en.wikipedia.org/wiki/Configuration_management
- Chef website: https://www.chef.io/
- SaltStack website: http://saltstack.com
- Ansible website: http://www.ansible.com
- Puppet website: https://puppetlabs.com
- What is puppet web page: https://puppetlabs.com/puppet/what-is-puppet

Summary

In this chapter, we introduced configuration management and its benefits for system administrators, especially when working in a big computer environment. We introduced in brief some of the well-known open source solutions used to carry out configuration management on Linux servers, especially CentOS 7. Then we chose Puppet as our candidate to show in a step-by-step tutorial how to set up and configure master/client architecture. And, finally, we have tested some commands on the client nodes.

In the final chapter, we will show you a few things that we believe every system administrator using Linux in general and CentOS more specifically should know, to better manage and secure their infrastructure in the best-practice ways.

9
Some Additional Tricks and Tools

For daily Linux usage, most system administrators/users must master a few techniques to help them use their Linux machine to its full potential. It is like having a Swiss Army knife and using it to just cut vegetables. Linux hides many useful techniques for daily-life tasks, and CentOS 7 is one of the latest and most reliable OS that many users can use to solve tons of problems.

Through this chapter, we are going to show some of the most needed tools that we believe any system administrator should know how to use. We will be showing how to use these tricks and tools to better manage a CentOS 7 server infrastructure.

Within this chapter, we are going to present the following topics:

- Connecting to multiple Linux machines using SSH
- Securing SSH and root login configurations
- SSH key-based authentication
- Installation and configuration of SpamAssassin
- Setting up the Clamav antivirus
- Configuration of Mytop for a MySQL database
- Setting up Samba and NFS for file sharing
- Introduction to some Linux system and network monitoring tools

SSH for remote connection

As we all know, SSH is the Secure Shell connection that we use to connect remotely to a Linux machine. It is the main tool used by system administrators for remote management of their infrastructure. It is one of the essential tools that we find in a basic installation of CentOS 7 and almost all Linux distributions by default.

Usually, SSH is only installed as a client, so you can only remotely connect to other machines; but this is not the case for a basic system installation. When installing the CentOS 7 server, it should already have the SSH server installed and running.

To install the SSH server, we can just rely on the default package repository without adding any extra third-party repository:

```
$ sudo yum install openssh-server
```

After having the SSH server installed, we should start the service and enable it for default system startup services:

```
$ sudo systemctl start sshd.service
$ sudo systemctl enable sshd.service
```

For security, most machines have the default SSH port closed, so we need to open it from the default firewall manager:

```
$ sudo firewallcmd permanent zone=public addport=ssh/tcp
$ sudo firewallcmd reload
```

That's all we need to do to make a machine remotely accessible.

To access this machine, we only need to type `ssh` followed by the username and the IP address or the hostname (if the machine is stored at the DNS server or listed at the local `/etc/hosts` file) of the machine desired to connect to:

```
$ ssh user1@server1.packt.co.uk
$ ssh user1@10.0.0.10
```

Usually, if the server is running and the `sshd` service is listening, then there should be an exchange of public keys upon the first ever connection to that server using this machine. Otherwise, the server will just ask for the desired user password to allow the login.

When we connect to a remote machine using SSH, it is like us having an open window to that machine, and we are kind of stuck to that, which is a network-consuming way of connecting if we are using it for a long period, and especially if we are just connected without really typing any commands. So we need to close the terminal window to leave the remote connection session and free the resources reserved. SSH offers some useful options such as `-t`. Through this option, we can send a command to be executed on the remote machine and send back the output:

```
$ ssh -t user1@server1.packt.co.uk cat /etc/hosts
```

This command will only show the containment of the `/etc/hosts` file without keeping the windows open.

We can also use SSH to send files between two machines to or from a remote machine, using the `scp` command:

```
$ scp user1@server1.packt.co.uk:/home/user1/Desktop/file1.txt   ./Desktop/
```

In the next section, we will show you how to secure SSH and manage a root login.

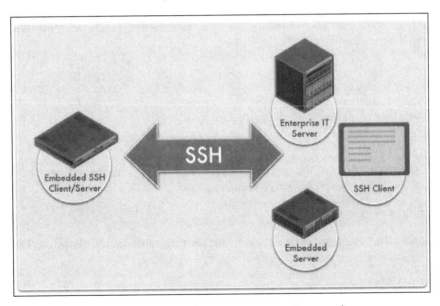

Source: `https://www.allegrosoft.com/`

Securing SSH and the root login configuration

For this section, we are going to show some basic and advanced ways to secure the SSH service to mitigate more threats. We will need to make some minor changes to the `/etc/ssh/sshd_config` file. We will explain every line as we change it gradually:

```
$ sudo nano /etc/ssh/sshd_config
```

Uncomment the SSH version 2 line to use only the newer version of SSH, which is more secure and reliable. The line should look like the following:

```
Protocol 2
```

We can limit users' access to restrict some users from accessing the server. We do this using SSH:

```
DenyUsers Baduser1 baduser2
```

Then we can set up the time out for the SSH connection to always close the sessions that are not active for a defined period of time. We need to set the countdown to start from the moment the session became idle:

```
ClientAliveInterval 360
ClientAliveCountMax 0
```

Then we can disable the root login using SSH:

```
PermitRootLogin no
```

In addition, we can disable empty password usage, whereby users do not have the right to log in if they don't have a password:

```
PermitEmptyPasswords no
```

In addition to that, we can do the same thing for password authentication. We can force all logins to happen via generated keys:

```
PasswordAuthentication no
```

Then a warning banner is always useful. So, if we need to create one, we should edit `/etc/issues` and add any kind of banner:

```
$ sudo nano /etc/issue
```

Then we should restart the service so that it can take effect:

```
$ sudo systemctl restart sshd
```

Some servers are publicly accessible, so they may need an extra reinforcement to their SSH service. For this task, we will be installing a tool called **Fail2Ban**, which is a very reliable tool that helps protect many services from brute-force attacks. It basically scans the log file for the specific service and looks for failed login attempts in order to block them. To have it installed, we need to install the EPEL repository first:

```
$ sudo yum install epel-release
```

Then we need to install it with **Rsyslog**, since it scans the log output taken from Rsyslog:

```
$ sudo yum install fail2ban rsyslog
```

To have it working fine, we can update it or update the SELinux policy.

Then we go ahead to configure it in order to secure SSH. We need to create a file named sshd.local in the jail folder of Fail2Ban:

```
$ sudo nano /etc/fail2ban/jail.d/sshd.local
```

Then we add the following code inside it:

```
[sshd]
enabled   = true
filter    = sshd
#action   = firewallcmd-ipset
maxretry = 8
bantime   = 172800
```

This will ban attacks for 48 hours. Then we start the service and enable it for system startup services:

```
$ sudo systemctl start fail2ban
$ sudo systemctl enable fail2ban
```

We can now say that we are done with securing SSH. Let's try to manage root login access. We have already shown how we can disable root login using SSH. Let's manage the Sudoers file a little to have a user execute superuser commands without the need to type in a password.

First, we need to install sudo on the server. Usually, most CentOS 7 server installations have sudo installed.

Then we can just use the group wheel. If needed, we can create a new one:

```
$ sudo nano /etc/sudoers
```

And we go to the line describing the group wheel:

```
%wheel ALL=(ALL)    ALL
```

Here, we need to add a word to make the users under this group gain root access using sudo, and they don't need to use passwords every time:

```
%wheel ALL=(ALL)    NOPASSWD: ALL
```

 Some system administrators do not advise this option, because if there is an error that gets typed, there is no turning back. It is always a choice to take for this option depending on the need.

SSH key-based authentication

As we have noticed by using SSH every time, we need to type the password, which is not something recommended in many security policies. This is where we will use the SSH feature to use authentication by using public/private keys.

SSH provides a tool for creating public/private keys to use for remote connection authentication, without the need to use a password. How do we do that? It's simple. For this test example we are going to create a new RSA key, a little bit more secure than the usual (we can create different types of keys such as dsa, ecdsa, ed25519):

```
$ ssh-keygen -t rsa -b 2048 -v
```

Then we follow the steps presented by the command. For a default installation, we can just keep typing *Enter*. Otherwise, we can always add some kind of passphrase to make it more secure. We may need to specify the key file name so we can use it later.

Then we need to copy the newly created keys file to the host that we want to connect to. There are two ways of doing this. The traditional way, which is to literally copy the key file into the server that we want to remote connect to without using a password. Where we need to put the file in the subfolder .ssh located at the current user folder. Or, we can simply use the ssh-copy-id command that does the same job without the pain:

```
$ ssh-copy-id user1@server1.packt.co.uk
```

Then we need to type the password for the last time.

After that, any SSH remote connection or file transfer can be done without the need for a password.

Source: `https://www.digitalocean.com/`

Installing and configuring SpamAssassin

SpamAssassin is one of the most powerful spam filters that work with Postfix to filter all mails that may present a threat.

We will use it to filter all Postfix mails on our mail server (as we described in *Chapter 4, Mail Server with Postfix,* about how to get one up and running).

First, we need to install it using the default package manager:

```
$ sudo yum install spamassassin
```

Then it is installed. Now we move on to the configuration part:

```
$ sudo nano /etc/mail/spamassassin/local.cf
```

We have some lines that we need to make sure are in the file. So, we'd rather write them or uncomment them if they are commented:

```
rewrite_header Subject ***SPAM***
required_hits 5.0
report_safe 0
required_score 5
```

Next, we create a new user group and a user to manage the service:

```
$ sudo groupadd spamd
$ sudo useradd -g spamd -s /bin/false -d /var/log/spamassassin spamd
$ sudo chown spamd:spamd /var/log/spamassassin
```

Then we have our service well configured. We move on to the Postfix part, where we should make some minor changes to its master configuration file:

```
$ sudo nano /etc/postfix/master.cf
```

We need to go to the line of the SMTPD configuration and add the following line:

```
-o content_filter=spamassassin
```

Therefore, it should look like this:

```
smtp      inet  n     -      n     -     -        smtpd -o content_
filter=spamassassin
```

After that, we add the following line:

```
spamassassin unix - n n - - pipe flags=R user=spamd argv=/usr/bin/spamc
-e /usr/sbin/sendmail -oi -f ${sender} ${recipient}
```

We save the file and quit. Now we need to update the SpamAssassin rules by typing the following:

```
$ sudo sa-update --nogpg
```

Now, to make the change in the `SpamAssassin` service and the Postfix server, we need to restart it and then we are done:

```
$ sudo systemctl restart spamassassin
$ sudo systemctl restart postfix.service
```

Setting up the Clamav antivirus

Clamav is an open source antivirus tool. Its basic usage is for detecting viruses, malware, and malicious software on Linux-based machines.

To install Clamav, we need to install the EPEL repository:

```
$ sudo yum install epel-release
```

Then we can install Clamav with all its useful tools:

```
$ sudo yum install clamav-server clamav-data clamav-update clamav-
filesystem clamav clamav-scanner-systemd clamav-devel clamav-lib clamav-
server-systemd
```

Before we start configuring, we need to make sure that SELinux will let Clamav work without issues:

```
$ sudo setsebool -P antivirus_can_scan_system 1
```

To check whether the option is active, we need to type this:

```
$ sudo getseboot -a | grep virus
```

Then we remove the example configuration, so we can make our own configuration:

```
$ sudo sed -i '/^Example/d' /etc/clamd.d/scan.conf
```

After removing the example lines, we need to do some modifications to define the TCP server type and to define the user root to execute the antivirus:

```
$ sudo nano /etc/clamd.d/scan.conf
```

We uncomment the following line:

```
LocalSocket /var/run/clamd.scan/clamd.sock
```

We add those two lines at the end of the file and save:

```
User root
LocalSocket /var/run/clamd.<SERVICE>/clamd.sock
```

To keep the Clamav database up to date, we need to enable a tool called **Freshclam**. Therefore, we need to create a backup file from its configuration file:

```
$ sudo cp /etc/freshclam.conf /etc/freshclam.conf.bak
```

Again we remove the example lines:

```
$ sudo sed -i '/^Example/d' /etc/freshclam.conf
```

Otherwise, if needed, we can adjust the options for a more personalized solution. We need to run Freshclam to update the database manually and to check whether the configuration is successfully set:

```
$ sudo freshclam
```

We need to create the file that will act as the service file to run the **Freshclam** daemon:

```
$ sudo nano /usr/lib/systemd/system/clam-freshclam.service
```

Then we put the following code inside the file and save it:

```
[Unit]
Description = freshclam scanner
After = network.target


[Service]
Type = forking
ExecStart = /usr/bin/freshclam -d -c 4
Restart = on-failure
PrivateTmp = true


[Install]
WantedBy=multi-user.target
```

Next, we should check whether the service is well configured by running it and checking its status:

```
$ sudo systemctl start clam-freshclam.service
$ sudo systemctl status clam-freshclam.service -1
```

If everything is running fine and there is no problem, we add it to the system startup service:

```
$ sudo systemctl enable clam-freshclam.service
```

Now we need to create the Clamav service file. We have an example service file that we need to copy into the system services folder. We need to change its name to something understandable. Then, we need to make some minor modifications to it:

```
$ sudo mv /usr/lib/systemd/system/clamd@.service /usr/lib/systemd/system/clamd.service
```

Since we have changed the name, we need to change it at the file that uses this service as well:

```
$ sudo nano /usr/lib/systemd/system/clamd@scan.service
```

We change the first line by removing @ to look like this:

```
.include /lib/systemd/system/clamd.service
```

At the same location, we need to change the Clamd service file:

```
$ sudo nano /usr/lib/systemd/system/clamd.service
```

We add the following lines at the end:

```
[Install]
WantedBy=multi-user.target
```

And we remove `%i` from both the `Description` and `ExecStart` options. Then we change them to look like the following:

```
Description = clamd scanner daemon
ExecStart = /usr/sbin/clamd -c /etc/clamd.d/scan.conf --nofork=yes
```

Before running any service, we need to check whether we have any errors. We will run Clamd manually:

```
$ sudo /usr/sbin/clamd -c /etc/clamd.d/scan.conf –nofork=yes
```

Then, if everything goes fine, we start the services and add them to the system startup services:

```
$ sudo systemctl enable clamd.service
$ sudo systemctl enable clamd@scan.service
$ sudo systemctl start clamd.service
$ sudo systemctl start clamd@scan.service
```

For a final verification of the Clamav services, we check its status:

```
$ sudo systemctl status clamd.service -1
$ sudo systemctl status clamd@scan.service -1
```

For a test scan of the current folder, we run the following command:

```
$ sudo clamscan --infected --remove --recursive ./
```

This is the architecture how ClamAV should be located in our infrastructure:

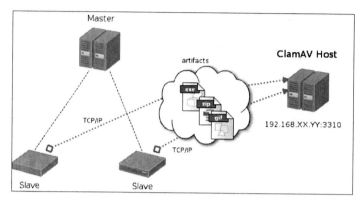

Source https://wiki.jenkins-ci.org/display/JENKINS/Home

The following figure shows a better description between the components of a mail server to explain how ClamAV help secure our mail service:

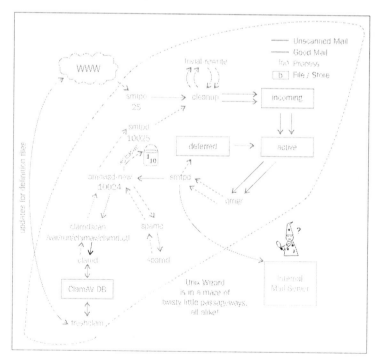

Source: https://aphyr.com/

Configuring Mytop for a MySQL database

Mytop is an open source solution that helps monitor the MySQL database's activities and performance, or what we now know as MariaDB for CentOS 7. It is a non-GUI monitoring tool. Therefore, it kind of provides an interphase through the shell command line.

To install Mytop, we should make sure that the installation is going to be at the same server where the MariaDB database server is installed. Then we add the EPEL repository, as follows:

```
$ sudo yum install epel-release
```

Next, we execute the installation using yum:

```
$ sudo yum install mytop
```

For the configuration, we only need to create a configuration file at the root folder:

```
$ sudo nano /root/.mytop
```

Then we type the following text inside it:

```
host=localhost
db=mysql
delay=3
port=3306
socket=
batchmode=0
color=1
idle=1
```

This is a personalized configuration that will be used during the execution of the program.

To run it, we need to type in the following command:

```
$ sudo mytop --prompt
```

Then we need to type in the MariaDB root password. Otherwise, if we are accessing using a non-root user, we can always type this:

```
$ sudo mytop -u user1 --prompt
```

Or if we need one specific database, we have the following:

```
$ sudo mytop -d packtdb--prompt
```

To know that it is working fine, you should see the following interface:

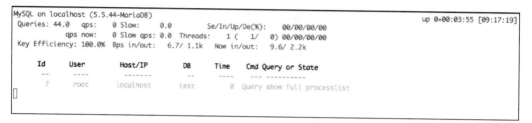

```
MySQL on localhost (5.5.44-MariaDB)                                            up 0+00:03:55 [09:17:19]
 Queries: 44.0   qps:    0 Slow:     0.0     Se/In/Up/De(%):    00/00/00/00
           qps now:    0 Slow qps: 0.0  Threads:    1 (   1/   0) 00/00/00/00
 Key Efficiency: 100.0%  Bps in/out:   6.7/ 1.1k   Now in/out:   9.6/ 2.2k


    Id      User        Host/IP      DB      Time   Cmd Query or State
    --      ----        -------      --      ----   --- ------------
     7      root        localhost    test       0   Query show full processlist
```

For more information on how to interact with the Mytop GUI, you can always check out its manual:

```
$ man mytop
```

```
MySQL on localhost (4.1.20)                                      up 11+11:03:03 [09:48:24]
 Queries: 123.8M  qps:   131 Slow:     11.4k         Se/In/Up/De(%):    78/04/06/03
           qps now:   108 Slow qps: 0.0   Threads:    31 (   1/   0) 78/03/07/03
 Cache Hits: 60.9M Hits/s:  64.5 Hits now:    53.4   Ratio: 63.1% Ratio now: 63.3%
 Key Efficiency: 100.0%  Bps in/out:   4.1k/599.8    Now in/out: 39.5k/567.9k

    Id       User       Host/IP      DB     Time    Cmd Query or State
    --       ----       -------      --     ----    --- ----------
  233817     user       localhost           0    Sleep
  233822     user       localhost           0    Sleep
  233851     user       localhost           0    Sleep
  233888     user       localhost           0    Sleep
  233910     user       localhost           0    Sleep
  233915     user       localhost           0    Query SELECT DISTINCT year(FROM_UNI
  233918     user       localhost           0    Query show full processlist
  233704     user       localhost           1    Sleep
  233907     user       localhost           1    Sleep
  233838     user       localhost           2    Sleep
  233854     user       localhost           2    Sleep
  233859     user       localhost           2    Sleep
  233875     user       localhost           2    Sleep
  233887     user       localhost           2    Sleep
  233894     user       localhost           2    Sleep
  233895     user       localhost           3    Sleep
  233853     user       localhost           4    Sleep
  233863     user       localhost           4    Sleep
  233890     user       localhost           4    Sleep
```

Source: http://i.gzn.jp

Setting up Samba and NFS for file sharing

Samba is an open source project with the goal of providing a secure and stable data and printer-sharing service across multiple operating systems (Windows, Linux, and Mac OS).

Samba works using the **Session Message Block (SMB)** protocol, which is a protocol supported by most Windows OS and Mac OS to serve those clients who have access to shared resources such as Linux storage media, printers, serial ports (hardware equipment).

For the tutorial, we are going to use a CentOS 7 Samba server and Mac OS machine to use the service to have access to a shared folder.

First, we will start by installing Samba on our CentOS 7 server:

```
$ sudo yum install samba samba-client samba-common
```

Before starting the configuration, we need to make some backup, environment creation, and firewall setup. So first, we need to create a backup for the Samba configuration file to make sure not to mess up the original configuration (this is useful in case of having many updated configurations). We better keep a backup of each stage in the update process:

```
$ sudo cp /etc/samba/smb.conf /etc/samba/smb.conf.backup
```

Then we need to create the folder that we need to share, or prepare it to be shared if it is already there. We need to set the user permissions to grant everything to that folder:

```
$ sudo mkdir /SharedFolder/
```

```
$ sudo chmod -R 755 /SharedFolder/
```

Finally, we need to open the Samba service port at the server firewall:

```
$ sudo firewall-cmd --permanent --zone=public --add-service=samba
$ sudo firewall-cmd --reload
```

Now we can start making the necessary configuration to the Samba configuration file:

```
$ sudo nano /etc/samba/smb.conf
```

We need to make sure that we set the appropriate workgroup (usually it is set as WORKGROUP):

```
workgroup = WORKGROUP
```

And we define a shared folder.

```
[Shared Folder]
path = /SharedFolder
read only = no
guest ok = yes
browsable =yes
writable = yes
create mask = 0755
directory mask = 0755
```

We save the file and create some Samba users:

```
$ sudo smbpasswd -a user1
```

Then we type in a password and retry typing it to create a new one.

If we want some folders to be shared with a specific user, we need to add the following line to the folder definition and we need to disable guest login by changing guest ok = yes to guest ok = no:

```
valid users = user1
```

For the testing phase, we need to start the services:

```
$ sudo systemctl enable smb.service
$ sudo systemctl enable nmb.service
$ sudo systemctl start smb.service
$ sudo systemctl start nmb.service
```

Then we go to the client side and type this link at the server connection:

```
smb://server_ip_address
```

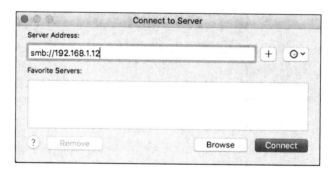

This test is used on a Mac machine. For a Windows machine, we type the following link at the Explorer address field:

`\\server_ip_address`

Then we will have a login screen, where we need to type the Samba user ID and password, like this:

After typing the correct user ID and password, there should be a screen showing the possible folder that this user can have access to, as follows:

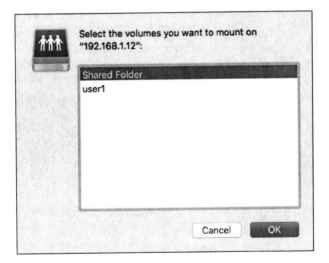

Then we will have our folder accessible with the rights as defined in the configuration folder. Since we have write permissions, we can create a folder and then check whether it did actually happen on the server.

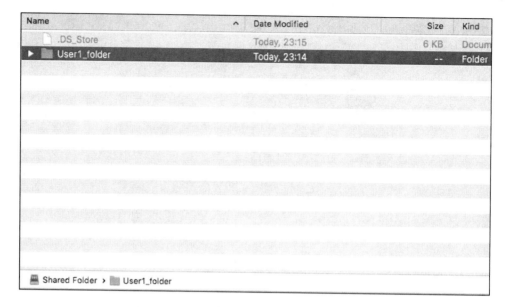

We can run our server to verify whether the change made by the client has been applied.

```
[user1@server /]$ ls -l /SharedFolder/
total 0
drwxrwxrwx 2 user1 user1 6 Nov 30 00:14 User1_folder
[user1@server /]$ 
```

If we ever need to change any of the folder-sharing configuration, we must restart the services to apply the change:

```
$ sudo systemctl restart smb.service
$ sudo systemctl restart nmb.service
```

Samba is good for multiple-environment file sharing, but we should not forget about Linux's most famous file-sharing solution—**Network File System** (**NFS**). NFS is a client-server tool used to share data between multiple Linux systems, via mounting many remote shared folders and drives across the network to directly access those files at the client side.

We are going to establish an NFS client-server test on CentOS 7 to show how it works.

First, we need to install the service at the server:

```
$ sudo yum install nfs-utils nfs-utils-lib
```

Then we start the service responsible for ensuring the functionality of the service:

```
$ sudo systemctl enable rpcbind
$ sudo systemctl start rpcbind
$ sudo systemctl enable nfs-server
$ sudo systemctl start nfs-server
$ sudo systemctl start nfs-lock
$ sudo systemctl start nfs-idmap
```

We prepare a folder to be shared:

```
$ sudo mkdir /NFSsharedFolder
$ sudo chmod -R 0755 /NFSsharedFolder
```

Then, to export this folder and make it accessible to be mounted on the client, we go ahead and edit the /etc/export file:

```
$ sudo nano /etc/export
```

And we add the following line:

```
/NFSsharedFolder 172.25.0.0/16(rw,sync,no_root_squash,no_all_squash)
```

This line means that we are exporting this folder to all IP addresses in the network. The rw option gives write permissions to the folder, sync makes sure that the folder is always in synchronization, no_root_squash gives root privileges for the folder at the client side, and finally, no_all_squash enables the user's authority.

After every change to the export file, we need to restart the NFS server:

```
$ sudo systemctl restart nfs-server
```

Finally, we need to open the NFS services' ports at the server firewall. Reload the firewall to apply the changes:

```
$ sudo firewall-cmd --permanent --add-port=111/tcp
$ sudo firewall-cmd --permanent --add-port=875/tcp
$ sudo firewall-cmd --permanent --add-port=2049/tcp
$ sudo firewall-cmd --permanent --add-port=20048/tcp
$ sudo firewall-cmd --permanent --add-port=42955/tcp
$ sudo firewall-cmd --permanent --add-port=46666/tcp
$ sudo firewall-cmd --permanent --add-port=54302/tcp
$ sudo firewall-cmd --reload
```

With this step, we can say that we are done configuring the server. Now we move to the client. Just like the server, we need to install the NFS utilities:

```
$ sudo yum install nfs-utils nfs-utils-lib
```

Then start the appropriate services:

```
$ sudo systemctl enable rpcbind
$ sudo systemctl start rpcbind
$ sudo systemctl enable nfs-server
$ sudo systemctl start nfs-server
$ sudo systemctl start nfs-lock
$ sudo systemctl start nfs-idmap
```

Before mounting the network-shared folder, we need to make sure that there is a location to mount on:

```
$ sudo mkdir /NFSfolder
```

```
$ sudo chmod -R 755 /NFSfolder
```

To test mount the folder, we can use the mount command or make the system mount it automatically by editing the /etc/fstab file:

```
$ sudo mount -t nfs 172.25.22.10:/NFSsharedFolder/ /NFSfolder/
```

```
$ sudo nano /etc/fstab
```

In addition, we insert the following line:

```
172.25.22.10:/NFSsharedFolder/ /NFSfolder/ nfs defaults 0 0
```

For a faster connection, we can always use the fourth version of NFS by typing the following:

```
172.25.22.10:/NFSsharedFolder/ /NFSfolder/ nfs4 defaults 0 0
```

NFS4 has more to offer than NFS3. We would recommend it for an environment that has Linux servers that do support NFS4.

Finally, if we need to check what we have mounted on a specific NFS client, we use mount:

```
$ sudo mount
```

Introducing the Linux system and network monitoring tools

In the final section of our chapter, we are going to present a number of very useful tools to monitor both systems and networks for our CentOS 7 server.

We will start by showing some system monitoring tools. We believe that most of these tools need the EPEL repository installed, so we can just install it before trying to install any of those tools:

```
$ sudo yum install epel-release
```

The first tool that we are going to talk about is Htop. It is kind of the same as the old `top` command, but it has a very user-friendly interface, wherein it is much more interactive with many shortcuts, a graphical colored presentation of the process, and the CPU, Memory, and SWAP Memory in a bar shaped way, to show how much of those are used. To install Htop, we just need to use Yum:

```
$ sudo yum install htop
```

And to run it, we simply need to type `htop`. There is no configuration needed:

```
$ htop
```

We should see this kind of interface:

```
  CPU[||||||||||||||||||||||||||||||||||||100.0%]   Tasks: 106, 140 thr; 4 running
  Mem[||||||||||||||||||||||||||||||1242/1816MB]    Load average: 1.93 1.63 1.58
  Swp[|                               5/2047MB]     Uptime: 03:22:30

   PID USER      PRI  NI  VIRT   RES   SHR S CPU% MEM%   TIME+  Command
   645 root       20   0  4372   576   496 S  1.8  0.0  0:07.53 /sbin/rngd -f
   675 root       20   0  303M  3812  3036 S  1.8  0.2  0:00.44 /usr/sbin/rsyslogd -n
 22599 root       20   0  119M  2108  1440 R  0.0  0.1  0:01.98 htop
  3101 alibi      20   0  314M  5940  4496 S  0.0  0.3  0:00.40 /usr/libexec/goa-identity-service
  1624 postgres   20   0  187M  1684   560 S  0.0  0.1  0:00.08 postgres: stats collector process
  3098 alibi      20   0  314M  5940  4496 S  0.0  0.3  0:00.49 /usr/libexec/goa-identity-service
   470 root       20   0 43016  3432  3232 S  0.0  0.2  0:08.98 /usr/lib/systemd/systemd-journald
  1213 haproxy    20   0 49640  1320   308 R  0.0  0.1  0:05.95 /usr/sbin/haproxy -f /etc/haproxy/
   673 root       20   0  303M  3812  3036 S  0.0  0.2  0:01.12 /usr/sbin/rsyslogd -n
     1 root       20   0  138M  5768  3616 S  0.0  0.3  0:07.07 /usr/lib/systemd/systemd --switche
  3105 alibi      20   0 1553M  225M 33400 S  0.0 12.4  0:22.75 /usr/bin/gnome-shell
  5560 alibi      20   0  132M  2196  1012 S  0.0  0.1  0:00.09 sshd: alibi@pts/0
   671 root       20   0  362M  3448  2756 S  0.0  0.2  0:00.62 /usr/libexec/accounts-daemon
   629 root       20   0  303M  3812  3036 S  0.0  0.2  0:01.56 /usr/sbin/rsyslogd -n
  1623 postgres   20   0  227M  2844  1160 S  0.0  0.2  0:00.07 postgres: autovacuum launcher proc
  1345 postgres   20   0  226M  8860  7796 S  0.0  0.5  0:00.09 /usr/bin/postgres -D /var/lib/pgsq
   756 root       20   0  429M  6712  4792 S  0.0  0.4  0:00.86 /usr/sbin/NetworkManager --no-daem
   705 root       20   0  537M 17604  5084 S  0.0  0.9  0:00.93 /usr/bin/python -Es /usr/sbin/tune
F1Help  F2Setup F3Search F4Filter F5Tree  F6SortBy F7Nice - F8Nice + F9Kill  F10Quit
```

The second system-monitoring tool on the list is Iotop. It does look like the old top command, but it specializes in showing the system available disk input and output access in real time. It shows each process activity, and how much it is using the hard disk (read/write speed and actual usage). To install it, we need to use YUM again, but usually it is installed on most CentOS 7 servers by default:

```
$ sudo yum install ioptop
```

To use it we need to type the name:

```
$ ioptop
```

We will have the following interface:

```
Total DISK READ :      0.00 B/s | Total DISK WRITE :      3.80 K/s
Actual DISK READ:      0.00 B/s | Actual DISK WRITE:     11.40 K/s
  TID  PRIO  USER      DISK READ  DISK WRITE  SWAPIN     IO>    COMMAND
  675 be/4 root        0.00 B/s    3.80 K/s  0.00 %   0.00 % rsyslogd -n [rs:main Q:Reg]
    1 be/4 root        0.00 B/s    0.00 B/s  0.00 %   0.00 % systemd --switched-m --deserialize 24
    2 be/4 root        0.00 B/s    0.00 B/s  0.00 %   0.00 % [kthreadd]
    3 be/4 root        0.00 B/s    0.00 B/s  0.00 %   0.00 % [ksoftirqd/0]
    5 be/0 root        0.00 B/s    0.00 B/s  0.00 %   0.00 % [kworker/0:0H]
    6 be/4 root        0.00 B/s    0.00 B/s  0.00 %   0.00 % [kworker/u2:0]
    7 rt/4 root        0.00 B/s    0.00 B/s  0.00 %   0.00 % [migration/0]
    8 be/4 root        0.00 B/s    0.00 B/s  0.00 %   0.00 % [rcu_bh]
    9 be/4 root        0.00 B/s    0.00 B/s  0.00 %   0.00 % [rcuob/0]
```

Just before going to the network monitoring tools, we should take a quick look at this tool that performs monitoring for both systems and networks. Monitorix is an open source, lightweight monitoring tool for systems and network monitoring. It collects system and network activities on a regular basis in order to show them in a well-presented graph through a web-based interface. It is very helpful for detecting bottlenecks and system failures for better management.

To install Monitorix, we need to install a few necessary packages first:

```
$ sudo yum install rrdtool rrdtool-perl perl-libwww-perl perl-MailTools
perl-MIME-Lite perl-CGI perl-DBI perl-XML-Simple perl-Config-General
perl-HTTP-Server-Simple
```

Then we install Monitorix:

```
$ sudo yum install monitorix
```

It is kind of a service, so we need to start it and enable it for the login service startup:

```
$ sudo systemctl start monitorix
$ sudo systemctl enable monitorix
```

We may need to disable SELinux or set it to permissive to make our service work fine. In addition, since Monitorix serves at port 8080, we need to open that at the firewall, as follows:

```
$ sudo firewall-cmd --permanent --zone=public —add-port=8080/tcp
$ sudo firewall-cmd --reload
```

Then we can start using it by using a browser. We type the following at the address section:

```
http://Server_IP_address:8080/monitorix
```

Thus, we will have the following interface:

We will get to see a variety of graphs for multiple pieces of information, as follows:

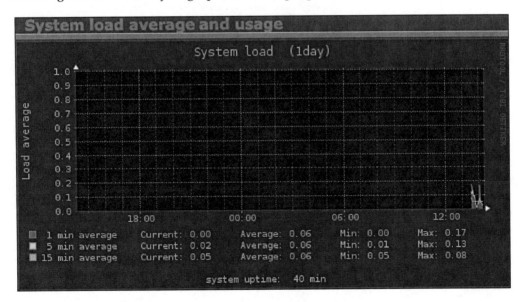

This was about system load average usage and the next one is about the network status:

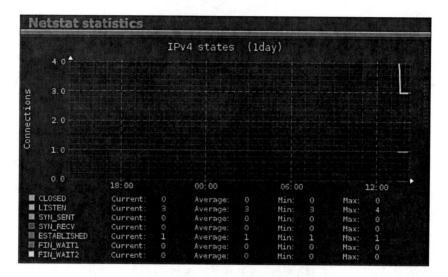

Now, let's talk about some useful network monitoring tools. We will first talk about Netstat, which is one of the most common tools for monitoring a network's incoming and outgoing traffic. It is very useful for network troubleshooting. It is usually installed on the system, so we only need to execute it:

```
$ netstat -a
```

Then we will have this kind of output:

```
[root@webserver3 alibi]# netstat -a
Active Internet connections (servers and established)
Proto Recv-Q Send-Q Local Address          Foreign Address         State
tcp        0      0 0.0.0.0:webcache       0.0.0.0:*               LISTEN
tcp        0      0 0.0.0.0:ssh            0.0.0.0:*               LISTEN
tcp        0      0 webserver3:smtp        0.0.0.0:*               LISTEN
tcp        0      0 webserver3.windows.:ssh mohameds-macbook-:52084 ESTABLISHED
tcp6       0      0 [::]:ssh               [::]:*                  LISTEN
tcp6       0      0 localhost:smtp         [::]:*                  LISTEN
udp        0      0 0.0.0.0:bootpc         0.0.0.0:*
udp        0      0 0.0.0.0:ntp            0.0.0.0:*
udp        0      0 0.0.0.0:62658          0.0.0.0:*
udp        0      0 0.0.0.0:mdns           0.0.0.0:*
udp        0      0 webserver3:323         0.0.0.0:*
udp        0      0 0.0.0.0:57157          0.0.0.0:*
udp6       0      0 [::]:ntp               [::]:*
udp6       0      0 localhost:323          [::]:*
udp6       0      0 [::]:60093             [::]:*
raw6       0      0 [::]:ipv6-icmp         [::]:*                  7
raw6       0      0 [::]:ipv6-icmp         [::]:*                  7
```

After this, we have IPTraf, which is a real-time network-monitoring tool. It gathers information about network traffic activity, such as TCP, UDP, IP, and ICMP statistics, and then presents them in its interface. To install it, we need to use YUM:

```
$ sudo yum install iptraf
```

Then we just type its name to run it.

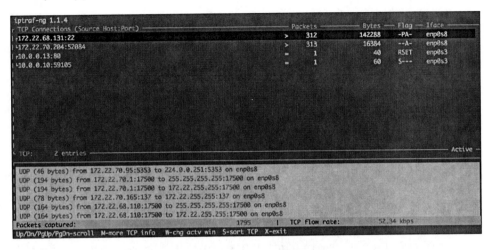

Finally, there is IfTop, which is an open source tool that reports network activities in real time. It is very useful for troubleshooting connections with outside servers, since it uses the `Pcap` library to capture incoming and outgoing packages on the desired network interface. To install it, we use yum again:

```
$ sudo yum install iptop
```

Then, to use it, we need to type the command with the desired interface to listen to:

```
$ sudo iptop -i eth0
```

References

Now, let's have a look at the references used throughout the chapter:

- OpenSSH website: `http://www.openssh.com`
- SpamAssassin website: `http://spamassassin.apache.org/`
- Clamav website: `http://www.clamav.net/`
- Mymap manual: `http://jeremy.zawodny.com/mysql/mytop/`
- Samba website: `https://www.samba.org/`
- NFS wiki: `http://nfs.sourceforge.net/nfs-howto/ar01s03.html`
- Trafshow wiki: `https://www.freshports.org/net/trafshow/`
- Monitorix home page: `http://www.monitorix.org/`

Summary

This chapter was a summary of topics that we believe should be mentioned to any system administrator willing to administrate CentOS 7. We started by presenting a way to easily access multiple machines from one place. We saw how to protect services, and it is a kind of best practice to make sure that the server is configured and secured. Then we presented a way to share data across multiple servers, which is very useful for both the installation phase and daily usage. Finally, we covered how to monitor our services' activities on both the system and the network.

The job of a system administrator varies from time to time. Sometimes it gets easier and sometimes it gets harder, especially during a new installation. So, we have covered those tools that help soften the hard times and make them more manageable.

We believe that this book is equivalent to Mastering Red Hat or Scientific Linux, which are resources that are very much in demand in the field of Linux system administration. As system administrators and as open source users, we believe that mastering this field requires more than just reading the book. You need to explore the part that we talked about briefly on making your own scenarios of testing and try to make it more complex. After all, we always learn from the hard experiences in our careers and not from the easiest ones.

Index

Thank you for buying
Mastering CentOS 7 Linux Server

About Packt Publishing

Packt, pronounced 'packed', published its first book, *Mastering phpMyAdmin for Effective MySQL Management*, in April 2004, and subsequently continued to specialize in publishing highly focused books on specific technologies and solutions.

Our books and publications share the experiences of your fellow IT professionals in adapting and customizing today's systems, applications, and frameworks. Our solution-based books give you the knowledge and power to customize the software and technologies you're using to get the job done. Packt books are more specific and less general than the IT books you have seen in the past. Our unique business model allows us to bring you more focused information, giving you more of what you need to know, and less of what you don't.

Packt is a modern yet unique publishing company that focuses on producing quality, cutting-edge books for communities of developers, administrators, and newbies alike. For more information, please visit our website at www.packtpub.com.

About Packt Open Source

In 2010, Packt launched two new brands, Packt Open Source and Packt Enterprise, in order to continue its focus on specialization. This book is part of the Packt Open Source brand, home to books published on software built around open source licenses, and offering information to anybody from advanced developers to budding web designers. The Open Source brand also runs Packt's Open Source Royalty Scheme, by which Packt gives a royalty to each open source project about whose software a book is sold.

Writing for Packt

We welcome all inquiries from people who are interested in authoring. Book proposals should be sent to author@packtpub.com. If your book idea is still at an early stage and you would like to discuss it first before writing a formal book proposal, then please contact us; one of our commissioning editors will get in touch with you.

We're not just looking for published authors; if you have strong technical skills but no writing experience, our experienced editors can help you develop a writing career, or simply get some additional reward for your expertise.

Troubleshooting CentOS

ISBN: 978-1-78528-982-8   Paperback: 190 pages

A practical guide to troubleshooting the CentOS 7 community-based enterprise server

1. Gain exposure to insider tips and techniques to quickly detect the reason for poor network/ storage performance.

2. Troubleshooting methodologies, defining, and isolating problems.

3. Identify key issues that impact performance, storage, scalability, capacity.

Learning RHEL Networking

ISBN: 978-1-78528-783-1   Paperback: 216 pages

Gain Linux administration skills by learning new networking concepts in Red Hat Enterprise Linux 7

1. Discover how to deploy the networks services Chrony, Network Time Protocol (NTP), Domain Name System (DNS), and Dynamic Host Configuration Protocol (DHCP).

2. Deploy RHEL 7 into your Microsoft Active Directory Domain to utilize Single-Sign in Linux and Active Directory with a single account.

3. Master firewalling your network and server with Firewalld.

Please check **www.PacktPub.com** for information on our titles

CPSIA information can be obtained
at www.ICGtesting.com
Printed in the USA
FFOW04n1413300917
40556FF